AF556048

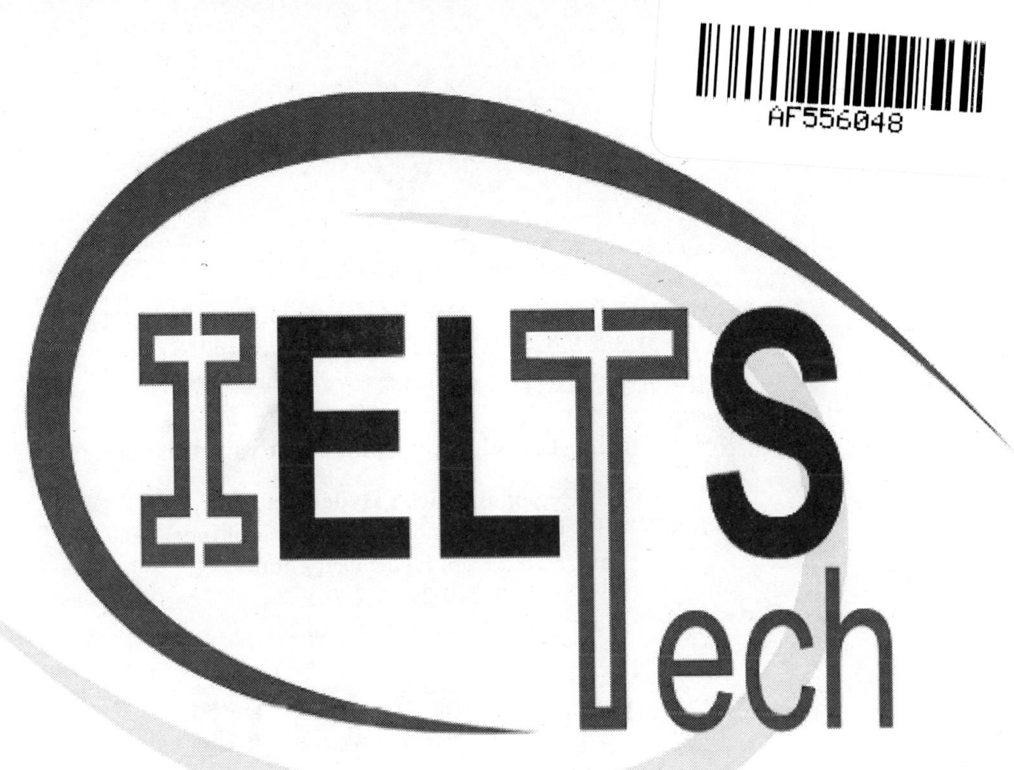

ACADEMIC MODULE

(A Smarter & Technical Solution for IELTS)

Jyoti Malhotra
(B.A Hons. M.A., NET-1, E-Commerce)

V&S PUBLISHERS

Published by:

F-2/16, Ansari road, Daryaganj, New Delhi-110002
☎ 23240026, 23240027 • *Fax:* 011-23240028
✉ info@vspublishers.com • 🌐 www.vspublishers.com

Online Brandstore: amazon.in/vspublishers

Regional Office : Hyderabad
5-1-707/1, Brij Bhawan (Beside Central Bank of India Lane)
Bank Street, Koti, Hyderabad - 500 095
☎ 040-24737290
✉ vspublishershyd@gmail.com

Follow us on:   

BUY OUR BOOKS FROM: AMAZON FLIPKART

© Copyright: Author

ISBN 978-93-505712-5-5
New Edition

DISCLAIMER

While every attempt has been made to provide accurate and timely information in this book, neither the author nor the publisher assumes any responsibility for errors, unintended omissions or commissions detected therein. The author and publisher makes no representation or warranty with respect to the comprehensiveness or completeness of the contents provided.
All matters included have been simplified under professional guidance for general information only, without any warranty for applicability on an individual. Any mention of an organization or a website in the book, by way of citation or as a source of additional information, doesn't imply the endorsement of the content either by the author or the publisher. It is possible that websites cited may have changed or removed between the time of editing and publishing the book.
Results from using the expert opinion in this book will be totally dependent on individual circumstances and factors beyond the control of the author and the publisher.
It makes sense to elicit advice from well informed sources before implementing the ideas given in the book. The reader assumes full responsibility for the consequences arising out from reading this book.
For proper guidance, it is advisable to read the book under the watchful eyes of parents/guardian. The buyer of this book assumes all responsibility for the use of given materials and information.
The copyright of the entire content of this book rests with the author/publisher. Any infringement/transmission of the cover design, text or illustrations, in any form, by any means, by any entity will invite legal action and be responsible for consequences thereon.

Printed at : Param Offsetters, Okhla, New Delhi–110020

Dedication

I, with due respect and profound privilege, serene dignity and folded hands dedicate my small piece of research program to my devoted and dedicated parents, Mrs. Kiran Malhotra and Mr. Pradeep Malhotra for their wholesome support and their dignified ambience which they offered me to sail the boat of my life on the path of hardwork and determination. I am really very thankful to both of them for blooming my life with their humble ambience.

Acknowledgement

There is a big vote bank of thanks in my whole projection of this project to my worthy parents, Mrs. & Mr. Deep Birla, My Guide, Mr. Parminder Singh Bhogal, Caring Brothers & Sisters - Mrs. & Mr. Rohit Gandhi, Mrs. & Mr. Aman Malhotra and Mrs. & Mr. Sandeep Malhotra.

My heartiest thanks to my life partner, Mr. Deepak Malhotra (husband) and the little steps of my Angel, Ditya Malhotra (daughter).

I am really grateful to be a part of the V & S Publishers who support my research analysis with their expert team of publishing. I am really very thankful to Mr. Sahil Gupta (Director) and Mr. Binay Srivastava for their wholesome cooperation to convert my research program to a complete masterpiece.

Regards

Jyoti Malhotra

Publisher's Note

V&S Publishers has recently ventured into the field of *Academic Books* with the launch of the *Gen X Series*. 'Gen X' stands for 'Excellence in Generation 'X'. The series comprises books for aspirants of various competitive examinations. Hence, following the success of our previous books in this series, we decided to launch a **series of IELTS or the International English Language Testing System books** under this series. The subject has been divided into five main parts which has been grouped into five books by the author, such as: ***IELTS Tech-Academic Module*, *IELTS Tech-Writing Essentials*, *IELTS Tech-Vocal Cosmetics*, *IELTS Tech- General Module*** and ***IELTS Tech- Speaking Essentials*** for the students, who aspire to study, work or settle abroad.

The books in this exclusive Series are written especially for the Indian students who wish to appear in the IELTS exams. Most of the foreign books available in the market on this subject have been written keeping in view the foreign readers and at times, may appear *Greek* to the students from India, primarily because of issues related to accent, grammatical aspects, spellings, etc. Therefore, the need for these books was felt by V&S Publishers and the author's extensive research on this subject was carefully moulded to present it in the form of five perfect books on IELTS, specifically for Indian students.

Each book contains **Skills, Strategies and Guidelines** written in a simple manner. Unique feature of this book is additional content accompanied with the book, available online on dropbox: https://www.dropbox.com/sh/05un0xu58pg5x08/AAAiBIBGKxpChzFGhNXH7bCSa?dl=0. The content here is **interactive and illustrative** and presented in a manner that even an average student can grasp the contents and master the language easily and quickly. V&S Publishers hopes that through these books, we can offer the IELTS aspirants--**A Smarter Way to Learn Technical English nationwide.**

Scan Dropbox QR Code : 

Contents

Listening Module

Preface

IELTS- TECH - A complete Toolkit for learning, practising and knowing about IELTS. As the world is growing smarter, the ways of its learning and getting education is also getting smarter day by day. IELTS-TECH (A TECHNICAL TOOLKIT OF LEARNING INTERNATIONAL LANGUAGE TESTING SYSTEM) acts as a smarter way to learn IELTS via Presentations on its Strategies. This Book is 4 in 1 which completes the wholesome package of READING, WRITING, LISTENING & SPEAKING skills, strategies (on DROPBOX) and its practice sessions. Undoubtedly, you get practice sessions and strategies online, or via some other books or media, but this book is unique because here you get everything in a single book, i.e., *skills, strategies, practice sessions and smart tech presentation* on IELTS.

This will really prove to be boon for the students.

The book is specially designed to investigate what skills and strategies are required in writing and speaking modules that distinguish the IELTS proficiency levels. There are a number of factors like *Word Stress, Intonation, Rhythm, Cohesive Devices* which are required on behalf of the IELTS candidates in order to determine their assessment s over four band scales: Fluency, grammatical range and accuracy, lexical resource and pronunciation. But how to attain all these skills is still a matter of discussion. Without understanding these technical aspects of English language, it is difficult for the IELTS candidates to score good grades in the IELTS Speaking Test as this is the criteria for their oral proficiency. In non-native English country like India and China, no preference is given to learn all these skills. Only few study materials are provided to them to memorize the answers. No preference is to be laid in building of Rhetoric among the candidates. The major objective of the book is:

- ✯ Making the IELTS candidates proficient in the Speaking Test by teaching them all the Rhetorical devices like *Word Stress, Intonation, Rhythm, Cohesive Devices, Fluency and Lexical Resource*.
- ✯ All these techniques should be properly designed and provided to the students in the form of study materials.
- ✯ Sound recorder (self-created by students in bobile phones) software should be used to maintain the Rate of Speech in the IELTS Speaking Task 2.

★ Speech Therapies should be given to the students to twist their tongues in L2.

In 2001, the IELTS interview format and criteria were revised. A major change was the shift from a single global scale to a set of four analytic scales focussing on different aspects of oral proficiency. This study is concerned with the validity of the analytical rating scales. It aims to verify the descriptors used to define the score points on the scales by providing empirical evidence for the criteria in terms of their overall focus, and their ability to distinguish levels of performance.

The Speaking Test band descriptors and criteria key indicators were analyzed in order to identify relevant analytical categories for each of the *four band scales: fluency, grammatical range and accuracy, lexical resource and pronunciation.*

The Speaking Skills Checklist is like this:

Production Skills, Pronunciation: Rhythm, Number and Length of Pauses, Stress, Intonation Contours.

Communication Skills: Fluency, Clarity, Coherence, Confidence Cultural Appropriateness

Language Skills: Grammatical Accuracy, Grammatical Range, Vocabulary

But how an IELTS student will build these skills is still the matter of discussion. The IELTS Books/Instructors or even the organization of IELTs are mum in this matter. No doubt, we can get this matter by netsurfing over different websites but what about the authenticity of the study material. The main problem in non –native English Country, how students twist their tongue in L2 (English Language) because while learning the language, they automatically get the influence of L1 (Mother Tongue) because it is their native language and this is natural. Nobody avoids it but learning global (English) Language with the help of Vocal Cosmetics/Rhetorical Devices will improve their tongue twisting into L2 (Second Language Acquisition) which automatically improve the proficiency of the candidate in the IELTS Speaking and Writing Test.

Keeping this viewpoint in mind, I have decided to put forth some technical aspects of learning, writing & speaking English through the medium of this book.This will truly help the students to speak good and perfect English.

Constructive suggestions are welcome. For any of your queries, please contact the author, Ms. Jyoti Malhotra.

Why IELTS-Tech is a Big Requirement:

- ✯ Candidates are not scoring more than 5.5 to 6.5 bands (A type of scoring system in which you are scored from 0-9 on a scale)
- ✯ Not able to speak English fluently
- ✯ Institutions are providing only practice sessions and not techniques to appear in the IELTS
- ✯ Lack of knowledge of Grammatical rules
- ✯ Speak more but score less
- ✯ Lack of standardised words, while speaking English
- ✯ Lack of ideas for attempting TASK 2 in Writing as well as the Speaking Task 1, 2 and 3
- ✯ Influence of Mother Tongue over the Second Language

IELTS-Tech Tool Kit

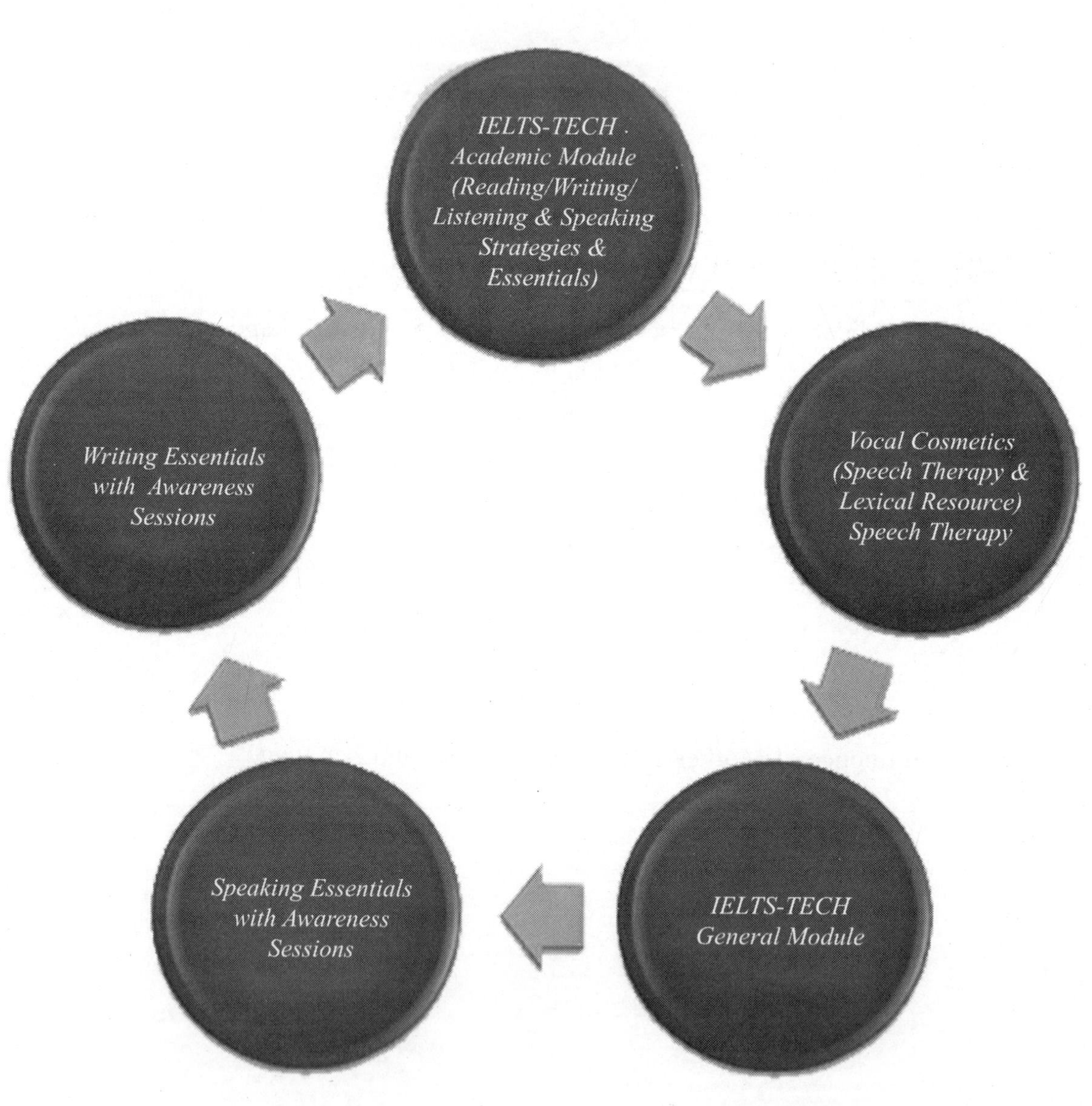

Meanings of Important Terms

VOCAL COSMETICS

A cosmetic for improving your voice. This product will fulfill the technical requirements of the candidate's English which includes understanding of Words, Stress, Intonation and Syllable.

Speech Therapy

This product will enhance the tongue-twisting abilities of the candidate.

Awareness Sessions

This product will improve the exposure of the candidate to the current affairs. This also offers the candidate, complete choice of words, proverbs, etc. For this purpose, chapters are designed in the PowerPoint format to improve the writing and speaking skills of the candidate.

Lexical Resource

This product will help the candidate to improve the usage of words at different levels of speaking and writing.

Band Descriptors

Reading Description

- ☆ 40 Questions
- ☆ 40 Marks

Listening Description

- ☆ 40 Questions
- ☆ 40 Marks

Writing Band Description

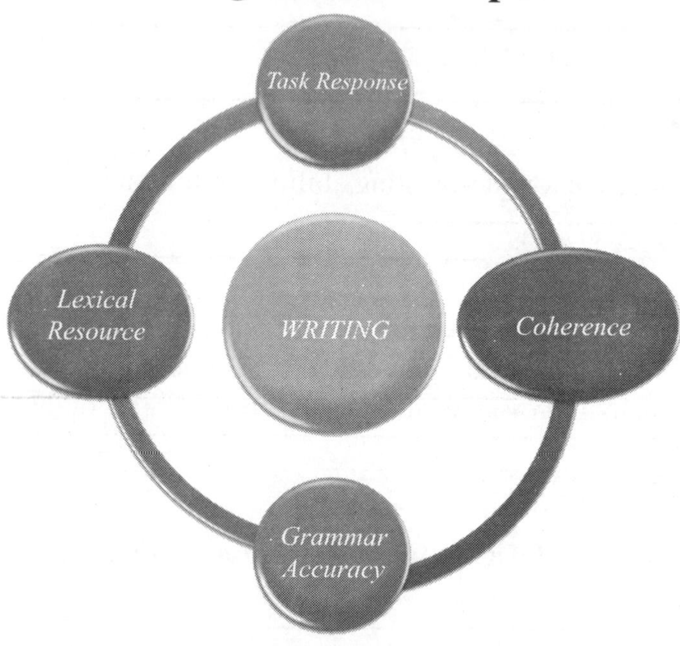

Speaking Band Description

Speaking Criteria	Bands
Fluency	1 Band
Word Stress Accent	2 Band
Intonation	3 Band
Rhythm	4 Band
Lexical Resource	5 Band
Coherence	6 Band
Grammar Accuracy	7 Band
L2	8 Band
Cultural Appro	9 Band

Note: *L2* – It's a level of listening proficiency

Cultural Appro – It is appropriate culturally according to the English language culture and traditions

IELTS Exam Criteria

Listening-40 Minutes	*Reading-60 Minutes*
Writing-60 Minutes	*Speaking-15 Minutes*

ABSTRACT

READING MODULE

This chapter helps the candidate to know about the strategies and skills for cracking the IELTS Reading Test, which includes its two basic techniques i.e., Skimming & Scanning along with different types of questions involved in the reading test. At the end of the module students will be able to practise those questions which are essential for the reading test.

Skimming and Scanning

Meaning: Skimming refers to a General Overview of the Reading Passage.

How to Approach Skimming in Reading Passage

A. Tensions are an inseparable part of our existence. If we have to live, we must be ready to face tensions. There is no panacea to get rid of them. Modern life has become so hectic that we cannot dream of life without tensions.

B. First of all, we should analyse our problems and find out the causes of the problems that we face in our daily life. If we diagnose the problems, it would be easy to seek a solution. Sharc your problems with your relatives because it is a common saying – 'Grief shared is grief halved'. The other way to reduce your tensions is to keep yourself busy. It is rightly said: 'The busiest person is the happiest person'. Apart from our daily routine, we should do some social welfare activities. In isolation, our grief is doubled. We should go for walks and participate in group activities.

C. Meditation, especially in the modern materialistic world, has become the last resort for the human beings of today. It purifies and enlightens our Mind and Body.

Skimming

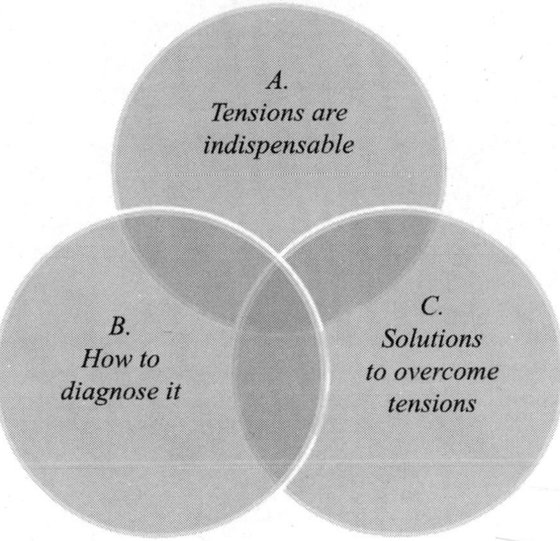

Meaning: Scanning means to reach the corridors of the reading passage.

How to Approach Scanning in the Reading Passage Test

A. Tensions are an inseparable part of our existence. If we have to live, we must be ready to face tensions. There is no panacea to get rid of them. Modern life has become so hectic that we cannot dream of life without tensions.

B. First of all, we should analyse our problems and find out the causes of the various problems that we face in our day-to-day life. If we diagnose the problem, it would be easy to seek a solution. Share your problems with your relatives because it is a common saying- 'Grief shared is grief halved'. The other way to reduce your tension is to keep yourself busy. It is rightly said: 'The busiest person is the happiest person.' Apart from our daily routine, we should do some social welfare activities. In isolation, our grief is doubled. We should go for walks and participate in group activities.

C. Meditation, especially in the modern materialistic world, has become the last resort for the human beings of today. It purifies and enlightens our Mind and Body.

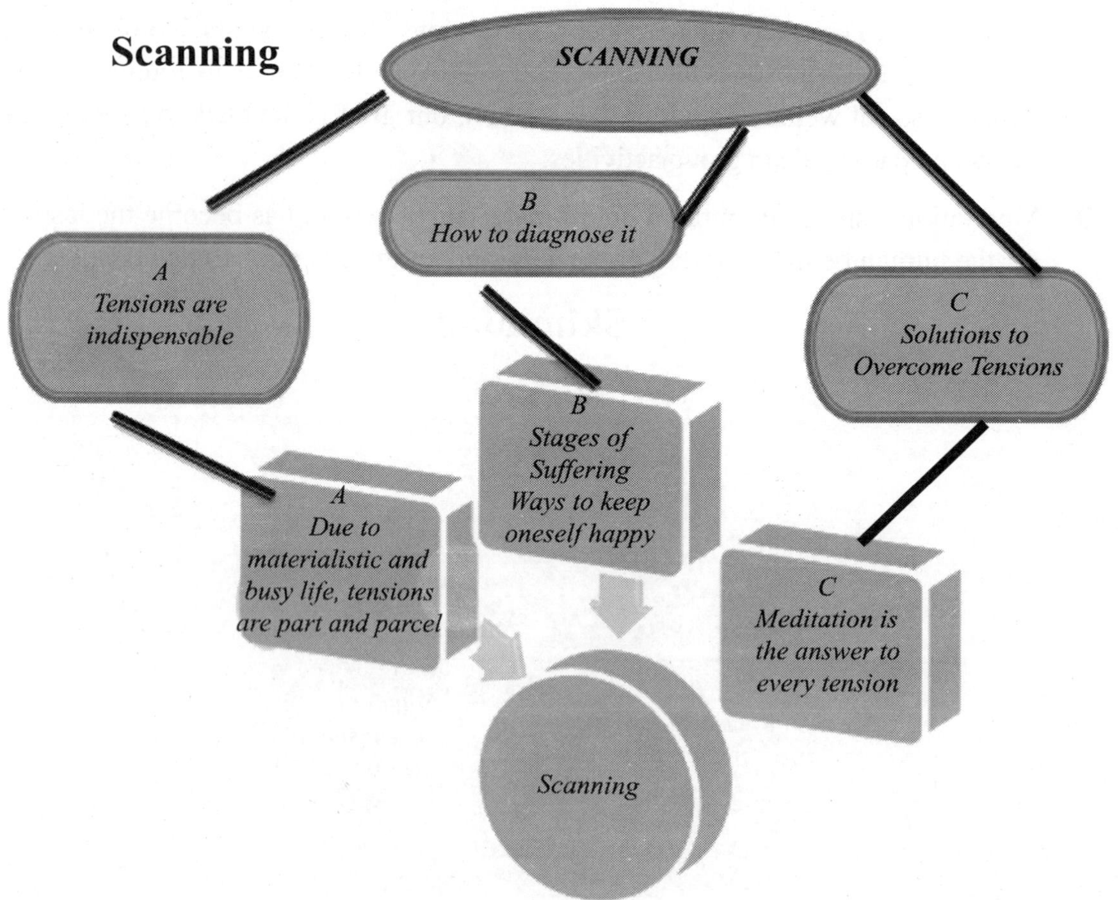

- *Read the paragraph only once using the technique of Skimming and Scanning.*
- *Always remember, Scanning is the consequence of Skimming interrogation. It is an answer to the query that occurs in Skimming.*
- *Always manage to get the general idea of each paragraph and then try to get the real meaning. In simple words, Do "POST MORTEM" of each paragraph.*

Different Types of Questions in Reading Test:

1. *Summary Completion*
2. *Multiple Choice Questions*
3. *Table Completion*
4. *Sentence Completion*
5. *Short Answer Questions*
6. *Choosing Headlines*
7. *Say True or False*

Type No. 1
Summary Completion

Hints

• *Meditation*	• *Tension*	• *Happy*
• *Busy*	• *Face*	• *Existence*
• *Grief*	• *Happiest*	

Example: *Modern Life is full of .... In order to live life one has to .... tensions. Tensions problems can be overcome if we share our .... with our kith and kin. One should be .... in their daily life. Then definitely they lead the .... life. The last resort to keep oneself happy is ....*

Solution: *Modern Life is full of .... **tensions** .... In order to live life one has to ... **face** ...... tensions. Tensions can be overcome if we share our ... **Grief**.............. with our kith and kin. One should be ...... **Happy** .... in their daily life. Then definitely they lead ... the **Happiest** .... Life. The last resort to keep oneself happy is .... **Meditation** ....*

Passage

A. Tensions are an inseparable part of our existence. If we have to live, we must be ready to face tensions. There is no panacea to get rid of them. Modern life has become so hectic that we cannot dream of life without tensions.

B. First of all, we should analyse our problem and find out the cause of the problem. If we diagnose the problem, it would be easy to seek a solution. Share your problems with your relatives because it is a common saying- 'Grief shared is grief halved'. The other way to reduce your tensions is to keep yourself busy. It is rightly said: 'The busiest person is the happiest person'. Apart from our daily routine, we should do some social welfare activities. In isolation, our grief is doubled. We should go for walks and participate in group activities.

C. Meditation, especially in the modern materialistic days, has become the last resort for modern human beings. It purifies and enlightens our Mind and Body.

Points to Remember

- *Always look for the right word from the given passage.*
- *Understanding of passage is must for solving the summary completion type questions.*

Type No. 2

Multiple Choice Questions

Choose the appropriate one from the following options:

A. **Tensions are due to**

a. Materialism

b. Life

c. Hectic Life

d. Grief

B. **Tensions can be overcome by**

a. Sharing

b. Crying

c. Being happy

d. Purifying

C. **Meditation helps to**

a. Enlighten the heart

b. Enlighten the Mind

c. Enlighten the Human Beings

d. Enlighten both the Mind and the Body

Passage

A. Tensions are an inseparable part of our existence. If we have to live, we must be ready to face tensions. There is no panacea to get rid of them. Modern life has become so hectic that we cannot dream of life without tensions.

B. First of all, we should analyse our problem and find out the cause of the problem. If we diagnose the problem, it would be easy to seek a solution. Share your problems with your relatives because it is a common saying – 'Grief shared is grief halved'. The other way to reduce your tensions is to keep yourself busy. It is rightly said: 'The busiest person is the happiest person'. Apart from our daily routine, we should also do some social welfare activities. In isolation, our grief is doubled. We should go for walks and participate in group activities.

C. Meditation, particularly in the modern materialistic days, has become the last resort for the modern human beings. It purifies and enlightens our Mind and Body.

Answers: c, a, d

Points to Remember

While choosing an option, make sure the option must have the description in the paragraph. For example, in the first question, 'A' 'B' 'C' seem to be the right option. But 'C' is the right answer as that option is mentioned in the first paragraph of the passage.

Sometimes the answer is hidden in the SYNONYMS and the ANTONYMS of the words mentioned in the options.

Type No. 3
Table Completion

Example: Complete the table by filling in the suitable option.

Causes	Effects	Voluntary Suggestions	Compulsory Suggestions
1.	Isolation	3.	5. ....
Hectic Life	2.	4.	

A. Tensions are an inseparable part of our existence. If we have to live, we must be ready to face tensions. There is no panacea to get rid of them. Modern life has become so hectic that we cannot dream of life without tensions.

B. First of all, we should analyse our problem and find out the cause of the problem. If we diagnose the problem, it would be easy to seek a solution. Share your problems with your relatives because it is a common saying- 'Grief shared is grief halved.' The other way to reduce your tensions is to keep yourself busy. It is rightly said: 'The busiest person is the happiest person'. Apart from our daily routine, we should do some social welfare activities. In isolation, our grief is doubled. We should go for walks and participate in group activities.

C. Meditation, especially in the modern materialistic world, has become the last resort for the human beings of today. It purifies and enlightens our Mind and Body.

Solution:

Causes	Effects	Voluntary Suggestions	Compulsory Suggestions
1. Materialistic Life	Isolation	3. Sharing	5. Meditation
Hectic Life	2. Grief	4. Participation	

Points to Remember

Always remember to divide the whole passage into 'Rhetorical Devices', i.e., each passage contains the following inputs: Introduction, Meaning, Causes, Effects, Solutions, Conclusion.

Type No. 4

Short Answer Questions

A. Tensions are an inseparable part of our existence. If we have to live, we must be ready to face tensions. There is no panacea to get rid of them. Modern life has become so hectic that we cannot dream of life without tensions.

B. First of all, we should analyse our problem and find out the cause of the problem. If we diagnose the problem, it would be easy to seek a solution. Share your problems with your relatives because it is a common saying- 'Grief shared is grief halved'. The other way to reduce your tensions is to keep yourself busy. It is rightly said: 'The busiest person is the happiest person'. Apart from our daily routine, we should do some social welfare activities. In isolation, our grief is doubled. We should go for walks and participate in group activities.

C. Meditation, especially in the modern materialistic world, has become the last resort for the modern human beings. It purifies and enlightens our Mind and Body.

Questions:

1. Why can't we think life without tensions?

   ....

2. How do our grief get doubled?

   ....

3. Why is meditation necessary in modern times?

   ....

Solution:

Q. Why can't we think life without tensions?

A. Tensions are indispensable...

Q. How do our grief get doubled?

A. When Not Shared...

Q. Why meditation is necessary in modern times?

A. It enlightens our Mind and Body.....................

Points to Remember

Always choose three words from the paragraph to complete the sentences.

Type No. 5

Sentence Completion

A. Tensions are the inseparable part of our existence. If we have to live, we must be ready to face tensions. There is no panacea to get rid of them. Modern life has become so hectic that we cannot dream of life without tensions.

B. First of all, we should analyse our problems and find out the cause of the problem. If we diagnose the problem, it would be easy to seek solutions. Share your problems with your relatives because it is a common saying- 'Grief shared is grief halved'. The other way to reduce your tensions is to keep yourself busy. It is rightly said: 'The busiest person is the happiest Person'. Apart from our daily routine, we should do some social welfare activities. In isolation our grieve are doubled.We should go for walks and participate in group activities.

C. Meditation, especially in the modern materialistic days, has become the last resort for modern human beings. It purifies and enlightens our Mind and Body.

Questions:

1. Existence of life can be possible only with

   ....

2. Reduce your tensions with

   A...................... B........................ C.......................

3. Meditation purifies

   ....

Solution:

1. Existence of life can be possible only with tensions.
2. Reduce your tensions with

   A. Participation B. Sharing C. Keep busy

3. Meditation purifies and enlightens the Mind and Body.

Type No. 6

Choosing and Matching Headlines

A. Tensions are an inseparable part of our existence. If we have to live, we must be ready to face tensions. There is no panacea to get rid of them. Modern life has become so hectic that we cannot dream of life without tensions.

B. First of all, we should analyse our problems and find out the cause of our problems. If we diagnose the problem, it would be easy to seek a solution. Share your problems with your relatives because it is a common saying 'Grief shared is grief halved.' The other way to reduce your tensions is to keep yourself busy. It is rightly said: 'The busiest person is the happiest person'. Apart from our daily routine, we should do some social welfare activities. In isolation, our grief is doubled. We should go for walks and participate in group activities.

C. Meditation, especially in the modern materialistic world, has become the last resort for the human beings of today. It purifies and enlightens our Mind and Body.

MATCHING HEADLINES

1. Meditation for Body and mind

2. Doubling of Grief

3. Busiest Person is the Happiest Person

4. Tension is part and parcel

5. Diagnoses of Tension

Solutions

A. ....4.............. **B.** ....5........ **C.** ....1.......

Points to Remember

Always try to find the 'BAG' (School Bag) for choosing the headlines for each paragraph. Then it becomes easy to find its copies. For example, sometimes, it is confusing because our thinking strikes at three or four options for one headline. At that point, keep all the confusing aspects at one side and try to find the "father" (means Priority Option/Primary Options) among those confusing options. Like in the above example for 2nd para, three options are suitable: 1. Doubling of Grief 2. The Busiest Person is the Happiest Person 3. Diagnoses of Tension. If chosen 1 and 2 options, some injustification is there with the third one but if the candidate chooses the 3rd option, i.e., Diagnoses of Tension, then other two are automatically adjusted.

Type No. 7
Say True or False

A. Tensions are an inseparable part of our existence. If we have to live, we must be ready to face tensions. There is no panacea to get rid of them. Modern life has become so hectic that we cannot dream of life without tensions.

B. First of all, we should analyse our problem and find out the cause of the problem. If we diagnose the problem, it would be easy to seek a solution. Share your problems with your relatives because it is a common saying- 'Grief shared is grief halved.' The other way to reduce your tensions is to keep yourself busy. It is rightly said: 'The busiest person is the happiest person'. Apart from our daily routine, we should do some social welfare activities. In isolation, our grief is doubled. We should go for walks and participate in group activities.

C. Meditation, especially in the modern materialistic world, has become the last resort for human beings of today. It purifies and enlightens our Mind and Body.

1. *TRUE:* **If the statement is correct**

2. *FALSE:* **If the statement is incorrect**

3. *NOT GIVEN:* **If the statement is not given**

A. Tension causes stress ....

B. Tension brings happiness ....

C. Tension involves grief ....

Points to Remember

Why True for 1. *The statement is said to be 'TRUE' when it is mentioned in paragraph and when the substance is according to the passage.*

Why False for 2. *The statement is said to be 'FALSE' when it is not according to the passage. When the matter is in the form of antonyms and synonyms then the substance is called false. As in the above example- 'Tension Brings Happiness', here happiness is the opposite of grief, so this is false as it has been mentioned, but conveys a wrong information.*

Why NG for 3. *The statement is said to be 'NOT GIVEN', when actually the matter is right but it is not mentioned in the paragraph. For example, in 'Tension causes stress' ...it is true that tension always causes stress, but it has no mention in the whole passage. Not even the word, 'STRESS' is used. So it is a NOT GIVEN or (NG) option.*

Reading Test - 1

PASSAGE 1

You should spend about 20 minutes on Questions 1-15 which are based on Passage 1 given below.

Lemon

.........nature's invaluable gift.

An innocuous, clear light yellow coloured fruit with a tangy sour taste known as the lemon should not be easily dismissed. The lemon is one of the richest sources of vitamin C available to man (the others being the gooseberry and the orange) and possesses invaluable anti-infection properties. Vitamin C is undoubtedly one of nature's all purpose remedies which helps the body fight off health challenges.

Regular intake of vitamin C, otherwise known as Ascorbic Acid, keeps the body well-toned, active and strong by refusing to let bacterial and viruses invade its defenssces. Vitamin C is extremely necessary for the proper functioning of the immune system, especially during an illness.

A very interesting and unique feature of this particular vitamin is that in a healthy body, it is absorbed in moderate amounts – so much and no more – while excesses are instantly rejected. But when a person automatically is deficient of the Vitamins, the body's need of Vitamin C increases tremendously and having it in greater amounts being beneficial, the body miraculously starts absorbing large quantities of it. But even while needing extra supplements, it is better to take it in smaller doses several times in the day to facilitate absorption rather than a lot at one time.

Vitamin C is also an indispensable ingredient in the forming of cologne – the protein that helps to form the connective tissue in the skin – consequently, people with burn injury need more of it to help recover quickly. Lemon with its high natural acid content helps in digestion and acts as an *efficacious counter-irritant*. When a meal has been too rich in fats, the easiest, cheapest, least dangerous and the most natural antedote is the juice of a lemon diluted with water, which immediately corrects the body's discomfort by coughing fat.

The juice of a freshly squeezed lemon in a glass of warm water goes a long way in keeping a person "slim' n 'thin" and is an ideal way to reduce excess weight.

When fagged out or feeling low on stamina, one of the simplest ways to get energy is to squeeze a quarter of a lemon into a glass of cold water, add to it a pinch of salt and two spoonfuls of honey and one has a fresh, natural healthy tonic that will have one zipping off again.

For those who might find it too sour, add tangy to be taken with water, a dash of lemon over fresh salad, cooked vegetables or lentils will ensure the daily quota of Vitamin C. Where then is the need for pills and capsules?

Apart from its aids to one's inside, externally too, the multifaceted lemon has innumerable uses. Fresh lemon juice rubbed on the scalp just half-an–hour before washing the hair helps to effectively control dandruff. Rubbed over teeth, it lightens stains and sets them sparkling. *To curb a nauseous feeling, lemon is a boon taken with a little salt and pepper.*

Besides its mild, healthy bleaching properties, lemon juice is an excellent natural cleanser. Diluted with a little water (for it should never be applied in a concentrated form) applied gently and left on for 8 to 10 minutes, it imparts a super glow, leaving even the dullest skin looking radiant. With its tingling freshness, it is one of the best astringents for an oily skin and being natural, costs a fraction of what others synthetic astringents cost. However, care should be taken to see that there is no broken skin, and wait until it is healed before applying.

Fresh salad greens when washed in highly diluted lemon water, stay fresh much longer than otherwise, as to fruits like apples, guavas and pears which otherwise turn a dull brown.

Silver jewellery that has lost its shine is best soaked in lemon juice and then see it looks as good as new. Copper cleansed with lemon juice glows brilliantly. Silk clothes dipped for a final rinse in cold water to which lime juice has been added, shimmer with an extra special sheen even as the dye is strengthened.Truly, the lemon is incredibly versatile and has a hundred different and supremely effective uses. So don't just give it a go-by, but stretch your hands towards it as often as possible.... it will not be in vain.

Caution: Lemon is contraindicated in cough, asthma, low blood pressure or chronic body-ache. One should consume less lemon in winter in comparison to summer. During the rainy season, one can use it liberally. Lemon can be taken with water, fruit juices, pulses, vegetables or salads. One should not consume pure undiluted lemon juice by itself. Because of its acidic and burning properties, it causes heartburn. Undoubtedly, lemon is a useful fruit. Every member of the family that consumes one lemon a day lives to be healthy, happy and cheerful.

QUESTIONS 1-6

Use NO MORE THAN THREE WORDS from the passage to complete each blank.

1. Rich in ....
2. Reduces ....
3. Contains ....
4. Necessary for ....
5. .... Proteins
6. Recover ....

QUESTIONS 7-9

Complete the text below by using NO MORE THAN THREE WORDS.

7. Lemon juice is an excellent cleanser for ....
8. Lemon is good for ....
9. Bad for ....

QUESTIONS 10-15

Do the following statements agree with the information given in the Reading Passage 1?

In the boxes, 10-15 on your answer sheet, write–

YES .... If the statement agrees with the information in the passage.
NO .... If the statement contradicts with the information in the passage.
NOT GIVEN .... If there is no information about the statement in the passage.

10. LEMON is a counter irritant when squeezed in warm water.
11. LEMON has bleaching properties that prove to be a boon when rubbed over the teeth and scalp.
12. LEMON is pungent, wormicidal and also alleviates stomach disorder.

13. LEMON is especially rich in vitamins 'B' 'C' and also in calcium.

14. LEMON, a boon for fruits, bane for salads.

15. LEMON is acidic in nature.

PASSAGE 2

You should spend about 20 minutes on Questions 16-27 which are based on the Reading Passage–2 given below.

Tablets *vs* Textbooks

........Education moves from Books to Tablets.......

A. As the popularity of tablets for education grows, parents and teachers are embracing technology's role in toddlers' development. When loaded with e-books, games and educational programming, the tablet becomes a great learning tool for young children. Parents or caregivers don't have to look a library of cardboard books around; they can store a library on their tablets, so reading can continue wherever they are. A child's favourite stories are easily found with e-reader apps, like Kindle for Android and NOOK for Android by B&N, each offering children's e-books with brilliant illustrations and playful features. Many e-books have a read-aloud function, allowing children to hear and see new words. 'The Pop Out!' 'Tale of Peter Rabbit' app, etc. even let children control characters.

B. Interactive games on a tablet's large, HD-quality screen, along with impressive sound quality, can help toddlers develop fine motor skills and correlate sound to vision. Games with bright, colourful graphics and fun noises make toddlers excited to play and learn. For example, in the game, *Pee ka boo Barn*, children open barn doors to find animals, learning about the cause and effect and becoming familiar with animal names and sounds in English or Spanish. Another game, *Number Hide and Seek*, helps toddlers learn numbers and counting through a rhyming story. Parents can stream educational television shows and movies from just about anywhere using apps like view Dini, a video portal that streamlines access to videos from a wide range of content providers. Popular shows and movies, including favourites, such as 'Bob the Builder' and 'Barney', are available with access to user ratings and plot summaries to ensure it is 'kid-friendly' programming. If Big Bird or Elmo is a favourite, there's the Sesame Street Video app that offers many educational videos featuring the lovable characters.

C. Publisher Houghton Mifflin Harcourt tested an interactive, digital version of an Algebra 1 textbook for Apple's iPad in California's Riverside Unified School District. Students who used the iPad version scored 20 percent higher on standardized tests versus students who learnt with traditional textbooks. The program, which replaced worn textbooks with interactive, digital versions with video, graphics and built-in quizzes that invited students to participate and give instant feedback, spurred positive comments that students using the iPad version were 'more motivated, attentive, and engaged' than those with the paper algebra books. This pilot program reveals when it comes to engaging today's students, it's not the content that matters, but the format. Students in the California experiment accessed the same content on the iPad as in a traditional book, but those who used the digital version tested higher. That may not be true for all subjects and over time. A small but growing number of researchers are uncovering evidence that readers are better able to remember what they read in printed books long-term when compared to materials read via an electronic screen, raising questions about tablets in the classroom.

For example, Kate Garland, a lecturer in psychology at the University of Leicester in England, conducted a study on the effects of e-books on memory, 'bombarding' psychology students with questions on economics on digital and printed versions of texts, and found learning differences.Students using digital versions of the unfamiliar material had to read the same information several times to gain the same level of knowledge as print readers. Students reading printed books seemed to more fully digest and understand the materials. Tablets' success in replacing textbooks will also come down to educational apps. Between them, Apple and Google offer over a millions apps, and educators will be challenged to curate the best and most appropriate for schools. Students with special learning needs may offer the most concrete evidence of the benefits of tablets in the classroom. Advocates, desperate to bridge the educational gaps in children with learning issues, are ahead of traditional educational leaders, since children with special learning needs used tablets and apps early on.

D. Apps help autistic children develop skills, but experts believe the wide spectrum of disorder and novelty of the technology needs to be tightly integrated and supported by sound educational research to more completely address the challenges facing children with special needs. Some tablet apps help give those with language delays a voice, while others help kids learn to navigate often bewildering social situations and reduce their stress. Yet some apps improve fine-motor skills to help children write and manipulate small objects, offering evidence that tablets do have concrete benefits in the classroom, at least for some students.

E. Though tablets are a recent phenomenon, many students in high school and college have been using smartphones for years, and are already well-acquainted with *touchscreen technology*. Because they've become so accustomed to using these devices, students are increasingly expecting to use them in the classroom setting. When classrooms don't implement what has now become 'everyday' technology, we're doing students a disservice. Additionally, students and consumers in general, are becoming more comfortable using tablets for advanced tasks. According to a new Nielsen survey, 35% of the tablet owners said they used their desktop computers less often or not at all now, and 32% of the laptop users said the same. Most tellingly, more than 75% of the tablet owners said they used their tablet for tasks they once used their desktop or laptop for. While tablets can't totally match laptops in terms of functionally (yet), they can get today's students most of the way there.

F. The appeal of tablets to a college student is obvious: They're thin, lightweight, and spring to life without delay, making them much easier to take it to and use in class than a laptop or a netbook. Longer battery life means students don't have to worry about carrying a charger with them. Forgot what the professor said at the end of class about the mid-term? Launch Tegrity, tap the lecture and replay it in just seconds. That's faster than texting a half-dozen classmates and waiting for what might be an inaccurate response.

G. Some of the most innovative software around is being developed specifically for tablets. In addition to the thousands of exciting educational apps available, tablets are fully compatible with online teaching and learning platforms, such as Blackboard, which are becoming the norm at colleges and universities. In fact, tablets' current shortcomings — limited multitasking — could be their greatest asset in education, as it forces students to focus on one task at a time.

H. Cloud-based solutions have become evern more popular with colleges and universities, which are looking to deliver synchronised experiences that are device agnostic. Tablets align well with this trend, given their portability and options for constant connectivity. With tablets and cloud-based systems, students can work anywhere on campus and make sure that their work is saved in a central location and accessible from all of their devices. They also don't have to pay for computing power that they no longer need.

I. One of the primary reasons that tablets have been slow to penetrate the higher education market was their limited availability. Apple's supply chain issues and the difficulty that some Android tablet manufacturers have faced in getting their products to market have made it difficult for schools to get serious about adopting it. As these issues are resolved over the coming year, expect to see more and more tablets popping up on campuses. Lower price points will make tablets even more appealing to colleges and universities. For close to a year, Apple went virtually unchallenged in the tablet market. Increased competition should drive down the prices. The wave of tablets introduced at CES in January is just the tip of the iceberg. With dozens to hundreds of offerings, many based on Google's open source Android OS, expect price points to fall quickly just as they have for laptops, smartphones and HDTV sets. Heck, Apple's original iPad can be had for as little as $349 if you get the timing right and don't mind a refurb. How close are we today to tablets displacing computers on campuses? Closer than you might think, I wrote this article on a tablet with a touchscreen keyboard.

QUESTIONS 16-22

Passage 2 has nine sections A-I

Choose the correct headline for each section from the list of headings below. Write the correct number, i –xi in the boxes 16-22 on your answer sheet.

List of Headings

i. Tablets are Becoming More Available
ii. Tablets have the Software to be Competitive
iii. Classrooms are Ready for Tablets
iv. Tablets Integrate with Educational IT Trends
v. Do Tablets Really Improve Learning?
vi. TABLETS are Inevitable
vii. Implications Related Tablets
viii. Tablets Fit Students' Lifestyles
ix. Spectrum of Tablet Apps
x. Tablets for Toddlers
xi. Tablets Replacing Textbooks

Example ………………… Answer

Paragraph A ………………… vi

16. Paragraph B …………………

17. Paragraph C …………………..

Example ………………… Answer

Paragraph D ………………… ix

18. Paragraph E ……………………

19. Paragraph F ……………………

20. Paragraph G ……………………

21. Paragraph H ……………………..

22. Paragraph I ……………………….

QUESTIONS 23- 27

Use information from the passage to complete the table below. Use no more than three words for each space.

Tablet Apps	Titles
KINDLE & NOOK	23 ....
DINI	A Video Portal
BOB THE BUILDER & BARNEY	24 ....
Algebera 1	25 ....
TEGRITY	26 ....
Blackboard	27 ....

PASSAGE 3

You should spend about 20 minutes on Questions 28-40 which are based on Passage 3 below.

Revolution in Radiation Therapy

A. Radiotherapy is one of the most effective treatments for the majority of cancers and with surgery, remains the most effective way of curing many cancers. As a hopeful world looks for a miracle that will cure cancer once and for all, a major revolution in cancer treatment has been quietly taking place in *Radiation Onocology*. The use of radiation for the treatment of cancer had its primitive beginnings at the turn of the 19th century and not long after the discovery of X-rays in 1895 by the German physicist, **Wilhelm Roentgen**. **Emil Grubbe** was the first person to use X-rays to treat a patient with breast cancer.

B. Radiation can destroy all tissues, both normal and tumour tissues. The goal of Radiotherapy is to maximise killing of the tumours and minimise normal tissue toxicity as well as preserve its functions. With conventional radiation therapy, X-ray pictures are taken and treatment areas are drawn on X-ray films. A large safety margin is given around the targeted area. But internal anatomy is not well-correlated with the external marking. Hence, there is always a risk of missing tumour and also damaging the normal tissues. New developments on computer technology led to an enormous evolution of radiotherapy techniques.

Advanced Radio Therapy techniques are:

Intensity Modulation Radiation Therapy(IMRT)

C. When using conventional radiotherapy, the intensity of beams throughout the radiation field is constant. The new technique called 'intensity modulated radiation therapy' allows modulation of beam intensity within the treatment field to obtain highly precise dose delivery and reduce the dose to normal tissues. It has two major benefits. The first is that a lesser dose to normal organs will cause lesser side effects. The second is that it allows an increased dose to be delivered to the tumour which in turn translates to better tumour control and survival.

Image Guided Radiation Therapy (IGRT)

D. Linear accelerators are equipped with various imaging modalities that allow acquiring high quality CTSCANS of the patient on the treatment table to locate the position of the tumour before delivering radiation dose. During a course of radiation treatment, the size and shape of the cancer tumour can change from one day to the next. The tumour location can also change as a patient breathes during treatment. Image Guided Radiation Therapy enables us to correct a patient's position or the radiation beams and thereby compensates for these changes.

In head and neck cancer patients, for example, the Intensity Modulated Radiation Therapy (IMRT) focusses treatment on the tumour reducing exposure of the nearby salivary glands. These patients treated with IMRT are thus less likely to develop dry mouth.We an deliver IMRT confidently if we have Image Guided Radiation Therapy (IGRT).

Hence *IMRT* and *IGRT* are complimentary.

Stereotactic Radiosurgery (SRS) & Stereotactic Body Radiation Therapy (SBRT)

E. Radiosurgery is a radiation delivery procedure that precisely delivers large radiation doses to tumours and other relevant anatomical targets in a single session or in a small fraction of sessions. Modern machines (e.g. Novalis Tx) can deliver this treatment at submillimeter accuracy. The goal of this non-invasive procedure is to destroy or make tumour inactive without harming nearby healthy tissues and without involving traditional surgery. This technique has drastically reduced the number of visits necessary for the treatment. Patients can go back to normal life quicker than before. Historically, radiosurgery began by treating targets in the brain and has now extended to targets in other organs like lung, liver pancreas, etc. This strategy can be more effective at killing or controlling certain types of cancer.

F. With the development of radiotherapy techniques, problematic disease sites, untreatable or restricted to inadequate treatment can now be routinely treated with radiation and with minimal risk of causing harm. We can now cure more cancers with fewer complications than ever before. Current developments in radiation therapy are commendable. If used judiciously, this already established modality will gain even greater importance in days to come.

QUESTIONS 28-35

Complete the following summary using information from the passage.

Choose your answers from the WORD LIST and write the appropriate alphabet from the word list to fill each of the blanks Write your answers in Boxes 28-35 on your answer sheet.

Radiotherapyisoneofthemostsignificant**28.**................inthehistoryofradiation**29.**................ . Its roots lie in the discovery of **30.** .... when it was first use to treat a patient with breast cancer. Killing of tumours and maintaining normal tissues toxicity are its **31.** .... and **32.** .... objectives. IMRT provides beam intensity. **33.** .... dose to tumour **34.** .... dose to normal organs. IGRT technique is used; for this purpose of **35.** .... of the patient has to be done.

WORD LIST

A. CT SCAN	**B.** Maximise	**C.** High
D. Conventional	**E.** Radiation	**F.** X-ray
G. Oncology	**H.** Minimise	**I.** Normal Tissues
J. Miracle	**K.** Lesser	**L.** Intensity
M. Radiotherapy	**N.** Surgery	

QUESTIONS 36-40

Complete the sentences below. Choose No More Than Three Words from the passage for each answer. Write your answers in boxes 36-40 on your answer sheet.

36. .... procedure that help to destroy tumour without disturbing normal healthy tissues.

RADIO SURGERY IS A **37.** ....

Modern Machine of RADIO SURGERY **38.** ....

Historically, it targets **39.** ....

Contemporarily, it targets **40.** ....

Reading Test 1

Answers

Passage 1

1. Vitamin C
2. Excess Weight
3. Ascorbic acid
4. Immune System
5. Cologne
6. Burn Injuries
7. Oily Skin
8. Fresh Salads
9. Fruits
10. No.
11. YES
12. Not Given
13. Not Given
14. No
15. YES

Passage 2

16. Vii
17. V
18. iii
19. Viii
20. ii
21. iv
22. i
23. E-books
24. Kid-friendly programming
25. Apple iPad textbook
26. Tapping the lectures
27. Online teaching platforms

Passage 3

28. J
29. G
30. F
31. B
32. H
33. C
34. K
35. A
36. Non-invasive
37. Radiation delivery procedure
38. Novalis Tx
39. Brain
40. Lungs, Liver and Pancreas.

Reading Test 2

PASSAGE 1

You should spend about 20 minutes on Questions 1-11 which are based on the Passage 1 below.

Neo-Luddites – Anti-Technology Extremists

A. Change causes problems, not least the anxiety it generates among those whose very livelihood is threatened. Yet there are people who seem to thrive on change, enjoying the constant flow of challenges. There is a bit of the Luddite in all of us when we are faced with adapting to the onslaught of technological developments at work. In the early 19th century, the luddites revolted against the introduction of what was new technology in their time by breaking machinery which was replacing workers. The pace of change today is much faster, a situation in which certain types of people flourish. To them the constant movement involved in change is like a drug. They become addicted very quickly, harnessing the power of technological advances and creating new opportunities, not just for themselves, but for others as well.

B. Neo-Luddite is someone who believes that the use of technology has serious ethical, moral and social ramifications. Operating under this belief, Neo-Luddites are critical of technology and cautious to promote its early adoption. While they are not necessarily opposed to technology, they would prefer to see a more serious discussion of the role of technology in society. Some Neo-Luddites actually dislike technology, opting for a life of 'voluntary simplicity', but this is not always the case.

C. The term, 'Luddite' comes from a political movement during the Industrial Revolution. The Luddites disliked the spread of mechanical devices, such as mechanised looms to accomplish tasks which were formerly performed by the people. They held marches, destroyed factories and engaged in other types of activism in an attempt to prevent further technological development. Ultimately, the Luddites were unsuccessful, but when people started to question technology in large numbers again in the 1970s, they revived the concept, calling themselves the 'New Luddites,' and the *Neo-Luddite Movement* was born.

D. In many cases, people who have questions about the use of technology do not necessarily refer to themselves as Neo-Luddites, although some do. Instead, it is often used in a deprecating way by the advocates of technology, to suggest that the thinking of Neo-Luddites is outdated and outmoded. *The fantastic failure of the original Luddite Movement is sometimes cited as an argument that opposition to technology is ultimately fruitless.*

E. The Neo-Luddite position is that rather than assuming that technology is always neutral or even beneficial, people should think about the ramifications of technology. For example, advanced life supporting systems now allow people to live much longer than was possible in previous eras, but these lives are not always fulfilling or happy. Technology is also used in a variety of ways which could be perceived as harmful; for example, several cities use extensive surveillance systems to keep an eye on the populace, which many people see as a breach of privacy. Members of this movement revolted against the introduction of new technology as it converted the old fashioned factories with computers and robots. Witnessing the conversion of world into 'Silicon Valleys' made them extremists.

F. Members of this movement are quite diverse, although many are activists and academics. These groups have been known to advocate or engage in criminal activity and plot acts of violence and terrorism in an attempt to advance their extremist goals. They have targeted college and university laboratories, scholars, biotechnology industries, U.S. corporations involved in the computer or airline industry, and others.

They share a similar distrust or wariness of technology, especially the role of corporate profit, rather than human need, in propelling technological change. Some Neo-Luddites are also opponents of globalisation for the same reasons.

G. Most people would not argue with the Neo-Luddite idea that technology is changing the human society, and sometimes even shifting what it means to be human. Stopping to think about the effect of technology on society is the main goal of many Neo-Luddites, some of whom freely admit that some technology can be very beneficial. As often happens with small movements which are critical of a larger social trend, the voices of Neo-Luddites are often overwhelmed by a fringe of minority, making difficult for the voice of reason to be heard. Proponents of technology criticise the Neo-Luddite position, arguing that the benefits of advances in technology far outweigh the potential problems and risks.

QUESTIONS 1-4

Choose the correct letter A, B, C or D. Write the correct letter in box, 1-4 on your answer sheet.

1. Writer hooked for what kind of change

A) Technological Advancements

B) Technological Work

C) Technological Machinery

D) Technological adoption

2. New technology

   A) Flourish fastly

   B) Creating new Opportunities

   C) Harnessing technological advances

   D) All of these

3. Neo-Luddittes

   A) Against the adoption of new technological advancements

   B) Cautious to promote technological advancements and its early adoption

   C) Limitise its usage on social, ethical and moral grounds

   D) Against sedentary life of Silicon Valleys

4. Who believes technology is always nothing but still beneficial, people should think about the modifications of technology?

   A) Luddite

   B) New–Luddite

   C) Neo–Luddites

   D) All of these

QUESTIONS 5-11

Do the following statements agree with the claims of the writer in the Reading Passage 1. In the boxes, 5-11 on your answer sheet, write:

YES ..... If the statement agrees with the information in the passage

NO ..... If the statement contradicts with the information in the passage

NOT GIVEN ..... If there is no information about the statement in the passage

5. Neo-Luddites are against the 'Silicon Valleys' ____________________.

6. Luddites were against in making human obsolete ____________________.

7. Technological advancements leaving the world to elites by extincting the humanity ____________________.

8. Corporate profits propelling due to technological advancements that lead to Luddites Movement more stronger ____________________.

9. Neo-Luddites are extremists ______________________________.

10. Luddites are against computers and robots ______________________.

11. Silicon Valleys propel to technological advancements ______________________ ______________________.

PASSAGE 2

You should spend about 20 minutes on Questions 12-26 which are based on Passage 2 below.

Acupuncture Doesnot Have Any Side Effects

Acupuncture originates from China and has been practised there for thousands of years. Although there are records of acupuncture being used hundreds of years ago in Europe, it was during the second half of the twentieth century that it began to spread rapidly in Western Europe, the United States and Canada. Acupuncture involves the insertion of very thin needles through the patient's skin at specific points on the body – the needles are inserted to various depths. We are not sure how acupuncture works scientifically. However, we do know that it does have some therapeutic benefits, including pain relief and alleviation from nausea caused by chemotherapy.

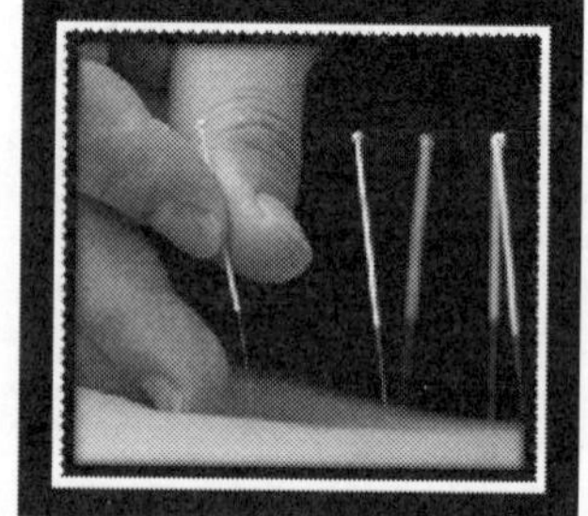

According to traditional Chinese medical theory, acupuncture points are located on meridians through which vital energy runs. There is no histological, anatomical or scientific proof that these *meridians or acupuncture points* exist. Acupuncture remains controversial among the Western medical doctors and scientists. Creating case studies that use proper scientific controls is difficult because of the invasive nature of acupuncture – a clinical study involves a *placebo* (sham product) compared to the targeted treatment. It is very hard to devise a sham acupuncture control that one can compare to proper acupuncture. While some studies have concluded that acupuncture offers similar benefits to a patient as a placebo, others have indicated that there are some real benefits. This article in a peer-reviewed British Medical Journal explains that the principles of acupuncture are firmly grounded in science, and you don't need Chinese philosophy either to make it work, or to practise it.

According to the WHO (World Health Organization) acupuncture is effective for treating 28 conditions, while evidence indicates it may have an effective therapeutic value for many more. People with tensions, headaches and/or migraines may find acupuncture to be very effective in alleviating their symptoms, according to a study carried out at the Technical University of Munich, Germany. Another study at The University of Texas,

M. D. Anderson Cancer Center found that twice weekly acupuncture treatments relieve debilitating symptoms of xerostomia – severe dry mouth – among patients treated with radiation for head and neck cancer.

A search in *The New York Times* shows that acupuncture was first reported in 1854, and about once yearly until 1971.

Acupuncture generally involves several weekly or fortnightly treatments. Most courses consist of up to 12 sessions. A visit to an acupuncturist will involve an exam and an assessment of the patient's condition, the insertion of needles, and advice on self-care. Most sessions last about 30 minutes. The patient will be asked to lie down, either face-up, face-down or on his/her side, depending on where the needless are inserted. The acupuncturist should use single-use disposable sterile needles. As each needle is inserted, the patient should feel them, but initially without pain. However, when the needle reaches the right depth, there should be a deep aching sensation. Sometimes, the needles are heated or stimulated with electricity after insertion. Once inserted, the needles will remain there for about 20 minutes.

Traditional Chinese medicine explains that health is the result of a harmonious balance of the complementary extremes of yin and yan of the life force known as *gi* or *chi*. Qi is said to flow through meridians (pathways) in the human body. Through 350 acupuncture points in the body, these meridians and energy flows may be accessed. Illness is said to be the consequence of an imbalance of the forces. If needles are inserted into these points with appropriate combinations, it is said that the energy flow can be brought back into proper balance. In Western societies and several other parts of the world, acupuncture is explained including concepts of neuroscience. Acupuncture points are seen by Western practitioners as places where nerves, muscles and connective tissue can be stimulated. Acupuncture practitioners say that the stimulation increases the blood flow, while at the same time triggering the activity of our own body's natural painkillers.

Even though acupuncture is commonly used on its own for some conditions, it is becoming very popular as a combination treatment by doctors in the Western Europe and North America. The use of acupuncture to alleviate pain and nausea after surgery is becoming more widespread. Even the US Air Force began teaching 'Battlefield Acupuncture' to physicians deployed to Iraq and Afghanistan in early 2009. Using acupuncture before and during surgery significantly reduces the level of pain and the amount of potent painkillers needed by patients after the surgery is over, a study revealed. Acupuncture is also beginning to make inroads into *veterinary medicine*. This article explains how a mare which had an infection in her ankle was treated by a vet at Virginia-Maryland Regional College of Veterinary Medicine at Virginia Tech with a combination of *acupuncture and traditional therapy*.

As more and more physicians accept acupuncture, a wider range of illnesses and conditions are being considered for acupuncture treatment. A study found that acupuncture may help in digestion symptoms commonly experienced by pregnant women. Some studies have revealed that there are conditions for which acupuncture appears to have no beneficial effect. A study carried out by researchers at Daejon, Busan, South Korea, and Exeter, as well as the United Kingdom, found that acupuncture cannot be shown to have any positive effect on hot flashes during the menopause. However, acupuncture does offer effective relief from hot flashes in women who are being treated with the anti-estrogen tamoxifen following surgery for breast cancer, another study found.

As it is very difficult to devise clinical studies that measure the effectiveness of acupuncture against a placebo, it is hard to create a definitive list of conditions in which acupuncture may be effective. However, some studies have indicated that acupuncture may help in treating low *back pain* (according to the SPINE trial), *fibromyalgia* (Mayo Clinic trials), migraines, *post-operative dental pain* (the Cochrane review), *hypertension* (Center for Integrative Medicine at UC Irvine Study) and *osteoarthritis* (according to researchers at the University Medical Center in Berlin, Germany), as well as chemotherapy-induced nausea and vomiting. Other studies have shown that acupuncture may help women with painful periods. A Cochrane trial found that although acupuncture helps people with headaches, fake acupuncture also seems to help them. Exercise and electro-acupuncture treatments can reduce sympathetic nerve activity in women with polycystic ovarian syndrome, a study found.

Generally, these treatments do not have any side effects. As energy is redirected in the body, internal chemicals and hormones are stimulated and healing begins to take place. Occasionally, the original symptoms worsen for a few days, or other general changes in appetite, sleep, bowel or urination patterns, or emotional state may be triggered. These should not cause concern, as they are simply indications that acupuncture is beginning to work. It is quite common with the first one or two treatments to have sensation of deep relaxation or even mild orientation immediately following the treatment. These pass within short time and never require anything more than a bit of rest to overcome.

QUESTIONS 12-16

Use information from the passage to complete the table below from 12-16. Use No More Than Three Words for each space.

NAME OF THE ORGANISATION/ THEORY/UNIVERSITY	OBSERVATIONS RELATED TO ACUPUNCTURE
Traditional Chinese Medical Theory	Acupuncture located on **12.** .... Through which **13.** .... runs.

The British Medical Journal	Roots of Acupuncture lies in **14.** ....
15.	Acupuncture has effective therapeutic value
Cancer Center of MD Anderson in the **16.**	acupuncture treatments relieve debilitating symptoms of xerostomia

QUESTIONS 17-22

Arrange the steps of acupuncture treatment as given in passage 2 and choose the appropriate letter from the Box to complete the steps mentioned from 17-22 on your answer sheet.

A. Needles are inserted	*Step 1:* **17.** ....
B. Advice on self care	*Step 2:* Visit to Acupuncturist (c)
	Step 3: **18.** ....
C. Visit to Acupuncturist	*Step 4:* **19.** ....
D. Needles are inserted for 20 minutes	
E. Initially, no pain but causing pain and aching sensation if inserted at right positions	*Step 5:* **20.** ....
F. 12 sessions in complete 30 minutes	*Step 6:* **21.** ....
G. Usage of disposable sterile needles	*Step 7:* **22.** ....

QUESTIONS 23-24

Choose the correct letter A, B, C or D. Write the correct letter in box 23-24 on your answer sheet.

23. During Acupuncture, needles are inserted which causes twists in the body parts that lead to the consequence of

A) Low back pain　　B) Illness

C) Headaches　　D) Migranes

24. .... sympathetic nerve activity in women with polycystic ovarian syndrome can be treated with

A) Chemotherapy　　B) Spinal Trials

C) Cochrane　　D) Electro-acupuncture

QUESTIONS 25- 27

Complete the following sentences from 25-27 on your answer sheet.

25. Changes in appetite, sleep, bowel or urination patterns or emotional state indicates

....

26. One or two treatments of acupuncture causes

....

27. Basic thing that is required after a short time is

....

PASSAGE 3

You should spend about 20 minutes on Questions 28-40 which are based on Passage 3 below.

Common Sense is Neither Common Nor Sense

Published on July 12, 2011 by Jim Taylor, Ph.D. in *The Power of Prime*

Common sense, defined as 'sound judgement derived from experience rather than study,' is one of the most revered qualities in America. It evokes images of early and simpler times in which industrious men and women built our country into what it is today. People with common sense are seen as reasonable, down to earth, reliable and practical. But here's the catch. *Common sense is neither common nor sense.* There's not a whole of sound judgement going on these days (though whether it is worse than in the past, I can't be sure), so it's not common. If common sense was common, then most people wouldn't make the kinds of decisions they do every day. People wouldn't buy stuff they can't afford. They wouldn't smoke cigarettes or eat junk food. They wouldn't gamble. And if you want to get really specific and timely, politicians wouldn't be tweeting pictures of their private parts to strangers. In other words, people wouldn't do the multitude of things that are clearly not good for them.

And common sense isn't real sense, if we define sense as being sound judgement, because relying on experience alone doesn't usually offer enough information to draw reliable conclusions. In fact, I think that the so-called common sense is a fallacy that has been foisted on us by our culture of ideology (any ideology that wants to tell us what we should think and do) that prefers us to be stupid, ill-informed and poor decision makers. Sorry to get a bit political here, but common sense is even used as an ideological cudgel by conservatives in which so-called coastal elites lack common sense and, as a result, are out of touch with 'real Americans' who apparently have an abundance of common sense. But, if we use our elected representatives as examples (though I can't vouch for how representative they actually are), I think it's safe to say that unsound judgement, that is, the absence of common sense, doesn't discriminate based on political ideology.

The word, common, by definition, suggests that common sense is held by a large number of people. But the idea that if most people think something makes sense then it must be a sound judgement which has been disproven time and again. Further, it is often people who might be accused of not having common sense who prove that what is common sense is not only sense, but also completely wrong. And, by the way, common sense is often used by people who don't have the real knowledge, expertise, or direct experience to actually make sound judgements.

The unfortunate reality is that trusting common sense, in fact, causes us to make poor rather than sound judgements. Perhaps, the biggest problem with common sense is that it falls prey to the clear limits of personal experience. Or, we don't even have any actual experience in the matter and rely simply on what we believe to be true or have been told is true, what we might label 'faith-based sense' (in the broadest sense of the word, faith). For example, when you're having a discussion about just about anything that requires taking a stand, for example, the weather, the economy, raising children, sports, what have you, how often do you hear some variation of, etc. "Well, it's been my experience that [fill in the blank]" and the person then draws a conclusion based on the said experience and how often is that conclusion wildly at odds with the facts? More often than not in my experience (though, of course, my experience may be insufficient to draw a truly sound conclusion).

I think we need to jettison this notion of the sanctity of common sense and instead embrace 'reasoned sense,' that is, a sound judgement based on rigorous study of an issue (which also includes direct experience). Of course, we can't do an in-depth scientific study of every issue for which we need to draw a conclusion or make a decision. We can't, in the formal sense, do a review of the literature that includes relevant theories and the scientific findings to date, prepare detailed hypotheses, design a formal methodology, collect data, and employ complex statistical analyses from which we draw conclusions. But we can, and should, apply many of these basic principles of the scientific methods in more informal ways in to our daily lives.

In fact, I think that a course in scientific thinking and methodology for everyday life should be a requirement for all students. Such proactive education about precise thinking and real sense might reduce the number of truly dunderhead things that subsequent generations will do (the current generations are probably beyond remediation).

Here are some ways in which people can engage in more 'sensical' thinking, whether common or otherwise (what does it matter where sense comes from as long as it does truly reflect a sound judgement?).

Firstly, we can begin our 'inquiry' with an open mind, something sorely lacking in matters both trivial (e.g., Who's better, Red Sox or Yankees. Red Sox, of course) and substantial (e.g., how to fix the budget deficit) these days. Without being receptive to answers that we may not want to hear, we might as well just ask ourselves what we want to be true and go with that, which is what many people with so-called common sense (most efficient, but often wrong) do.

Secondly, we all establish a hypothesis that we would like to see affirmed when we are asking questions in our lives, for example, about relationships (e.g., "I know she likes me.") or the economy (e.g. "It's definitely picking up."). But for hypothesis to be more than just foregone conclusions (e.g., the world is flat; oops!), it's important to also propose alternative hypothesis (e.g., maybe, the world is round or square). Just considering that there might be answers other than the ones we want to ensure that any 'experiment' we conduct isn't just an exercise in self-serving affirmation (e.g., drug trials done by pharmaceutical companies).

Thirdly, we can collect a sizable sample of data that is more likely to represent the population as a whole. So, instead of just asking a few friends their opinions on an issue (which are likely similar to our own), we ask others, particularly those we know to have differing views. Does that guarantee sound judgements? Of course, not. But does it make it more likely that whatever conclusion is drawn will be closer to reality? Absolutely.

Fourth, we can analyse the data as objectively as possible. Let's be realistic. No one likes to see their 'theories' disproven. And there's a cynical saying in the sciences, 'If the facts don't fit the theory, throw out the facts.' Also, don't forget 'GIGO' (Garbage In, Garbage Out) which describes the 'failures in human decision making due to faulty, incomplete, or imprecise data' (thanks to Wikipedia). The scientific method attempts to prevent both sayings from being realised by using statistical analyses that, at least in theory, don't allow for the intrusion of human biases (recent research has found this assumption presumptuous, but it's the best we have at this point).

The bottom line is that if we can learn to think in more open and rigorous ways, we can draw the most accurate conclusions and make the best decisions possible for the myriad of questions, concerns and issues we face every day, be they mundane or impactful. And we might just all get along a little better too.

QUESTIONS 28-35

Complete the summary using the list of words, A-L given in the word list. Write the correct letter, A-L from the box and complete the boxes, 28-35 on your answer sheet.

According to the American scientists, Common Sense is neither common nor sense. Moreover, it is not a sound judgement that comes from **28.** .... or **29.** .... because if it is combination of all these things, then everyone would be a good decision maker, nobody would commit crime, everybody would think twice or thrice before doing **30.** .... and tweeting with **31.** .... **32.** .... donot require experience. Most of the time, our common sense depends upon our ideological **33.** .... In real terms, common sense is the possession of ignorant and **34.** .... persons because giving sound judgement donot require any experience at all. Now it is the basic requirement among students to build common sense which can be possible by using the methodology of thinking which must be **35.** .... in nature.

WORD LIST

A. Culture	**B.** Sound Judgement	**C.** Experience
D. Proactive	**E.** Gambling	**F.** Politicians
G. Strangers	**H.** Scientific	**I.** Unexperienced
J. Reason	**K.** Study	**L.** Generations
M. Fallacy		

QUESTIONS 36-40

Look at the following hypothesis related to Common Sense. Which five of the statements from A-H are the steps of developing common sense? Write the correct letter A-H, in boxes 36-40 on your answer sheet.

HYPOTHESES

A. Alternative hypothesis are not confused with common sense

B. Do open thinking and believe in the rigorous ways of drawing conclusions.

C. Inquiry with open mind.

D. Acknowledge and confirm about certain facts and conclusions.

E. Believe in your thinking and go accordingly.

F. Analyse the data.

G. Sampling of data is to be done to draw more realistic judgements.

H. Collect realistic data based on facts, values and proper analysis.

36. Hypothesis 1 ....

37. Hypothesis 2 ....

38. Hypothesis 3 ....

39. Hypothesis 4 ....

40. Hypothesis 5 ....

Reading Test 2

Answers

Passage 1

1. A
2. D
3. C
4. C
5. No
6. Yes
7. Not Given
8. Yes
9. No
10. Yes
11. Not Given

Passage 2

12. Meridians
13. Gi vital energy
14. Science
15. World Health Organization
16. University of Texas
17. F
18. A
19. D
20. G
21. E
22. B
23. B
24. D
25. Acupuncture has started working
26. Deep relaxation and mild disorientation
27. A bit of rest

Passage 3

28. C
29. K
30. E
31. G
32. B
33. A
34. I
35. H
36. E
37. D
38. G
39. H
40. B

Reading Test - 3

PASSAGE 1

You should spend about 20 minutes on Questions 1-13 which are based on Passage 1 given below:

What is Biometrics?

'Biometrics' means 'life measurement' but the term is usually associated with the use of unique physiological characteristics to identify an individual. The application which most people associate biometrics with is 'security'. However, biometrics identification has eventually a much broader relevance as computer interface becomes more natural. Knowing the person with whom you are conversing is an important part of human interaction and one expects computers of the future to have the same capabilities.

A number of biometric traits have been developed and are used to authenticate the person's identity. The idea is to use the special characteristics of a person to identify him. By using special characteristics, we mean using the features such as face, iris, fingerprint, signature, etc.

The method of identification based on biometric characteristics is preferred over traditional passwords and PIN based methods for various reasons such as: The person to be identified is required to be physically present at the time-of-identification. Identification based on biometric techniques obviates the need to remember a password or carry a token. A biometric system is essentially a pattern recognition system which makes a personal identification by determining the authenticity of a specific physiological or behavioural characteristic possessed by the user. Biometric technologies are thus defined as the 'automated methods of identifying or authenticating the identity of a living person based on a physiological or behavioural characteristic'.

A biometric system can be either an 'identification' system or a 'verification' (authentication) system, which are defined below. Identification – One to Many: Biometrics can be used to determine a person's identity even without his/her knowledge or consent. For example, scanning a crowd with a camera and using face recognition technology, one can determine matches against a known database.Verification – One to One: Biometrics can also be used to verify a person's identity. For example, one can grant physical access to a secured area in a building by using *finger scans* or can grant access to a bank account at an ATM by using a *retinal scan*.

Biometric authentication requires to compare a registered or enrolled biometric sample (biometric template or identifier) against a newly captured biometric sample (for example, the one captured during a login). This is a three-step process (*Capture, Process, Enroll*) followed by a *Verification or Identification* process.

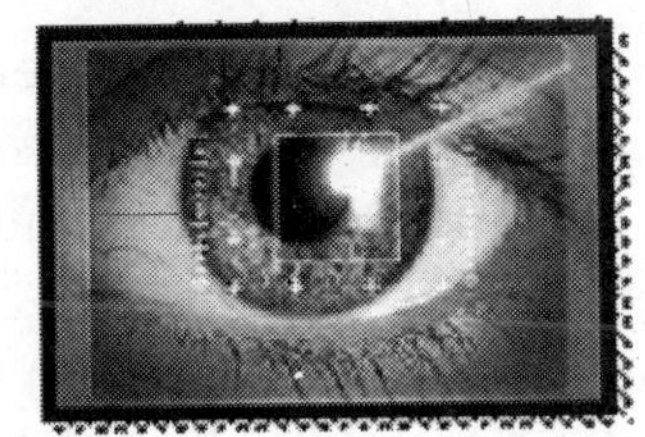

During Capture process, raw biometric is captured by a sensing device, such as a *fingerprint scanner* or *video camera*. The second phase of processing is to extract the distinguishing characteristics from the raw biometric sample and convert into a processed biometric identifier record (sometimes called biometric sample or biometric template). Next phase is the process of enrollment. Here the processed sample (a mathematical representation of the biometric – not the original biometric sample) is stored/registered in a storage medium for future comparison during an authentication. In many commercial applications, there is a need to store the processed biometric sample only. The original biometric sample cannot be reconstructed from this identifier.

A number of biometric characteristics may be captured in the first phase of processing. However, automated capturing and automated comparison with previously stored data requires that the biometric characteristics satisfy the following characteristics:

Universal: Every person must possess the characteristic/attribute. The attribute must be one that is universal and seldom lost to accident or disease.

Invariance of properties: They should be constant over a long period of time. The attribute should not be subject to significant differences based on age either episodic or chronic disease.

Measurability: The properties should be suitable for capture without wasting time and must be easy to gather the attribute data passively.

Singularity: Each expression of the attribute must be unique to the individual. The characteristics should have sufficient unique properties to distinguish one person from any other. Height, weight, hair and eye colour are all attributes that are unique assuming a particularly precise measure, but do not offer enough points of differentiation to be useful for more than categorising. **Acceptance:** The capturing should be possible in a way acceptable to a large percentage of the population. Excluded are particularly invasive technologies, i.e. technologies which require a part of the human body to be taken or which (apparently) impair the human body. **Reducibility:** The captured data should be capable of being reduced to a file which is easy to handle. **Reliability and tamper-resistance:** The attribute should be impractical to mask or manipulate. The process should ensure high reliability and reproducibility. **Privacy:** The process should not violate the privacy of the person. **Comparable:** Should be able to reduce the attribute to a state that makes it digitally comparable to others. The less probabilistic the matching involved, the more authoritative the identification. **Inimitable:** The attribute must be irreproducible by other means. The less reproducible the attribute, the more likely it will be authoritative.

Among the various biometric technologies being considered, the attributes which satisfy the above requirements are fingerprint, facial features, hand geometry, voice, iris, retina, vein patterns, palm print, DNA, keystroke dynamics, ear shape, odour, signature, etc.

QUESTIONS 1-6

Do the following statements agree with the information given in the Reading Passage 1 in the boxes 1- 6 on your answer sheet, write:

YES ..... If the statement agrees with the information in the passage

NO ..... If the statement contradicts with the information in the passage

NOT GIVEN ..... If there is no information about the statement in the passage

1. Biometrics is the mathematical calculation of human nature.
2. Biometrics is better than man-made identity card to ensure the uniqueness of the individual.
3. Biometrics based on behavioural and physiological characteristics.
4. Biometrics identification method does not require any password.
5. Retinal Scan is one to one biometrics.
6. Face recognition is one of the most flexible identification method of biometrics.

QUESTIONS 7-8

Choose the correct letter, A, B, C or D. Write the correct letter in box 7-8 on your answer sheet.

7. Biometrics Templates is the result of
   - A) Capture Process
   - B) Second Phase of Processing
   - C) Enrolment Process
   - D) Verification Process

8. Mathematical calculation of biometrics characteristics is done under

   A) Capture Process

   B) Second Phase of Processing

   C) Enrolment Process

   D) Identification Process

QUESTIONS 9-13

Use information from the passage to complete the sentences below from 9-13. Use No More Than One Word for each space.

9. Unique attribute of the individual ....
10. Biometrics captured data easy to handle in ....
11. Not easy to manipulate ....
12. No violation of confidential matters of the person ....
13. No replica of attribute of a person ....

PASSAGE 2

You should spend about 20 minutes on Questions, 14-25 which are based on Passage 2 given below.

Card Skimming

'Card skimming' is the illegal copying of information from the magnetic strip of a credit or ATM card. It is a more direct version of a *phishing scam*. The scammers try to steal your details so that they can access your accounts. Once scammers have skimmed your card, they can create a fake or 'cloned' card with your details on it. The scammer is then able to run up charges on your account. Card skimming is also a way for scammers to steal your identity (your personal details) and use it to commit *identity fraud*. By stealing your personal details and account numbers, the scammer may be able to borrow money or take out loans in your name. Cloning of cards can be done at shops, petrol pumps and at other places, where one swipes cards to make payments.

Cloning of cards takes place under three steps: Firstly for cloning a genuine credit or debit card, fraudsters use a device with a scanning slot, popularly known as a *data reader* and attach it with the *swipe machine*. These sophisticated devices can be easily procured from shops or ordered online. Then the swindler will then swipe a customer's credit card through the machine which is attached to the cloning device. The cloning device comes with a software that can store stolen information of more than 3,000 cards.

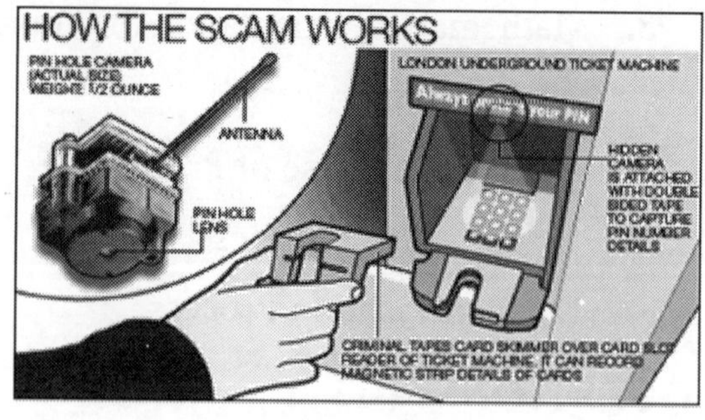

Lastly, once swiped, the secret of the card is transferred to the data reader device. The fraudster can now copy the stolen details on to the expired, black or stolen card to make a clone of the original credit or debit card. The fraudster can now start using the cloned card for shopping or other illegal transactions.

The Warning Signs of Card Skimming: A shop assistant takes your card out of your sight in order to process your transaction; you are asked to swipe your card through more than one machine; you see a shop assistant swipe the card through a different machine to the one you used; you notice something suspicious about the card slot on an ATM (e.g. an attached device).You notice unusual or unauthorised transactions on your account or credit card statement. It can be protected. Keep your credit card and ATM cards safe. Do not share your Personal Identity Number (PIN) with anyone. Do not keep any written copy of your PIN with the card. Check your bank account and credit card statements when you get them. If you see a transaction you cannot explain, report it to your credit union or bank. Choose passwords that would be difficult for anyone else to guess. Do your homework; if you are using an ATM, take the time to check that there is nothing suspicious about the machine. Ask yourself if you trust the person or trader who you are handing your card over to. If a shop assistant looks like they are going to take your card out of your sight, ask if it is really necessary. If an ATM looks suspicious, do not use it and alert the ATM owner. If you are in a shop and the assistant wants to swipe your card out of your sight, or in a second machine, you should ask for your card back straightaway and either pay with a cheque or cash, or not make the purchase at all.

Similar Scams: Requests for your account information ('phishing' scams)

Phishing e-mails are *fake e-mails* usually pretending to be from banks or other financial institutions. They make up some reason for you to give your account details and then use these details to steal your money.

Phoney Fraud Alerts: Scammers pretend to be from your bank or financial institution and tell you that there is a problem with your account. They ask for your account details to protect your money, but then use these details to steal your money.

Credit Card Scams: There are many types of scams that aim to steal your credit card details, either by taking the card itself or by tricking you into giving them the card's details. Spyware and key-loggers. Spyware is a type of software that spies on what you do on your computer. Key-loggers record what keys you press on your keyboard. Scammers can use them to steal your online banking passwords or other personal information.

QUESTIONS 14-25

Use information from the passage to complete the table below from 14-25. Use No More Than Three Words for each space.

Card Skimming	TERM used as a **14.** .... scam. Known as **15.** .... card	Executed by **16.** .... Filch **17.** .... Commit **18.**	Swipe at petrol pumps, Shops, etc.
STEPS	Used Data Reader **19.**	Pinch Information with the **20.** .... of the device.	Make a **21.** .... of the card.
Warning	Take place during **22.** .... Transactions.	Protection Save your **23.** .... **24.**	**25.** .... of your account and credit card.

QUESTIONS 26-28

Complete the following sentences from 26-28 on your answer sheet.

26. One who pretends and promises to keep your account safe ....
27. Key-loggers filch information ....
28. Scammers filch information by decoding ....

Passage 3

You should spend about 20 minutes on Questions, 29-40 which are based on Passage 3 given below.

Population Ageing – A Global Problem

A. Population ageing is a phenomenon that occurs when the median age of a country or region rises due to the rising life expectancy and/or declining birth rates. There has been, initially in the *More Economically Developed Countries (MEDC)* but also more recently in LEDCs (Less Economically Developed Countries), an increase in the life expectancy which causes ageing population. This is the case for every country in the world except the 18 countries designated as 'demographic outliers' by the UN. For the entirely of the recorded human history, the world has never seen as aged a population, as it currently exists globally. The UN predicts the rate of population ageing in the 21st century will exceed that of the previous century. Countries vary significantly in terms of the degree, and the pace, of these changes, and the UN expects populations that began ageing later to have less time to adapt to the many implications of these changes.

B. Population ageing is a shift in the distribution of a country's population towards older ages. This is usually reflected in an increase in the population's mean and median ages, a decline in the proportion of the population composed of children, and a rise in the proportion of the population that is elderly. Population ageing is widespread across the world. It is most advanced in the most highly developed countries. The Oxford Institute of Population Ageing, however, concluded that population ageing has slowed considerably in Europe and will have the greatest future impact in Asia, especially as Asia is in stage five of the demographic transition model.

C. Among the countries currently classified by the United Nations as more developed (with a total population of 1.2 billion in 2005), the overall median age rose from 29.0 in 1950 to 37.3 in 2000, and is forecasted to rise to 45.5 by 2050. The corresponding figures for the world as a whole are 23.9 in 1950, 26.8 in 2000, and 37.8 in 2050. In Japan, one of the world's most quickly ageing countries, in 1950 there were 9.3 people under 20 for every person over 65. By 2025, this ratio is forecasted to be 0.59 people under 20 for every person over 65.Population ageing arises from two (possibly related) demographic effects: increasing longevity and declining fertility. An increase in longevity raises the average age of the population by increasing the numbers of surviving older people. A decline in fertility reduces the number of babies, and as the effect continues, the numbers of younger people in general also reduce. A possible third factor is **migration**.

D. Of these two forces, it is 'declining fertility' that is the largest contributor to population ageing in the world today. More specifically, it is the large decline in the overall fertility rate over the last half century that is primarily responsible for the population ageing in the world's most developed countries. Because many developing countries are going through faster fertility transitions, they will experience even faster population ageing than the currently developed countries in the future. The rate at which the population ages is likely to increase over the next three decades; however, few countries know whether their older populations are living the extra years of life in good or poor health. A 'Compression of Morbidity' would imply reducing reduced disability in old age, whereas an expansion would see an increase in poor health with increased longevity. Another option has been posed for a situation of 'dynamic equilibrium' (Manton, 1982). This is crucial information for governments if the limits of lifespan continue to increase indefinitely, as some researchers believe it will.

The World Health Organization's suite of household health studies is working to provide the needed health and well-being evidence, including, for example, the World Health Survey, and the Study on Global Ageing and Adult Health (SAGE). These surveys cover 308,000 respondents aged 18+ years and 81,000 aged 50+ years from 70 countries. The Global Ageing Survey, exploring attitudes, expectations and behaviours towards later life and retirement, directed by George Leeson, and covering 44,000 people aged 40–80 in 24 countries from across the globe, has revealed that many people are now fully aware of the ageing of the world's population and the implications which this will have for their lives and the lives of their children and grandchildren.

E. Canada has the highest per capita immigration rate in the world, partly to counter population ageing. The C. D. Howe Institute, a conservative think-tank, has suggested that immigration cannot be used as a viable means for countering population ageing. This conclusion is also seen in the work of other scholars. Demographers Peter McDonald and Rebecca Kippen comment, "fertility sinks further below replacement level, increasingly higher levels of annual net migration will be required to maintain a target of even zero population growth".

F. The economic effects of an ageing population are considerable. Older people have higher accumulated savings per head than younger people, but spend less on consumer goods. Depending upon the age ranges at which the changes occur, an ageing population may thus result in lower interest rates and the economic benefits of lower inflation. Some economists (Japan) see advantages in such changes, notably the opportunity to progress automation and technological development without causing unemployment. They emphasise a shift from the GDP to personal well-being.

G. However, population ageing also increases some categories of expenditure, including some met from public finances. The largest area of expenditure in many countries is now healthcare, whose cost is likely to increase dramatically as populations age. This would present governments with hard choices between higher taxes, including a possible reweighing of tax from earnings to consumption, and a reduced government role in providing health care.The second-largest expenditure of most governments is education and these expenses will tend to fall with an ageing population, especially as fewer young people would probably continue into tertiary education as they would be in demand as part of the work force.

Social security systems have also begun to experience problems. Earlier defined benefit pension systems are experiencing sustainability problems due to the increased longevity. The extension of the pension period was not paired with an extension of the active labour period or a rise in pension contributions, resulting in a decline of replacement ratios. In recent years, many countries have adopted policies to strengthen the financial sustainability of pension systems, although the challenges regarding pension adequacy remain.

QUESTIONS 29-35

Passage 3 has seven sections, A-G. Choose the correct headline for each section from the list of headings below. Write the correct number, i –vii in the boxes, 29-35 on your answer sheet.

LIST OF HEADINGS

A. Expenditure upon Senior Citizens

B. Immigration Countering Ageing Population

C. Rising Demographic Effects of Ageing Population

D. Rise of Ageing Population Globally

E. Decline in Fertility Rate

F. Increase of Longevity in Life Expectancy

G. Demographic Position of Ageing Population

H. UN Records the Highest Ageing Population

I. Surveys of Population Ageing

J. Ageing Population is More Economical

29. Paragraph A ....

30. Paragraph B ....

31. Paragraph C ....

32. Paragraph D ....

33. Paragraph E ....

34. Paragraph F ....

35. Paragraph G ....

QUESTIONS 36-40

Choose the correct letter A, B, C or D. Write the correct letter in box, 36-40 on your answer sheet.

36. Demographic Outliers Countries by the UN:

A) Europe B) Canada

C) Japan D) Asia

37. Increase in ageing population

A) Decline in Fertility Rate

B) Migration Factor

C) Increasing Longevity

D) All of the above

38. A Compression of Morbid is the state of

A) Increased Life Expectancy with Decline in Fertility Rate

B) Longevity in Older Age without Disability

C) Increase in Longevity with Poor Health

D) Dynamic Equilibrium

39. In order to counter population ageing, which factor is most important:

A) High Immigration Rate

B) Decline in Life Expectancy Rate

C) Migration

D) None of these

40. Major portion of economic expenditure on Senior Citizens

A) Pension System B) Social Security

C) Health Care D) Savings

Reading Test 3

Answers

Passage 1

1. Not Given	2. Not Given	3. Yes
4. No	5. Yes	6. Not given
7. B	8. C	9. Singularity
10. Reducibility	11. Reliability	12. Privacy
13. Inimitable	14. Phishing	15. Cloned

Passage 2

16. Scammers	17. Identity details	18. Identity fraud
19. Device	20. Scanning slot	21. Clone
22. Transactions	23. PIN	24. ATM
25. Passwords	26. Phoney Fraud Alerts	

27. By keeping the records of the keys/record keys which you press

28. Online banking passwords

29. D

Passage 3

30. G	31. C	32. I
33. B	34. A	35. J
36. D	37. D	38. B
39. A	40. C	

Reading Test – 4

PASSAGE 1

You should spend about 20 minutes on Questions, 1-15 which are based on Passage 3 given below:

Euthanasia – Right to Die

Euthanasia is the termination of a very sick person's life in order to relieve them of their suffering. A person who undergoes euthanasia usually has an incurable condition. But there are other instances where some people want their life to be ended. In many cases, it is carried out at the person's request, but there are times when they may be too ill and the decision is made by the relatives, doctors in some instances, the courts. The term is derived from the Greek word, *euthanatos* which means easy death. Euthanasia is against the law in the UK, where it is illegal to help anyone kill themselves. *Voluntary euthanasia* or *assisted suicide* can lead to imprisonment of up to 14 years. The issue has been at the centre of very heated debates for many years and is surrounded by religious, ethical and practical considerations.

The Ethics of Euthanasia: Euthanasia raises a number of agonising moral dilemmas: Is it ever right to end the life of a terminally ill patient who is undergoing severe pain and suffering? Under what circumstances can euthanasia be justifiable, if at all? Is there a moral difference between killing someone and letting them die? At the heart of these arguments are the different ideas that people have about the meaning and value of human existence. Should human beings have the right to decide on issues of life and death? There are also a number of arguments based on practical issues. Some people think that euthanasia shouldn't be allowed, even if it was morally right, because it could be abused and used as a cover for murder.

Killing or letting die Euthanasia can be carried out either by taking actions, including giving a lethal injection, or by not doing what is necessary to keep a person alive (such as, failing to keep their feeding tube going on). *'Extraordinary' medical care:* It is not euthanasia if a patient dies as a result of refusing extraordinary or burdensome medical treatment. It's not euthanasia to give a drug in order to reduce pain, even though the drug causes the patient to die sooner. This is because the doctor's intention was to relieve the pain, and not to kill the patient. This argument is sometimes known as the *Doctrine of Double Effect*. *Mercy killing*: Very often, people call euthanasia as 'mercy killing', perhaps thinking of it for someone who is terminally ill and suffering prolonged, unbearable pain.

Why People Want Euthanasia? Most people think unbearable pain is the main reason people seek euthanasia, but some surveys in the USA and the Netherlands showed that less than a third of requests for euthanasia were because of severe pain. Terminally, ill people can have their quality of life severely damaged by physical conditions, such as *incontinence, nausea and vomiting, breathlessness, paralysis and difficulty in swallowing.* Psychological factors that cause people to think of euthanasia include depression, fearing loss of control or dignity, feeling a burden, or dislike of being dependent, etc.

Forms of Euthanasia: Euthanasia comes in several different forms, each of which brings a different set of rights and wrongs.

Active and Passive Euthanasia: In active euthanasia, a person directly and deliberately causes the patient's death. In passive euthanasia, they don't directly take the patient's life, they just allow them to die. This is a morally unsatisfactory distinction, since even though a person doesn't 'actively kill' the patient, they are aware that the result of their inaction will be the death of the patient. *Active euthanasia is when death is brought about by an act – for example, when a person is killed by being given an overdose of painkillers.*

Passive Euthanasia: It is when death is brought about by anomission - i.e., when someone lets the person die. This can be by withdrawing or withholding treatment.Withdrawing treatment: for example, switching off a machine that is keeping a person alive, so that they die of their disease.Withholding treatment: for example, not carrying out surgery that will extend life for a short time. Traditionally, **passive euthanasia** is thought of less bad than **active euthanasia**. But some people think active euthanasia is morally better.

Voluntary and Involuntary Euthanasia: Voluntary Euthanasia occurs at the request of the person who dies. **Non-voluntary Euthanasia** occurs when the person is unconscious or otherwise unable (for example, a very young baby or a person of extremely low intelligence) to make a meaningful choice between living and dying, and an appropriate person takes the decision on their behalf. Non-voluntary euthanasia also includes cases where the person is a child who is mentally and emotionally able to take the decision, but is not regarded in law as old enough to take such a decision, so someone else must take it on their behalf in the eyes of law. Involuntary euthanasia occurs when the person who dies chooses life and is killed anyway. This is usually called *murder*, but it is possible to imagine cases where the killing would count as being for the benefit of the person who dies.

Indirect Euthanasia: This means providing treatment (usually to reduce pain) that has the side effect of speeding the patient's death. Since the primary intention is not to kill, this is seen by some people (but not all) as morally acceptable. A justification along these lines is formally called the *doctrine of double effect.*

Assisted Suicide: This usually refers to cases where the person who is going to die needs help to kill himself/herself and asks for it. It may be something as simple as getting drugs for the person and putting those drugs within their reach.

People have the right to die. Human beings have the right to die when and how they want to.

In...cases, where there are no dependents who might exert pressure one way or the other, the right of the individual to choose should be paramount. So long as the patient is lucid, and his or her intent is clear beyond doubt, there need be no further questions. (*The Independent*, March 2002).

Many people think that each person has the right to control his or her body and life and so should be able to determine at what time, in what way and by whose hand, he or she will die. Behind this lies the idea that human beings should be as free as possible – and that unnecessary restraints on human rights are a bad thing. And behind that lies the idea that human beings are independent biological entities, with the right to take and carry out decisions about themselves, providing the greater good of society doesn't prohibit this. Allied to this is a firm belief that death is the end.

Religious opponents disagree because they believe that the right to decide when a person dies belongs to God.

Secular Objections: Secular opponents argue that whatever rights we have are limited by our obligations. The decision to die by euthanasia will affect other people – our family and friends, and healthcare professionals – and we must balance the consequences for them (guilt, grief, anger) against our rights. We should also take account of our obligations to the society, and balance our individual right to die against any bad consequences that it might have and for the community, in general. These bad consequences might be practical, such as making involuntary euthanasia easier and so putting vulnerable people at risk. There is also a political and philosophical objection that says that our individual right to autonomy against the state must be balanced against the need to make the sanctity of life an important, intrinsic, abstract value of the state. Secular philosophers put forward a number of technical arguments, mostly based on the duty to preserve life because it has value in itself, or the importance of regarding all human beings as ends rather than means.

End of Life Assistance Bill rejected by the Scottish Parliament:

In December 2009, the Independent MSP Margo Macdonald, who has Parkinson's Disease, put forward a bill in the Scottish Parliament to legalise assisted suicide. *The End of Life Assistance Bill* would have allowed people whose lives become intolerable through a progressive degenerative condition, a trauma or terminal illness to seek a doctor's help in dying. It also proposed a series of safeguards which would prevent abuse of the legislation.

The vote took place in December 2010 and MSPs were permitted to vote freely based on their consciences rather than along party lines. After a number of legal challenges by Debbie Purdy, a *multiple sclerosis* sufferer who wanted to know if her husband would be prosecuted for helping her to die, the law on assisted suicide in England and Wales was clarified in September 2009. It was ruled that the decision to prosecute would be based on factors including the nature of the victim's illness. All cases would be investigated by the police but discretion will still be used.

QUESTIONS 1-8

Do the following statements agree with the information given in the Reading Passage 1? In the boxes, 1-8 on your answer sheet, write:

YES ..... If the statement agrees with the information in the passage

NO ..... If the statement contradicts with the information in the passage

NOT GIVEN ..... If there is no information about the statement in the passage

1. Ending the suffering of fellow human beings is an art of mercy.

2. The Doctrine of Double Effect is the intentional killing of a person under the name of mercy.

3. Euthanasia patient is psychologically weak but physically fit.

4. Is it right to call euthanasia if a patient refuses to get medical treatment?

5. Non-voluntary euthanasia patients emotionally are not good decision makers.

6. Voluntary euthanasia is called murder.

7. Euthanasia means sure death.

8. Right to die is a human right.

Choose the correct option from A, B, C & D

9. Which euthanasia is morally better?

A. Voluntary Euthanasia

B. Involuntary Euthanasia

C. Passive Euthanasia

D. Active Euthanasia

QUESTIONS 10-15

Complete the following summary from the passage and complete the boxes, 10-15 on your answer sheet.

Human Beings are free as far as **10.** .... matters are concerned. Nobody can prohibit him from their **11.** .... right. Everybody knows **12.** .... is the end. So putting unusual **13.** .... upon this right is a bad thing. No doubt many religious and **14.** .... objections are upon it because some rights are bound with obligation. Similarly, Right to die completely **15.** .... on God.

PASSAGE 2

You should spend about 20 minutes on Questions 16-28 which are based on Passage 3 below:

The World's Economies

Rather than take the three-world view, economists classify the world's economies as: Industrial or Developed Nations, Newly Industrialised Nations, Developing Nations.

Industrialised Nations: Growing and Growing Old

An industrialised economy has a large base of productive capital, sophisticated banking systems and financial markets, a variety of industries producing a broad range of products, and vigorous and varied international trade. Industrialised nations also have well established systems of government and law, and provide educational opportunities for their people.

Econo Tip

The G-8 includes the G-7 plus Russia, which may best be described as an economy in transition. The transition will take Russia from a *planned economy* to a *free-market, capitalist economy*. The central planning structure has been dismantled, but the transition to a successful market economy is still in progress. In that sense, *Russia is also a developing economy*.

Econo Talk

The term, 'sustainable growth' refers to economic growth based on renewable resources (and efforts to renew them) with minimal environmental degradation. You will often hear about efforts to achieve sustainable growth in an economy or in the global economy.

The countries in the **Group of Seven (G-7)** have the most industrialised economies. The G-7 are the *United States, Canada, Japan, Germany, France, the United Kingdom* and the *Italy* (with Germany, France, the United Kingdom, and Italy comprising Europe's so-called **Big Four**). However, the entire **EU**—which also includes Austria, Belgium, Finland, Greece, Ireland, Luxembourg, the Netherlands, Portugal and Spain—and some European nations outside the EU, such as Switzerland, Sweden and Denmark, are also industrialised. So are Australia, New Zealand and Taiwan. Less than 20 percent of the world's population lives in industrial nations, and they account for about 70 percent of the world output. That fact – and the income inequality that it generates – creates some of the questions these countries face, such as: What is the realistic and responsible role for developed nations to play in the economies of less developed nations? What are the moral and ecological implications of using such a large share of the earth's resources (relative to the share other nations use) to sustain the levels of production and growth that industrial nations have achieved? What, in fact, constitutes sustainable growth, and is it achievable?

Industrialised economies also face the problems of maintaining low unemployment and inflation, choosing the optimal mix of public and private goods, and coping with domestic poverty, crime and disease. Also, the United States, Japan and Western Europe are experiencing record low birth rates coupled with longer life expectancies. This translates to a 'greying' of the population, in which older people will come to outnumber younger people. This holds serious implications for funding their retirement and healthcare, as we saw in our look at the U.S. Social Security system in Hey, Big Spender! **The Federal Budget:** On top of all this, the threat of terrorism, mainly from Islamic extremists from less developed countries, may well represent the most difficult and dangerous problem for industrialised nations, particularly the United States.

Newly Industrialised Nations: Getting Going

Newly industrialised nations (NICs) have a rapidly growing base of productive capital and rising incomes. Most of these nations have sound governments and banking and financial systems, although they may occasionally be subject to financial or political dislocation. For instance, Brazil is weighed down with international debt and must work hard to control inflation. Pakistan may face political instability and a shaky relationship with neighboring India. Newly industrialized nations include *Hong Kong*, *Singapore*, *Taiwan*, and *South Korea* – which are known as Asia's **"Four Tigers"** – *Pakistan, Malaysia, Indonesia, Thailand, Mexico, Brazil, Chile, Venezuela, Israel, South Africa,* and *Hungary* are also coming into limelight days. Less than 5 percent of the world's population lives in the NICs, and they earn less than 5 percent of the world's income.

The Four Tigers followed a strategy of export-oriented industrialisation, in which they moved from the status of developing country to that of NIC in the 1970s and 1980s. These nations ambitiously took Japan as a role model, but concentrated on light manufacturing. The Tigers have been held up by the **World Bank** and the International Monetary Fund (IMP) as models for other *developing* and *underdeveloped nations*. However, export-oriented growth isn't possible for every nation, especially when other nations, including China and some industrialised nations, still engage in protectionism. The NICs face a variety of problems, depending on their specific situations. One common issue is financing growth. How much can and should they rely on foreign borrowing? How much money for capital investment can they reasonably expect to generate themselves?

A number of newly industrialised countries need more sophisticated banking and financial systems, and more stable governments. Some NICs are moving from economies based on producing and exporting natural resources to producing and exporting manufactured goods. Diversity of exports is both the mark of an industrial economy and a stabilizer of any economy. But this transition can be difficult, especially for nations, such as Venezuela and Mexico, which export oil and have come to depend on the large revenues that oil exports produce.

Developing Nations

Developing nations range from the poorest in the world to those that have begun to build an industrial base, but have yet to achieve stable growth in production and income. These economies are also called *underdeveloped*, *undeveloped*, and, most commonly, *Less Developed Countries* (LDCs). A number of these nations have large, growing urban populations and serious difficulties with unemployment, crime and poverty in the cities.

The Organization for Economic Cooperation and Development includes all countries of Africa except the Republic of South Africa, all the countries of Asia except Cambodia, China, Japan, Laos, North Korea, and Vietnam, all the countries in Latin America, except Cuba, also includes countries in the Middle East, the Malta, Portugal, Spain, Greece, and Turkey. The *People's Republic of China (PRL)* could be considered an LDC. However, most economists view the PRC as a special case because it this beginning to industrialise but still relies heavily on small farms. This list literally covers a lot of ground, and includes some nations that some economists would classify elsewhere. For example, Cuba is by many measures a less developed country, and while Portugal, Spain and Greece are poor by European standards, they are wealthy compared with most nations of Africa. Regarding the Middle East, many economists think of Israel as an industrialised nation, albeit one that uses significant amounts of foreign aid.

Most economists also place the *Oil Producing Nations of the Middle East (OPNEC)* in a separate category. The OPEC nations suffer serious internal income in equality and have not diversified their industrial base significantly beyond oil production. But it's difficult to think of Saudi Arabia, with per capita income of about $7,000 as being in the same category as Ghana, with the per capita income of $400. Many less developed nations experience intense periodic political upheaval, including war, as well as natural disasters, such as *droughts* and *hurricanes*. Most of them depend on small-scale commercial farming, which produces exports such as coffee, bananas and timber, and on subsistence farming, in which people grow their own food.

The staggering array of economic problems in truly less developed nations includes lack of skills, productive capital, organised financial markets, commercial diversification, transportation and communication infrastructure, technological infrastructure, capital formation, stable currency and stable government. The poverty in many of these nations results in lack of food, clothing, housing, healthcare, education, and even drinkable water and basic sanitation. Virtually, all less developed nations receive some forms of economic aid and assistance. Yet the extent and persistence of their internal economic and political problems render this help almost symbolic.

QUESTIONS 16-28

Use information from the passage to complete the table below from 16-28. Use No More Than Three Words for each space.

	BEST	WORST	MENACE
INDUSTRIALISED	Productive capital Banking & Financial Capital **16.** .... Trade. **17.** .... & Order	Low unemployment Inflation Domestic **18.** .... Disease & Crime **19.** ..... Population	**20.** .... by Islamic Extremists.

NEWLY INDUSTRIALISED NATIONS	Rising Income Role Model Of Newly Developed Industrailised nations are **21.** .... Who followed the approach of **22.** .... Industrialisation	Financial Growth Capital **23.**	
DEVELOPING NATIONS	Stable Growth Commercial and **24.** .... farming.	Crime, Poverty, Disease, Unemployment Growing **25.** .... Population Internal Income **26.** .... Political Upheaval Natural Disasters	Lack of Skills Productive capital Technological & **27.** .... Infra-structure Poverty Sanitation and **28.** ....

PASSAGE 3

Quality of Empathy

A. Emotional Intelligence (EQ) is the ability to identify, use, understand and manage emotions in positive ways to relieve stress, communicate effectively, empathise with others, overcome challenges, and defuse conflicts. Emotional intelligence impacts many different aspects of your daily life, such as the way you behave and the way you interact with others. If you have a high emotional intelligence, you are able to recognise your own emotional state and the emotional states of others and engage with people in a way that draws them to you. You can use this understanding of emotions to relate better to other people, form healthier relationships, achieve greater success at work, and lead a more fulfilling life.

B. Emotional Intelligence consists of four attributes: **Self-awareness** – you recognize your own emotions and how they affect your thoughts and behaviour, know your strengths and weaknesses, and have self-confidence. **Self-management** – You're able to control impulsive feelings and behaviour, manage your emotions in healthy ways, take initiative, follow through your commitments, and adapt to the changing circumstances. **Social**

awareness – You can understand the emotions, needs and concerns of other people, pick up on emotional cues, feel comfortable socially, and recognise the power dynamics in a group or organisation. **Relationship management** – You know how to develop and maintain good relationships, communicate clearly, inspire and influence others, work well in a team, and manage conflict. Why is **Emotional Intelligence** or **Emotional Quotient** (EQ) so important? As we know, it's not the smartest people that are the most successful or the most fulfilled in life. You probably know people who are academically brilliant and yet are socially inept and unsuccessful at work or in their personal relationships. Intellectual Intelligence or Intellectual Quotient (IQ) isn't enough on its own to be successful in life. IQ can help you get into college but it's EQ that will help you manage the stress and emotions of sitting your final exams. Emotional Intelligence affects your performance at work. It can also help you to navigate the social complexities of the workplace, lead and motivate others, and excel in your career. In fact, when it comes to gauging job candidates, many companies now view Emotional Intelligence as being as important as technical ability and require *EQ testing before hiring.*

C. Your Physical Health: If you're unable to manage your stress levels, it can lead to serious health problems. Uncontrolled stress can raise blood pressure, suppress the immune system, increase the risk of heart attack and stroke, contribute to infertility, and speed up the ageing process. The first step to improving Emotional Intelligence or Emotional Quotient is to learn how to relieve stress.

Your Mental Health: Uncontrolled stress can also impact your mental health, making you vulnerable to anxiety and depression. If you are unable to understand and manage your emotions, you'll also be open to mood swings, while an inability to form strong relationships can leave you feeling lonely and isolated.

Your Relationships: By understanding your emotions and how to control them, you're better able to express how you feel and understand and how others are feeling. This allows you to communicate more effectively and forge stronger relationships, both at work and in your personal life.

How to Raise your Emotional Intelligence: All information to the brain comes through our senses and when this information is overwhelmingly stressful or emotional, instinct will take over and our ability to act will be limited to the flight, fight, or flee response. Therefore, to have access to the wide range of choices and make good decisions, we need to be able to bring our emotions into balance at will.

D. Memory is also strongly linked to emotions. By learning to use the emotional part of your brain as well as the rational, you'll not only expand your range of choices, when it comes to responding to a new event, you'll also factor emotional memory into your decision-making. This will help prevent you from continually repeating earlier mistakes. To improve your Emotional Intelligence – and your Decision-making Abilities – you need to understand and control the emotional side of your brain. This is done by developing four key skills. By mastering the first two skills, you'll find the skills, 3 and 4 much easier to learn.

E. Developing Emotional Intelligence through Four Key Skills: Emotional Intelligence consists of five key skills, each building on the last: Emotional Intelligence or Emotional Quotient (EQ) skill 1: The ability to quickly reduce stress. Emotional Intelligence (EQ) skill 2: The ability to recognise and manage your emotions. Emotional Intelligence (EQ) skill 3: The ability to connect with others using non-verbal communication. Emotional Intelligence (EQ) skill 4: The ability to use humour and play to deal with challenges.

Emotional intelligence (EQ) skill 1: Rapidly Reduces Stress

High levels of stress can overwhelm the mind and the body, getting in the way of your ability to accurately 'read' a situation, hear what someone else is saying, be aware of your own feelings and needs, and communicate clearly. Being able to quickly calm yourself down and relieve stress helps you stay balanced, focussed, and in control – no matter what challenges you face or how stressful a situation becomes. **Stress Busting:** Functioning well in the heat of the moment.

F. Develop your stress busting skills by working through the following three steps: Realise when you're stressed – The first step to reducing stress is recognising what stress feels like. How does your body feel when you're stressed? Are your muscles or stomach tight or sore? Are your hands clenched? Is your breath shallow? Being aware of your physical response to stress will help regulate tension when it occurs.Identify your stress response – Everyone reacts differently to stress. If you tend to become angry or agitated under stress, you will respond best to stress relief activities that quiet you down. If you tend to become depressed or withdrawn, you will respond best to stress relief activities that are stimulating. If you tend to freeze – speeding up in some ways while slowing down in others – you need stress relief activities that provide both comfort and stimulation. Discover the stress-busting techniques that work for you – The best way to reduce stress quickly is by engaging one or more of your senses: sight, sound, smell, taste, and touch. Each person responds differently to sensory input, so you need to find things that are soothing and/ or energizing to you. For example, if you're a visual person you can relieve stress by surrounding yourself with uplifting images. If you respond more to sound, you may find a wind chime, a favourite piece of music, or the sound of a water fountain helps to quickly reduce your stress levels.

G. Emotional Intelligence (EQ) Skill 2: This is emotional awareness, i.e., being able to connect to your emotions—having a moment-to-moment awareness of your emotions and how they influence your thoughts and actions—is the key to understanding yourself and others. Many people are disconnected from their emotions–especially the strong core emotions, such as anger, sadness, fear and joy. This may be the result of negative childhood experiences that taught you to try to shut off your feelings. But although we can distort, deny, or numb our feelings, we can't eliminate them. They're still there, whether we're aware of them or not. Unfortunately, without emotional awareness, we are unable to fully understand our own motivations and needs, or to communicate effectively with others.

H. What Kind of a Relationship do you have with your Emotions? Do you experience feelings that flow, encountering one emotion after another as your experiences change from moment to moment? Are your emotions accompanied by physical sensations that you experience in places like your stomach or chest? Do you experience discrete feelings and emotions, such as anger, sadness, fear, joy, each of which is evident in subtle facial expressions? Can you experience intense feelings that are strong enough to capture both your attention and that of others? Do you pay attention to your emotions? Do they affect your decision making? If any of these experiences are unfamiliar, your emotions may be turned down or turned off. In order to be emotionally healthy and emotionally intelligent, you must reconnect to your core emotions, accept them, and become comfortable with them.

I. Emotional Awareness can be learnt at any time of life. If you haven't learnt how to manage stress, it's important to do so first. When you can manage stress, you'll feel more comfortable reconnecting to the strong or unpleasant emotions and changing the way you experience and respond to your feelings. You can develop your emotional awareness by learning the *mindfulness meditation* in Helpguide's free: *Bring Your Life into Balance Toolkit* that helps you to get in touch with the difficult emotions and manage uncomfortable feelings.

J. Emotional Intelligence Skill (EQ) 3: Non-verbal Communication

Being a good communicator requires more than just verbal skills. Often, what you say is less important than how you say it or the other non-verbal signals you send out—the *gestures you make, the way you sit, how fast or how loud you talk, how close you stand, how much eye contact you make*. In order to hold the attention of others and build connection and trust, you need to be aware of and in control of this body language. You also need to be able to accurately read and respond to the non-verbal cues that other people send you.These messages don't stop when someone stops speaking. Even when you're silent, you're still communicating non-verbally. Think about what you are transmitting as well, and if what you say matches with what you feel. If you insist, 'I'm fine', while clenching your teeth and looking away, your body is clearly signalling the opposite. Your non-verbal messages can produce a sense of interest, trust, excitement and desire for connection – or they can generate fear, confusion, distrust and disinterest.

Successful non-verbal communication depends on your ability to manage stress, recognise your own emotions, and understand the signals you're sending and receiving. When communicating: focus on the other person. If you are planning what you're going to say next, daydreaming, or thinking about something else, you are almost certain to miss non-verbal cues and other subtleties in the conversation. Make eye contact. Eye contact can communicate interest, maintain the flow of a conversation, and help gauge the other person's response. Pay attention to non-verbal cues you're sending and receiving, such as facial expression, tone of voice, posture and gestures, touch and the timing and pace of the conversation.

K. Emotional Intelligence (EQ) Skill 4: Use Humour and Play to deal with Challenges

Humour, laughter and play are natural antidotes to life's difficulties. They lighten your burden and help you keep things in perspective. A good hearty laugh reduces stress, elevates mood, and brings your nervous system back into balance.

Playful communication broadens your Emotional Intelligence and helps you. Taking hardships in stride. By allowing you to view your frustrations and disappointments from new perspectives, laughter and play enable you to survive annoyances, hard times and setbacks smoothly. Using gentle humour often helps you say things that might be otherwise difficult to express without creating a flap. Simultaneously, relax and energise yourself. Playful communication relieves fatigue and relaxes your body, which allows you to recharge and accomplish more. It also makes you more creative. When you loosen up, you free yourself of rigid ways of thinking and being, allowing you to be more innovative, creative and see things in new ways.

QUESTIONS 29-32

Use information from the passage to complete the sentences below from 29-32. Use No More Than three Words for each space.

29. EQ is better than IQ because it affects your ....

30. What kind of technical ability companies keep in mind while hiring employees for their company?

....

31. Emotional Intelligence is important for .... and .... health.

32. Raising the Emotional Intelligence. It is necessary that emotions must be ....

QUESTIONS 33-40

The passage includes four types of skills to raise the emotional Intelligence. Identify about which skill a writer is talking about in the given options. The number of the skills can be repeated more than once.

Example: Understanding our own motivations and needs .... Skill 2 ....

33. A skill of creative and visionary that teaches to see the new originality of life ....

34. A skill in which responses are necessary more than its requirement ....

35. A skill that teaches to face the trials and tribulations of life ....

36. To understand the discretionary feelings of anger, fear and joy. Which skill is required ....

37. Signal language teaches in which skill ....

38. A skill in which five senses are involved ....

39. Emotionally aware person is a focussed man ....

40. Emotional Intelligence teaches stress relieving techniques ....

Reading Test 4

Answers

Passage 1

1. .....Y	2. N	3. N
4. N	5. Y	6. N
7. NG	8. NG	9. D
10. Biological	11. Human	12. Death
13. Restraint	14. Secular	15. Belongs

Passage 2

16. International	17. Law	18. Poverty
19. Greying	20. Terrorism	21. Four Tigers of Asia
22. Export oriented	23. Investment	24. Farming
25. Urban	26. Equality	27. Communication
28. Water		

Passage 3

29. Performance at work
30. Emotional Intelligence
31. Physical and mental health
32. Linked with memory

33. Skill 4	34. Skill 1	35. Skill 4
36. Skill 2	37. Skill 3	38. Skill 1
39. Skill 3	40. Skill 1	

Abstract

WRITING MODULE

Here in this module, we endeavour to help the candidate with certain strategies and skills and practise essential for the writing task 1 & 2, which includes strategies related to graphical representation and essay topics along with their techniques how to utilise strategies for the wirting task 1 & 2. A set of four practice sessions are enclosed herewith for the IELTS candidates.

Task – 1 : Graphic Representation

IELTS ACADEMIC WRITING TASK 1 – GRAPHIC REPRESENTATION is an information transfer task related to the factual content of input texts, graphs, tables or diagrams. Sometimes, you will have to describe a process shown in the diagram.

Strategy No. 1: Introduction of the Graph

- ★ Do mention in the beginning that which **Type** of graph it is, i.e., whether the graph is BAR, LINE, PIE, TABLE.
- ★ Do write the **Title** of the graph, i.e., what type of information graph it is conveying.
- ★ Do mention the **Date, Month & Year** of the graph.
- ★ It is necessary to describe the **Scale** of the graph, i.e., whether the graph is marked in hundreds, thousands, millions, pounds, dollars, Kilograms, tons, meters, kilometers, or percentage and so on... .

Strategy No. 2: Description of the Graph

- ★ No need to write the whole data. For example: There is no need to give reasons for why figures are moving low or high. No specialised knowledge or individual opinions are required.
- ★ **Describe the Trends:** A trend needs to be described, i.e., how values change generally over time and it is important to describe the changes along with some sort of numerical values.
- ★ If there is only one graph and it does not have much numerical data in it, then it will be expected to include all or nearly all of the numerical details.
- ★ If there is an option with two graphs, then it is not necessary to describe every small or big detail of numerical data as in the writing text, the candidate has to write only 150 words to perform the Task-1. So just include the significant detail which is worth to mention and make it more reliable and stable to understand.

Example : Line Graph

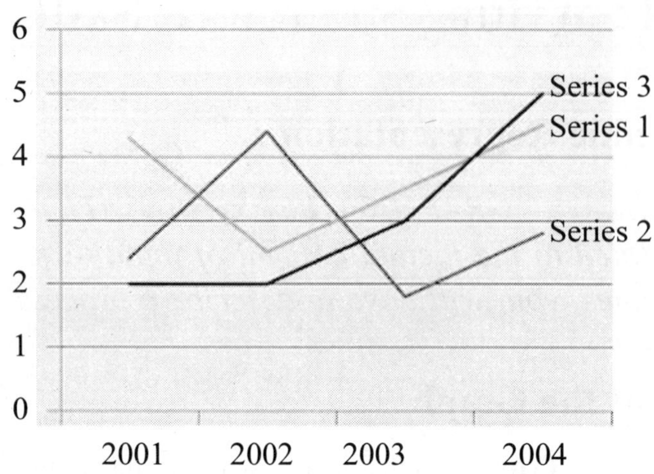

- ✯ Describe the trend pictorically.
- ✯ Describe the movement of the lines of the graph giving numerical details at the important points of the line.
- ✯ Use appropriate vocabulary.

Example : Bar Graph

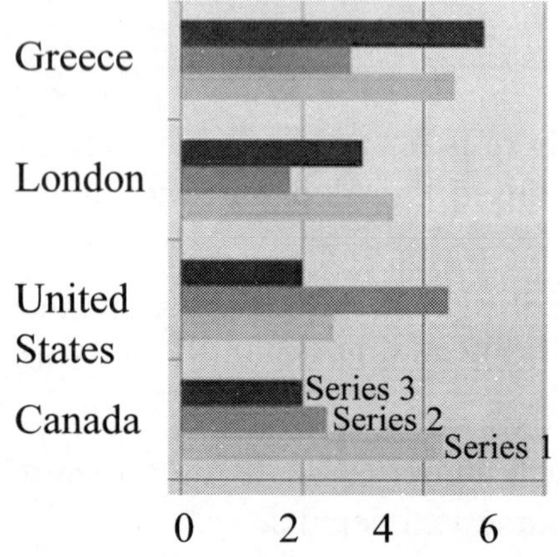

- ✯ Describe the highest value to the lowest value or the lowest value to the highest value if there are many bars. Individuals can sometimes group together for description 1 or 2 or 3 bars which have similar or the same values.
- ✯ If there are many bars and the individuals can't group them, then describe the ones that is most significant.

Example : Table Representation

Grade/Year	1999	2000	2001	2002	2003	2004
Kindergarten	2.4	2.5	2.6	2.7	2.8	2.9
Grades 1-2	1.5	1.2	1.3	1.5	1.8	2.1
Grades 3-4	1.6	1.7	1.8	1.9	2.1	2.2
Grades 5-6	1.5	1.3	1.3	1.6	2.1	2.6
Grades 7-8	1.6	1.6	1.6	2.2	2.4	2.5

TIPS

- ✭ Describe the highest value to the lowest value or the lowest value to the highest value
- ✭ Describe all the values and sections that are significant to mention.
- ✭ Use appropriate words to describe the graph.

Example : Pie Chart

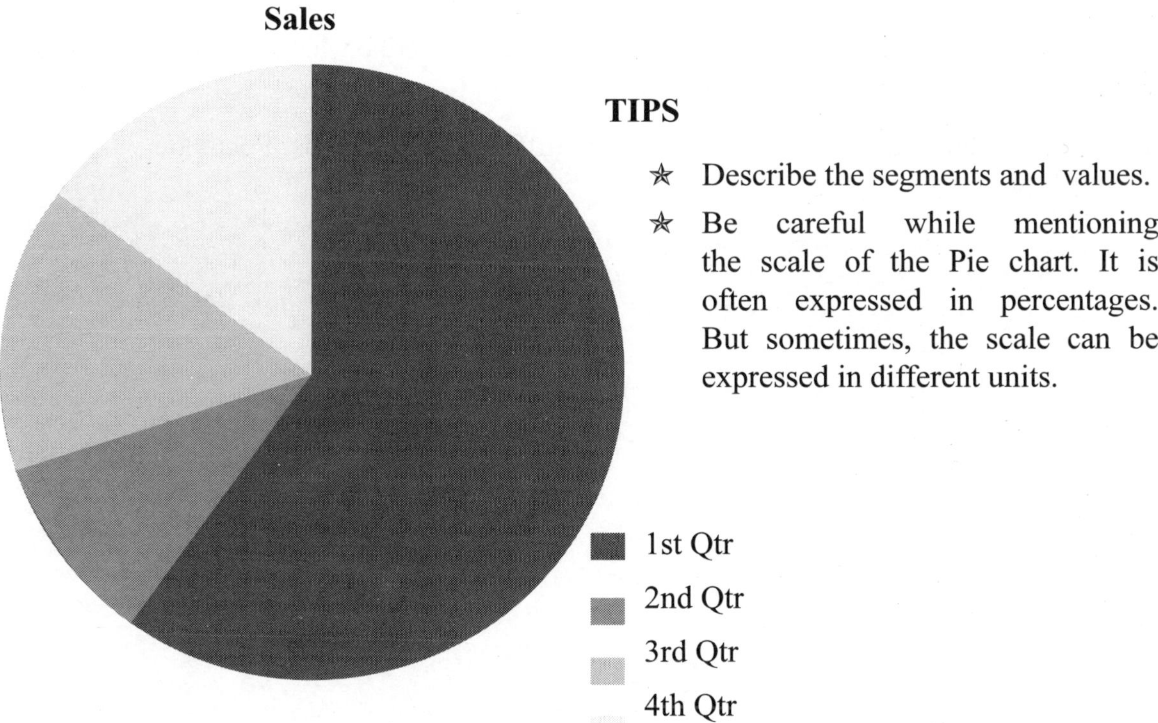

TIPS

- ✭ Describe the segments and values.
- ✭ Be careful while mentioning the scale of the Pie chart. It is often expressed in percentages. But sometimes, the scale can be expressed in different units.

Example : Description of the Process

1. Describe how solar radiation can be utilized to provide domestic hot water and lighting.

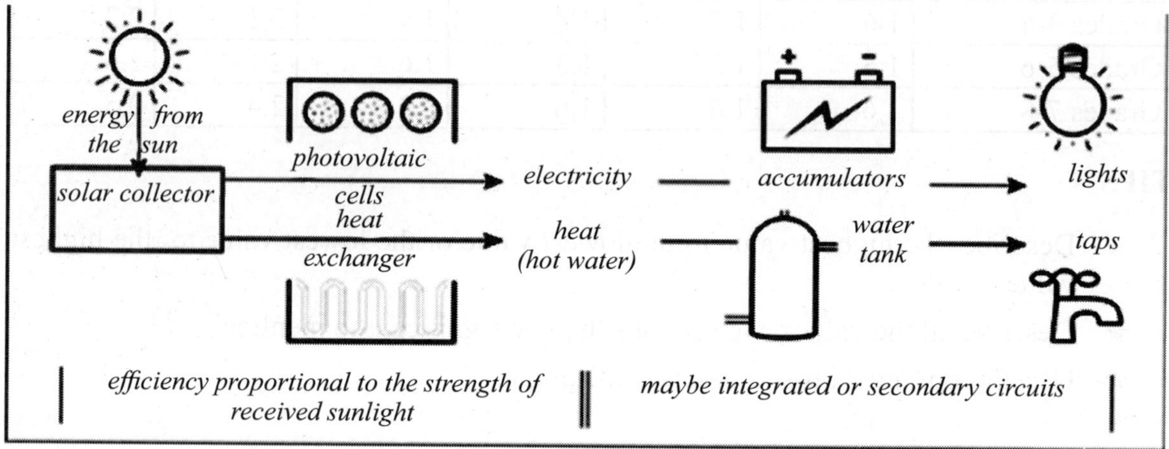

Process: With a process, you must describe how something works or how it is made or used.

Object: With an object or set of objects, candidates must describe what something is or what it does. Focus on the relationship between parts.

Data: With data, you must describe changes, differences or trends. Focus on what these are and why.

Strategy No. 3 : Ready-Made Structure of the Graph

How to Start the Graph

A. Presenting Visuals

As you will see from this graph…... On the line graph, you will note:

A strong upward trend in the sales of product A...

- ★ despite occasional fluctuations...
- ★ with a slight drop during the holiday season ...
- ★ with occasional variations due to ...

The overall performance of product B is good

- ★ the initial surge in sales was followed by a period of slower growth in the second half of the year
- ★ the instant success of the product was followed by a period of stabilisation in the level of sales

B. Commenting Trends

Increases:

- ★ a slight/constant/marked/substantial increase in sales
- ★ an increase of about/roughly/approximately/in the region of ...%
- ★ a little over/above what we predicted
- ★ the recovery/upturn began in (month)
- ★ an overall increase in...
- ★ an upward trend in the demand for...
- ★ sales reached record levels/reached a peak in (month)
- ★ a strong surge in the sales of ...
- ★ by (month) the figure had risen to ...
- ★ we predict that sales will soar in the coming year/over the next ...months.

Decreases:

- ★ just under our target
- ★ way below our expectations

- ☆ a slight/notable/significant decrease in
- ☆ a drop of about ...% in ...
- ☆ a slight/regular/dramatic decline/reduction in ...
- ☆ the downturn began in (month)
- ☆ the situation began to deteriorate in (month)
- ☆ the number has continued to fall

Fluctuations/Variations:

- ☆ a slow start developed into a steady progress in sales
- ☆ an initial upward trend was followed by ...
- ☆ we note slight fluctuations throughout the year
- ☆ normal seasonal variations are the cause of occasional downward trends
- ☆ sales have been (rather) irregular
- ☆ the level/the rate has been unstable since ...
- ☆ you will note a certain instability in the rate of ...

C. Conclusions

- ☆ Appropriate measures must be taken
- ☆ The only option we have is to ...
- ☆ These changes are inevitable.
- ☆ The result/outcome will be ...

Strategy No. 4 : Lexical-Resource for the Graphs

Vocabulary for Describing Graph

Verbs	Nouns	Verbs	Nouns
Rise (to)	A Rise	Reduce (to)	A Reduction (of)
Increase (to)	An Increase		A Slump
Go up (to)		Level out	A Levelling out
Grow (to)	Growth	No Change	No Change
Climb (to)	A Climb	Remain Stable (at)	
Boom	A Boom	Remain Steady (at)	
Peak (at)	(Reach) a peak (at)	Stay (at)	
Fall (to)	A Fall (Of)	Stay constant (at)	
Decline (to)	A Decline (of)	Maintain the same level	
Decrease (to)	A Decrease (of)		
Dip (to)	A Dip (of)		
Drop (to)	A Drop (of)		
Go Down (to)			

Vocabulary for Describing Graph

Adjectives	Adverbs	Adjectives	Adverbs
Dramatic	Dramatically	Rapid	Rapidly
Sharp	Sharply	Quick	Quickly
Huge	Hugely	Swift	Swiftly
Enormous	Enormously	Sudden	Suddenly
Steep	Steeply	Steady	Steadily
Substantial	Substantially	Gradual	Gradually
Considerable	Considerably	Slow	Slowly
Significant	Significantly		
Marked	Markedly		
Moderate	Moderately		
Slight	Slightly		
Small			
Minimal	Minimally		

Task – 2 : Strategies for Essay Writing

Strategy No. 5 : Magic of Rhetorical Devices
(The Art of Writing An Article)

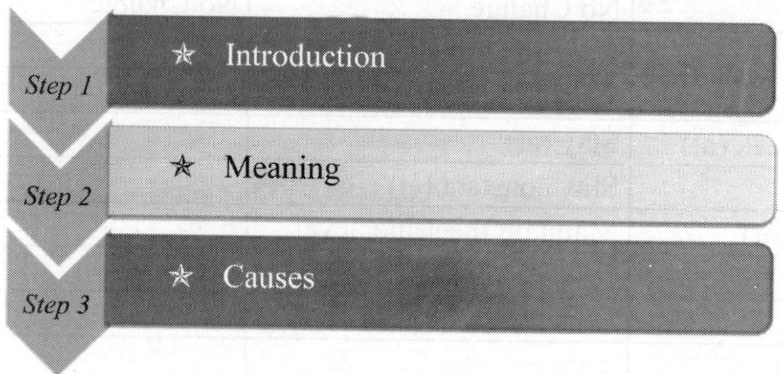

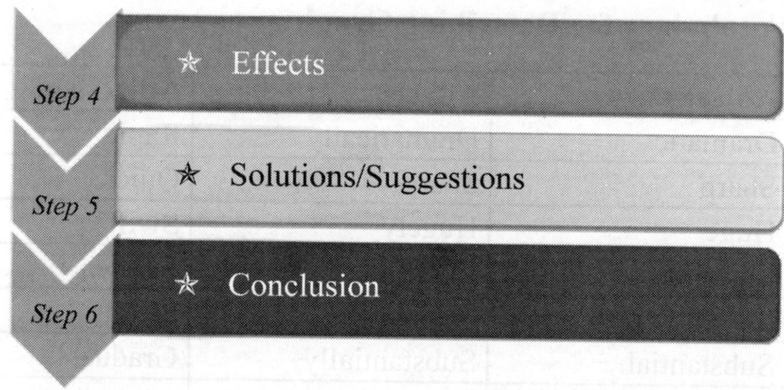

Example : Craze for Overseas Education among Indians

Introduction

- ✭ Overseas Education is the order of the day
- ✭ Better opportunities of development in abroad
- ✭ A trend and prestige issue
- ✭ Craze among Punjabi youngsters over a decade

Article: Overseas Education is the order of the day. The influx of Indian students to foreign universities and colleges is on the rise. So what propels students to study overseas? Is it because of too much of competition in India? Or is it because of better quality of education? Or is it a global exposure? It would be difficult to point out a specific reason for why the girl next door is packing her bags and leaving for the UK tomorrow. It might be the frustrating education system in India; it might be freedom from home; she might even be desire to add value to her CV.

Meaning

- ✭ Foreign Education
- ✭ Study Abroad
- ✭ Different From Academic Education

Article: Overseas education is different from academic education. In other words, it is foreign education. Foreign universities that provide internationally recognised qualifications of higher standards.

Causes

- ✭ Lack of Educational and Job Opportunities
- ✭ Defective Indian Educational System
- ✭ Proper due is not granted

Article: Now Let's discuss all those reasons why overseas education becomes a craze among the youngsters. It may be due to lack of educational and job opportunities for the Indian Youth, Defective Indian education, Proper due is not granted according to worth…, etc.

Positive

- ✯ Become a global player
- ✯ Opens up opportunities in international markets
- ✯ Add value to your CV
- ✯ Provide environment to acquire skills
- ✯ Broadens your horizon

Article: Moreover, foreign education offers international exposure, opens up opportunities in international job markets, adds value to your CV, provides environment to acquire skills that you might not learn in domestic environment, and finally, broadens your horizon. But it doesn't mean foreign education does not suffer from defects.

Negative

- ✯ Loss of talented youth and caliber
- ✯ Problem of Racialism
- ✯ Jobs are not according to their worth
- ✯ Ill-treatment
- ✯ Too many restrictions, rules and regulations

Article: The basic disadvantage of foreign education is the problem of racialism for example: Recent attack on Indians in which they were badly treated and stabbed by foreigners. Everyday Indians are losing their dignity on foreign grounds. Not only this they are also restricted with so many hard and fast rules which curtail their individual liberty at every step.

Effects

- ✯ Academic education will loose its gleam
- ✯ Talent goes waste
- ✯ Disgracing cultural dignity and humanity
- ✯ Geniusness of Indians disposed of in just few dollars

Article: Overseas Education affects academic education in india as India and there is brain-drain It will loss its gleam as indian talents of India are utilised by foreigners. In this way, genuineness of Indians dispose of in no time. Moreover, when they start doing job there, they are even ready to compromise with their worth and sell their labour in just few dollars. This reflects the cripple attitude of the Indian youth on foreign grounds.

Solutions

- ✯ Provide ample job opportunities to the Indian youth

- ✯ The government should make some particular strategy
- ✯ Be patriotic towards your nation
- ✯ Due according to the worth

Article: Here government can step forward and adopt some strategy or policy to save the talent and the caliber of the Indian Youth and provide them ample job opportunities so that they stop even thinking of settling abroad. Moreover, rules and regulations related to Visa Application should be revised.

Conclusion

- ✯ Go abroad just to learn, not to settle
- ✯ East or west India is the best
- ✯ Be patriotic

Article: In the end, I would like to say that Overseas Education is good but setting abroad not. One should not forget that education cannot be received but only achieved with intricate self-worth, then what matters if its an Indian education or foreign education? One should be devoted and dedicated towards the nation of birth and serve that country till his/ her last breath.

Nutshell

Introduction	Article
Meaning	Article
Causes	Article
Positive	Article
Negative	Article
Effects	Article
Solution	Article
Conclusion	Article

Strategy No. 6

W-FAMILY

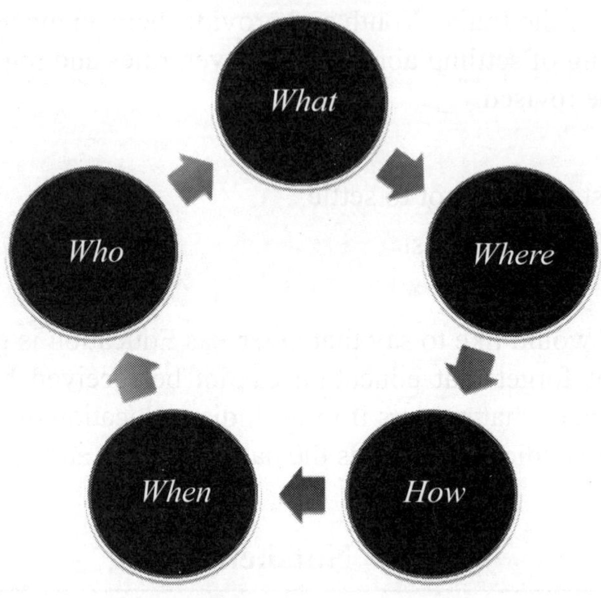

EVALUATION OF 'W' FAMILY

Whenever you want to write an article, just before writing, think over all the questions related to that topic.

TOPIC	CRAZE FOR OVERSEAS EDUCATION AMONG STUDENTS
Why...	Overseas Education?
Who...	Will provide you overseas education?
Where...	People go for overseas education?
What...	Are those reasons because of which they prefer to study abroad?
How...	Can you make your future secure by opting for overseas education?

Band Description

IELTS Task 2: Writing Band Description (public version)

Band	Task Response	Coherence & Cohesion
9	Fully addresses all parts of the task. Presents a fully developed position in answer to the question with relevant, fully extended and well supported ideas.	Uses cohesion in such a way that it attracts no attention. Skilfully manages paragraphing.
8	Sufficiently addresses all parts of the task. Presents a well-developed response to the questions with relevant, extended and supportive ideas.	Sequences information and ideas logically. Manages all aspects of cohesion well. Uses paragraphing sufficiently and appropriately.
7	Addresses all parts of the task. Presents, extends and supports main ideas, but there may be a tendency to overgeneralise and/or supporting ideas may lack focus.	Logically organises information and ideas; there is clear progression throughout. Uses a range of cohesive devices appropriately although there may be some under forever use. Presents a clear central topic within each paragraph.
6	Addresses all parts of the task although some parts may be more fully converted than others. Presents a relevant position although the conclusions may become unclear or repetitive. Presents relevant main ideas but some may be inadequately developed unclear.	Arranges information and ideas coherently and there is a clear overall progression. Uses cohesive devices effectively, but cohesion within and or between sentences may be faulty or mechanical. May not always use referencing clearly or appropriately. Uses paragraphing, but not always logically.
5	Addresses the task only partially, the format may be inappropriate in places. Expresses a position but the development is not always clear.	Presents information with some organisation but there may be a lack of overall progression. Makes inadequate, inaccurate or over-emphasises imformation.

Lexical Resource	Grammatical Range and Accuracy
Uses a wide range of vocabulary with very natural and sophisticated control of lexical features; rare minor errors occur only as 'slips'.	Uses a wide range of structures with full felexibility and accuracy; rare minor errors occur only as 'slips'.
Uses a wide range of vocabulary fluently and flexibly to convey precise meanings. Skilfully uses uncommon lexical items but there may be occasional inaccuracies in word choice and collocation. Produces rare errors in spellings and for word formations.	Uses a wide range of structures. The majority of sentences are error-free. Makes only very occasional errors or inappropriates.
Uses a sufficient range of vocabulary to allow some flexibility and precision. Uses less common lexical items with some awareness of style and collocation. May produce occasional errors in word choice, spellings and for word formations.	Uses a variety of complex structures. Produces frequent error-free sentences. Has good control of grammar and punctuation but may make a few errors.
Uses an adequate range of vocabulary for the task. Attempts to use less common vocabulary but with some inaccuracy. makes some errors in spellings and for word formations, but they do not impede communication.	Uses a mix of simple and complex sentence forms. Makes some errors in grammar and punctuation but they rarely reduce communication.
Uses a limited range of vocabulary, but this is minimally adequate for the task. May make noticeable errors in the task.	Uses only a limited range of structures. Attempts complex sentences but these tend to be less accurate than simple sentences.

Writing Practice Test-1

Task – 1

Write a report for the university lecturer describing the information in the graph below.

- ✯ You should write at least 150 words.
- ✯ Allow yourself 20 minutes for this task.

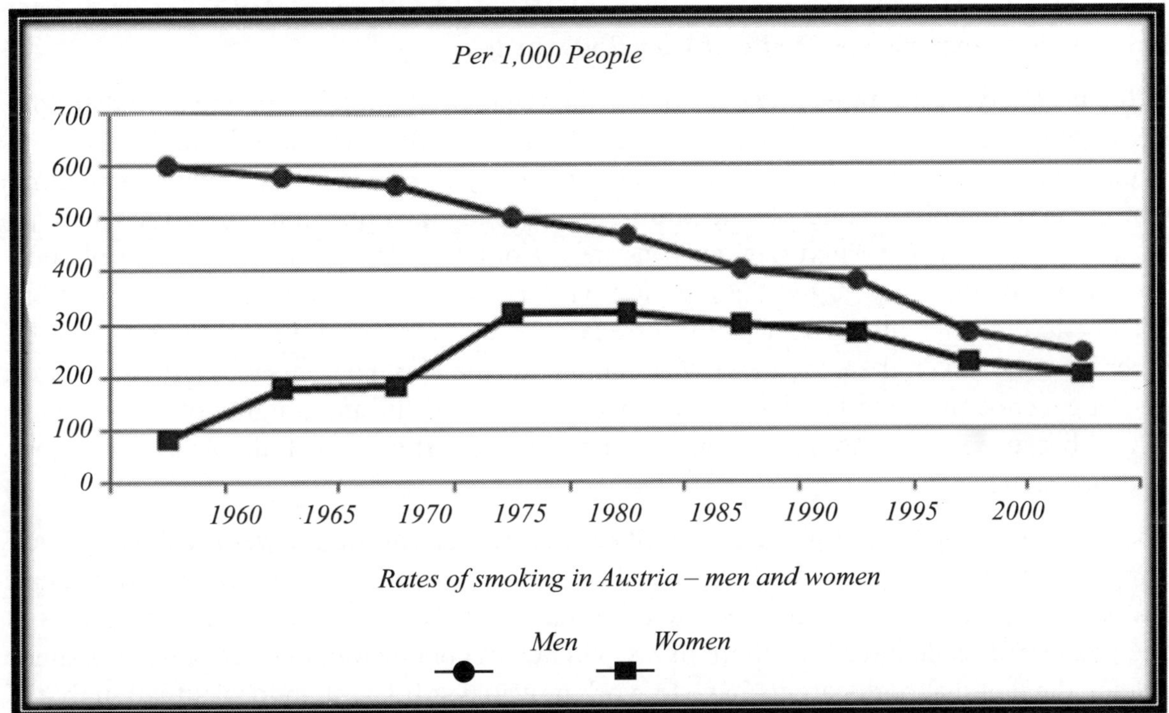

The graph compares the rate of smoking in men and women in Austria between the years, 1960 and 2000. It can be clearly seen that the rate of smoking for both men and women is currently declining and that fewer women have smoked throughout the period. In 1960, 600 men in every 1,000 were smoking. This number decreased gradually to 500 by 1974 and continued to decrease, but more steeply to 250 in 2000. In contrast, the rate of smoking in women in 1960 was very low at only 80 in every 1,000. By 1968, this increased to 170, and increased again but more steeply to 320 in 1977. The rate of female smokers then remained stable at 320 until 1984 at which point the figures began to decline and had dropped to 200 by 2000.In conclusion, we can see that the rate of smoking in men dropped throughout the whole period, but was always at a higher level than the female figures. The rate of smoking in women increased until 1977, but then decreased for the rest of the period.

Task–2

You should spend about 40 minutes on this task.

Write about the following topic:

In today's competitive world, many families find it necessary for both parents to go out to work. While some say the children in these families benefit from the additional income, others feel they lack support because of their parents' absence.

Give reasons for your answer and include any relevant examples from your own knowledge or experience. Write at least 250 words.

In the past, a typical family consisted of a father who went out to work and a mother who stayed at home and looked after the children. Nowadays, it is the norm for both parents to work. This situation can affect children both positively and negatively. Some people think that the children of working parents are in an advantageous position where their parents are able to afford more luxuries, such as new clothes, video games or mobile phones. Proponents of this view argue that children are able to enjoy and experience more from life due to their parents' extra wealth; for example, by going on foreign holidays. On the other hand, however, there are those who claim that when both parents work, their children do not get enough support and attention, meaning that the children might not do as well at school because there is no one at house to provide support with such things as homework or exam revision.

The absence of a parent at home could make it easier for children to get involved in such things as drugs or undertake drinking.When I was growing up, both my parents worked and I was always well provided for. On the other hand, I think that it would sometimes have been better if I could have seen more of my parents. In conclusion, I believe that we cannot change the fact that both parents have to work nowadays. It is not an ideal situation, but if parents devote time for their children in the evenings and at the weekends, then the children will not suffer in any way. It must be stated that the extra income generated by both parents working, makes for a much higher standard of living which benefits the whole family.

Writing Practice Test-2

Task–1

You should spend about 20 minutes on this task.

The diagram below shows how a central heating system in a house works. Summarise the information by selecting and reporting the main features, and make comparisons where relevant.

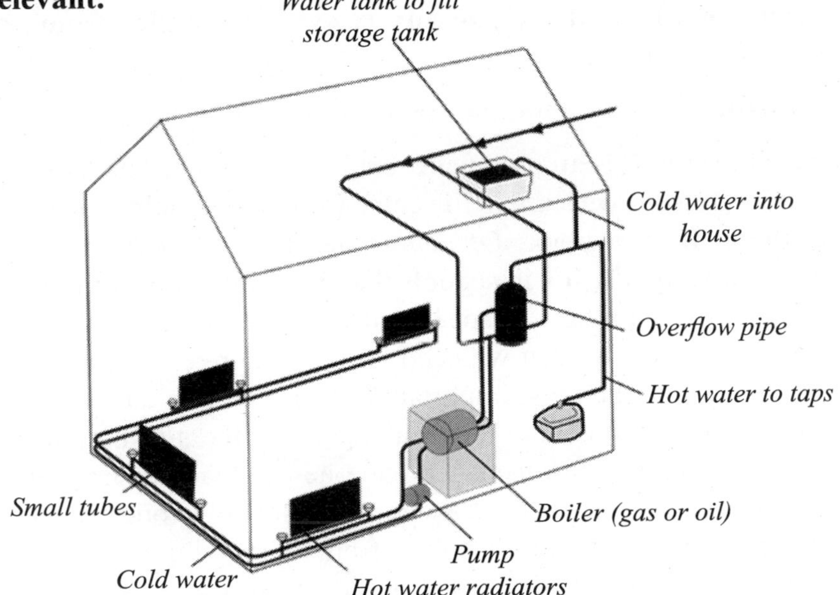

You should write at least 150 words.

This diagram provides an overview of a domestic central heating system. It shows how the tank, boiler and pipes ensure a constant flow of hot water to both the radiators and the taps.The cold water enters the house and is stored in a water storage tank in the roof. From there flows down to the boiler, located on the ground floor of the house.The boiler, which is fuelled by gas or oil, heats up the water as it passes through it. The hot water is then pumped around the house through a system of pipes and flows into the radiators, located in different rooms. The water circulates through the radiators, which have small tubes inside them to help distribute the heat, and this warms each of the rooms. Some of the water is directed to the taps to provide hot water for the house. Once the water has been through the pipes and radiators, it is returned to the boiler to be reheated and circulated around the house again.

Task–2

You should spend about 40 minutes on this task.

Write about the following topic:

It has been said, "Not every thing that is learnt is contained in books." Compare and contrast knowledge gained from experience with knowledge gained from books. In your opinion, which source is more important? Why?

Give reasons for your answer and include any relevant examples from your own knowledge or experience.

Write at least 250 words.

"Experience is the best teacher" is an old cliché, but I agree with it. The most important, and sometimes the hardest lessons we learn in life come from our participation in situations. You can learn everything from a book. *Of course, learning from books in a formal educational setting is also valuable.* It's in schools that we learn the information we need to function in our society. We learn how to speak and write and understand mathematical equations. This is all the information that we need to live in our communities and earn a living. Nevertheless, I think that the most important lessons can't be taught; they have to be experienced. No one can teach us how to get along with others or how to have self-respect. As we grow from children into teenagers, no one can teach us how to deal with peer pressure. As we leave adolescence behind and enter adult life, no one can teach us how to fall in love and get married.This shouldn't stop us from looking for guidelines along the way. Teachers and parents are valuable sources of advice when we're young. As we enter into new stages in our lives, the advice we receive from them is very helpful because they have already had similar experiences. But experiencing our own triumphs and disasters is really the only way to learn how to deal with life.

Writing Practice Test-3

Task–1

You should spend about 20 minutes on this task.

Eating sweet foods produces acid in the mouth, which can cause tooth decay.

(High acid levels are measured by low pH values) Describe the information below and discuss the implications for dental health.

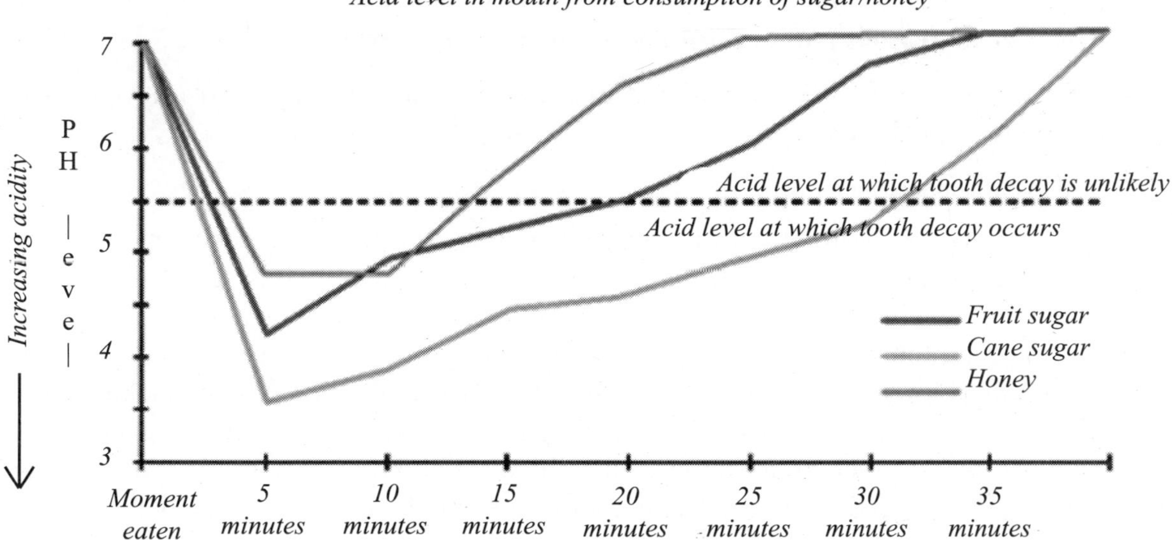

You should write at least 150 words.

Anyone who has visited a dentist has been told that eating excessive amounts of sweets risk harming the teeth. This is because sweets lower the pH levels in the mouth to dangerous levels.When the pH level in the mouth is kept above 5.5, acidity is such that teeth are unlikely to be in danger of decay. Sweet foods, however, cause pH in the mouth to drop for a time, and the longer pH levels remain below 5.5, the greater the opportunity for decay to occur. By comparing fruit sugar, cane sugar and honey, which are all common ingredients of sweet foods, we find that cane sugar lowers the pH levels for the longest period, thus producing the greatest risk of the three. Approximately, five minutes after consuming cane sugar, the pH levels drop to as little as 3.5. They then begin to rise slowly, but do not rise above 5.5, until at least 30 minutes have elapsed. By contrast, fruit sugar, which causes the mouth's acidity to fall to just above, poses a danger for a shorter period: tooth decay is unlikely within 20 minutes after consumption. Honey appears to be an even less risky substance. Though acidity falls to about 4.75 within five minutes of consumption, it returns to above 5.5 in under 15 minutes. The implications, then, are that people who insist on eating sweet foods should be aware of the ingredients, and that fruit sugar or honey appear preferable to cane sugar.

Task–2

You should spend about 40 minutes on this task.

Write about the following topic:

Nowadays, food has become easier to prepare. Has this change improved the way people live? Use specific reasons and examples to support your answer.

Give reasons for your answer and include any relevant examples from your own knowledge or experience.

Write at least 250 words.

The 20th century has brought with it many advances. With those advances, human lives have changed dramatically. In some ways, life is worse, but mostly it is better. Changes in food preparation methods, for example, have improved our lives greatly. The convenience of preparing food today is amazing. Even stoves have gotten too slow for us. *Microwave cooking is much easier*. We can press a few buttons and a meal is completely cooked in just a short time. People used to spend hours preparing an oven-cooked meal, and now they can use that time for other, better things. Plus, there are all kinds of portable, prepackaged foods we can buy. Heat them in the office microwave, and lunch at work is quick and easy.

Food preparation today allows for more variety. With refrigerators and freezers, we can preserve a lot of different foods in our homes. Since technology makes cooking so much faster, people are willing to make several dishes for even a small meal. Parents are more likely to let children be picky, now that they can easily heat them up some prepackaged macaroni and cheese on the side. Needless to say, adults living in the same house may have very different eating habits as well. If they don't want to cook a lot of different dishes, it's common now to eat out at restaurants several times a week. Healthful eating is also easier than ever now. When people cook, they use new fat substitutes and cooking sprays to cut fat and calories. This reduces the risk of heart diseases and high cholesterol. Additionally, we can buy fruits and vegetable fresh, frozen or canned. They are easy to prepare, so many of us eat more of those nutritious items daily. A hundred years ago, you couldn't imagine the process of taking some frozen fruit and ice from the freezer, adding some low-fat yogurt from a plastic cup and some juice from a can in the refrigerator, and whipping up a low-fat smoothie in the blender! Our lifestyle is fast, but people still like good food. What new food preparation technology has given us is more choices. Today, we can prepare food that is more convenient, healthier and of greater variety than ever before in history.

Writing Practice Test-4

Task–1

You should spend about 20 minutes on this task.

The graphs below show the numbers of male and female workers in 2000 and 2010 in several employment sectors of Australia.Write a report for the university teacher describing the information shown.

You should write at least 150 words.

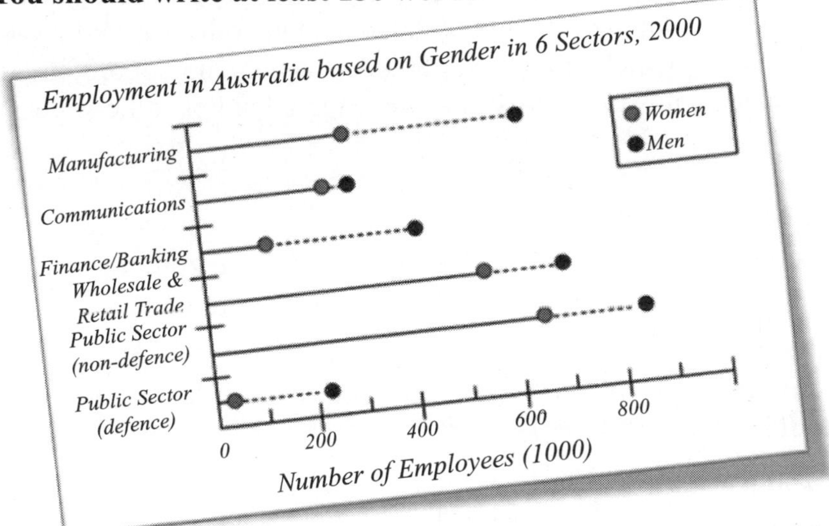

The two decades between 2000 and 2010 brought significant changes in the representation of women in Australia work force, according to the graphs. In 2000, for example, some 300,000 men and 250,000 women worked in the communication sector. Twenty years later, though the number of men remained unchanged, the number of women rose to 550,000.

A similar situation was seen in the wholesale and retail trade sector, where the number of women rose from about 550,000 in 2000 to almost 800,000, two decades later. The number of men in this sector remained stable over the period, at around 700,000. Women also made gains in both the finance/banking industries and in the defence-related public sector.

Whereas some 125,000 women worked in finance and banking institutions in 2000, the number increased to 450,000 by 2000. The number of men grew only marginally from 425,000 to 480,000 over the same period. In defence, the number of men declined from 225,000 to 200,000, while the number of women rose from 25,000 to over 100,000. Two sectors that retained stable employment numbers for both men and women were manufacturing, which had about 300,000 women and 650,000 men in both surveyed years, and the public sector (non-defence), which employed 650,000 women and 850,000 men. Thus, women appear to have made gains in the Australia work force but not at the expense of men.

Task–2

You should spend about 40 minutes on this task. Present a written argument or case to an educated reader with no specialist knowledge of the following topic:

People who have original ideas are of much greater value to the society than those who are simply able to copy the ideas of others well. To what extent do you agree or disagree with this statement?

You should write at least 250 words.

I certainly agree that people who come up with new ideas, i.e., in other words, those who 'invent' or 'discover' things are very important to the society as a whole. However, I also think there is a role in society for good imitators. No one would deny that the key individuals should be thanked for providing us with certain facilities that we use every day. Where, would we be, for example, without basic items, such as the washing machine, the television and more recently, the computer? These items are now used so regularly that we tend to take them for granted. In fact, the society we live in today has become increasingly consumer-oriented, and while it may be possible to constantly update and improve consumer goods, not everyone where I live can afford the prices of these innovations. Furthermore, not everyone lives in an area that has accessibility to the latest models on the market. For this reason, there is a value to be placed on being able to provide good copies of expensive items. Having said that, we can say that certain innovations have a more serious impact on our lives than consumer goods and cannot easily be replicated. Vital medicines like *penicillin* and *vaccines* against dangerous diseases also exist because people made continual efforts to develop them. Scientific ideas, such as these enable us to live longer and escape illnesses.

ABSTRACT

SPEAKING MODULE

IELTS speaking has three parts Part 1, II & III, which includes Interview Sessions, Cue Cards & Followup Queries. We endeavour to help the candidate with the collection of the most popular 50 questions for part I and most popular Cue Cards for part 2 alongwith extended discourse (Part 3) for IELTS candidate.

Chapter 6 : Speaking Strategies, Skills and Guidelines

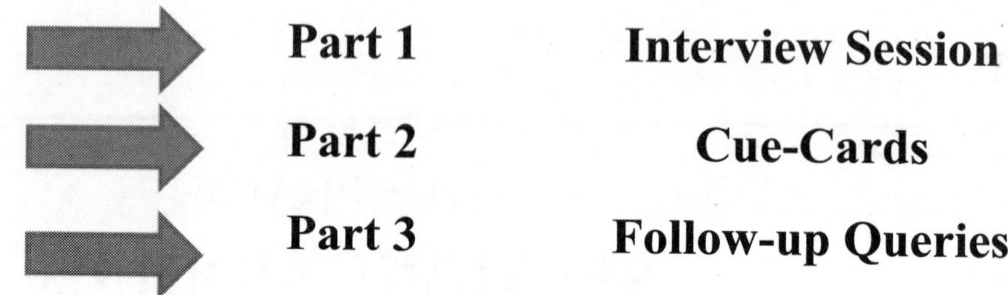

Paper Duration: 15 To 20 Minutes

PART 1

Phase A: Home/Study/Work

Phase B: Likes & Dislikes

Food/Shopping/Festivals/Markets/Books /Sports, etc.

SAMPLE QUESTIONS FOR PHASE A (WARM UP QUERIES)

Home/Study/Work

- ✯ Do you work or are you a student ?
- ✯ Can you tell me something about your studies?
- ✯ What is your favourite subject?
- ✯ What is your study plan ?

SAMPLE QUESTIONS FOR PHASE - B

What do you eat for breakfast?

STRATEGY NO. 1: BE CULTURAL APPROPRIATELY

For example: While answering this question, make sure that certain diet/breakfast must belong to the culture of your state.

Will people's diet change in future ?

STRATEGY NO. 2: BE VERSATILE IN ANSWERING

For example: Do discuss some other cuisines apart from your states cuisine.

Here examiner wants to see your exposure.

Do you have any hobbies ?

STRATEGY NO. 3: UPDATE YOUR ANSWER

It is necessary to be up to date in answering the questions. Don't follow rote memorization. Whatever present hobbies the candidate is adhered to answer only that.

What are the most popular sports in your country?

STRATEGY NO. 4: ALWAYS USE CURRENT UPDATES

For example: While answering this question, make sure that whatever is going on currently should be discussed. Try to use your IQ level.

How do you spend your spare time?

STRATEGY NO. 5: BE PRACTICAL IN ANSWERING

For example: Do the examiner come to know what exactly your way and standard of living is? Never try to be overconfident in answering.

What kind of music instrument do you enjoy in playing ?/Do you play a musical instrument ?

STRATEGY NO. 6: BE OPTIMISTIC IN APPROACH AND TRY TO COVER ANSWER IN INTRODUCTORY LINES

Sometimes questions are beyond once comprehension, so don't lose heart. That time, rather try to answer in introducing the topic. For example, playing an instrument is not the cup of every one's tea. While answering follow an optimistic approach and say presently, "I Don't know but I really wish to learn flute/piano, etc." or use some introductory lines for music for example: "Music is the food for the soul", etc.

PART 2

CUE-CARD 1

Describe Your Favourite Movie

You should say:

Which the movie it is

Why the movie impressed you so much

You can give your own suggestions

And explain, how it influenced you

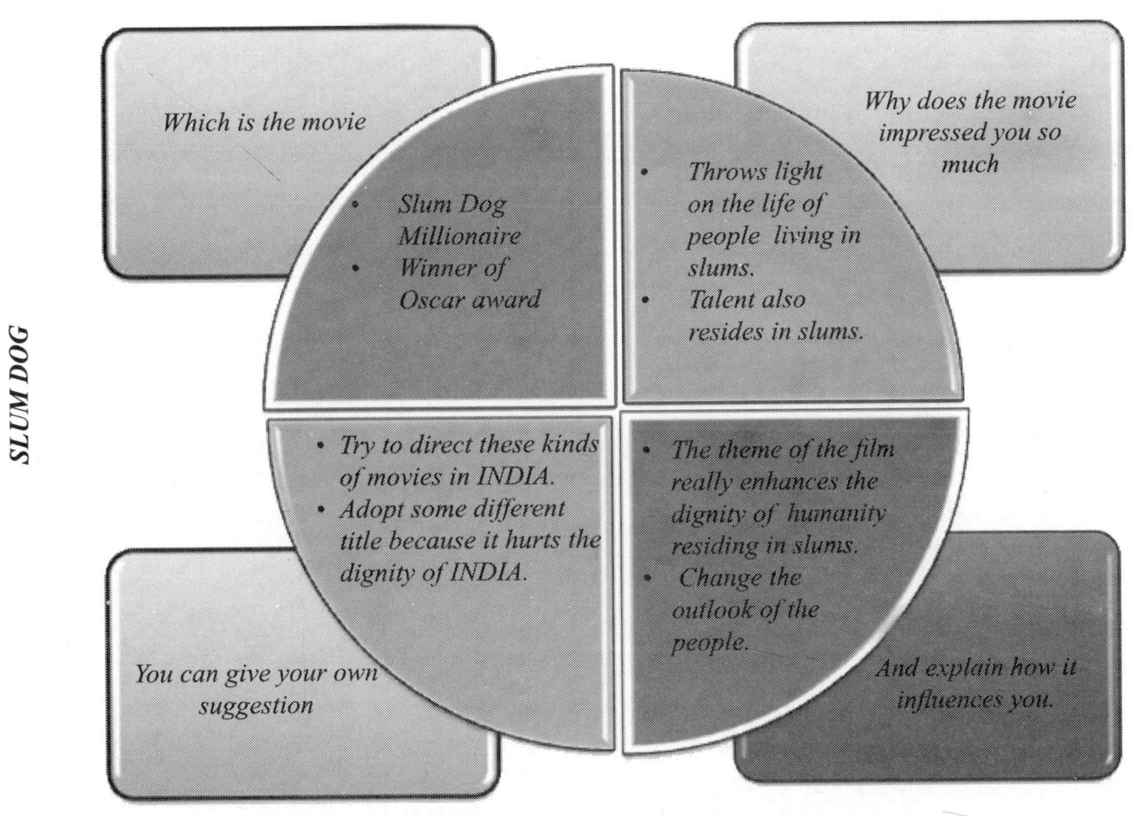

SUMMARIZATION: 'JOURNEY FROM RAGS TO RICHES'

STRATEGY NO. 7: TO CRACK CUE-CARDS

STEP NO. 1 MAKE A GRID: When the examiner offers 2 minutes to think over the topic, make a Grid, and decide the title of the Cue-Card.

STEP NO. 2 ANSWER THE QUERIES: Make the notes and answers of all the following questions of the CUE-CARD.

STEP NO. 3 SYNCHRONIZE THE NOTES WITH SUMMARIZATION: Now start speaking by using the pronouns like It, This, That, etc. You can use three types of pronouns that are utilised like the First Person, the Second Person, the Third Person, etc.

CUE-CARD 2

Describe Your Favourite Gadget

You should say:

Which is the gadget

Why you like that gadget

How it helps you

And explain, whether it brings change in to your life

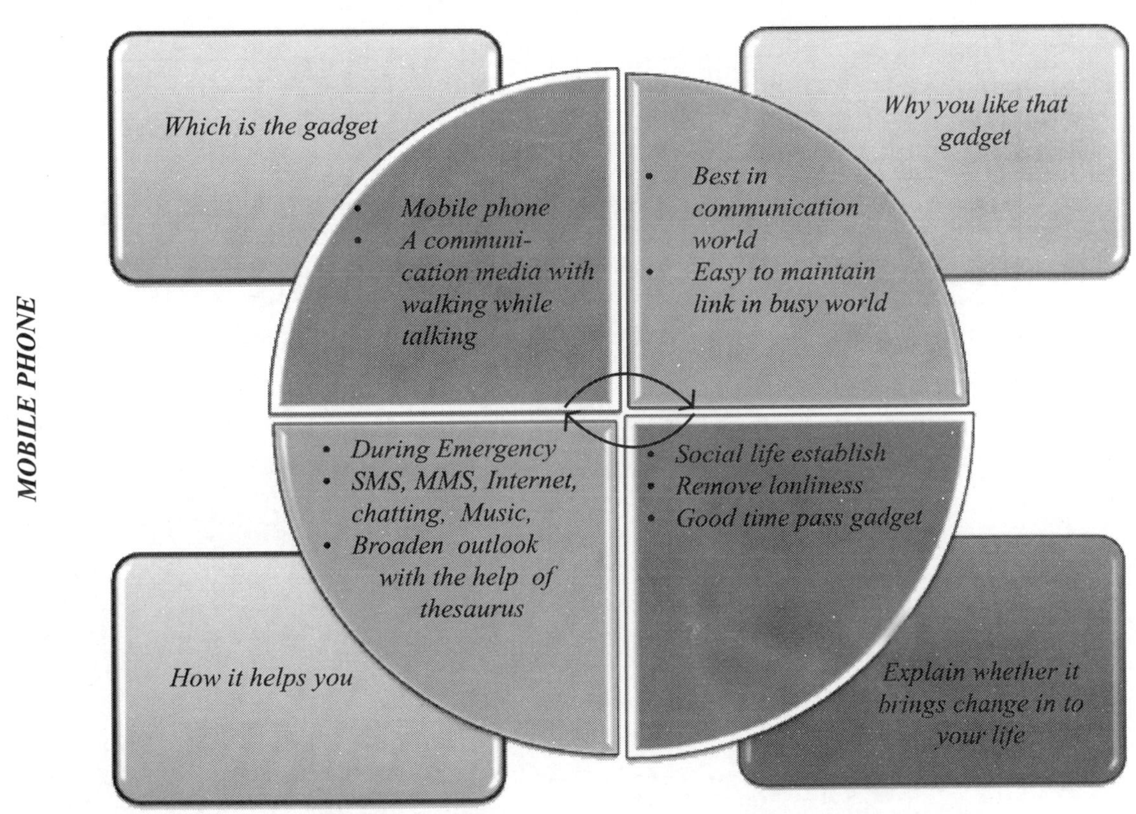

SUMMARIZATION: 'without this gadget life is handicapped'

CUE-CARD 3

Describe Any National Day

You should say:

Which is the day

Why it is celebrated

How it is celebrated

And explain, what you do on this day

Strategies to Approach The Cue-Cards

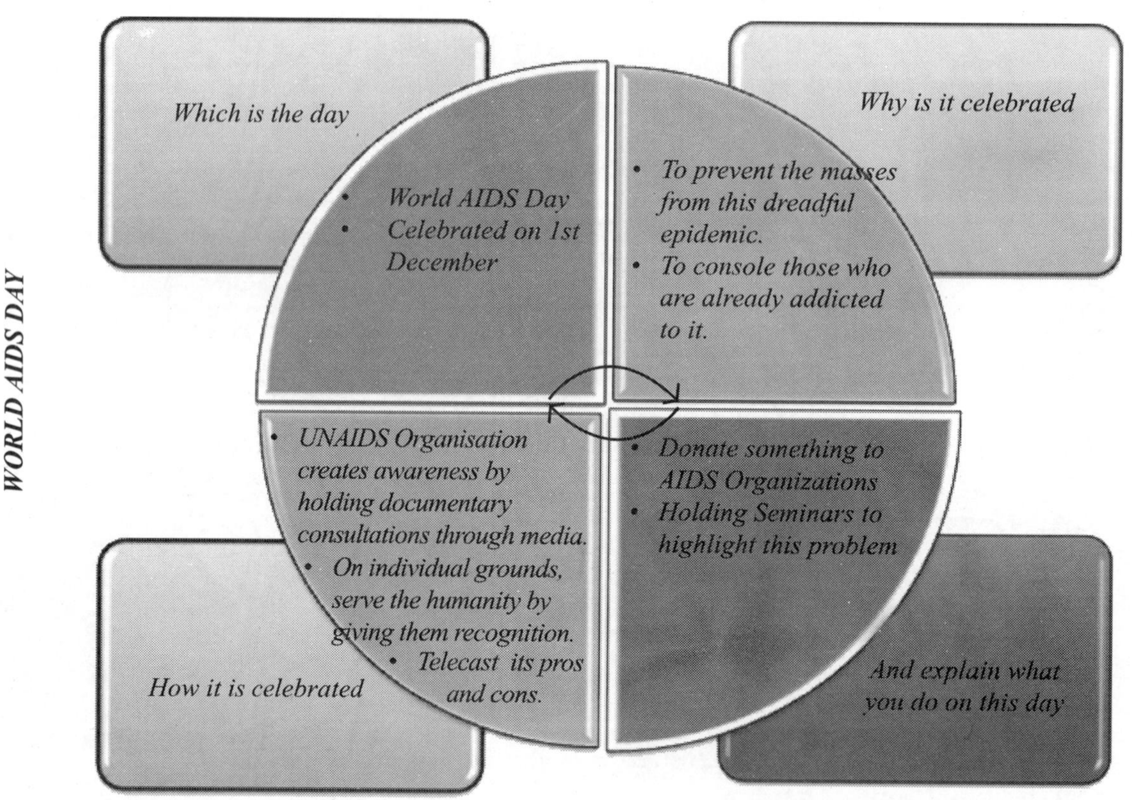

SUMMARIZATION: 'JOURNEY FROM HEAVEN TO HELL'

PART 3

FOLLOW-UP QUESTIONS

1. ***If the Cue-Cards are related to an ideal teacher, then in part 3, a follow on concept will be applied, i.e., all the questions are related to education, school and college.***

   JUST FOLLOW THIS EXAMPLE

   ✯ What is the importance of a teacher in our life?

   ✯ Should teacher be versatile?

   ✯ Do you think teacher should update their knowledge?

2. ***If the Cue-Cards is related to technology in part 3 follow on concept will be applied, i.e., all questions are related to science, communication & inventions.***

   JUST FOLLOW THIS EXAMPLE

   ✯ What are the important inventions of the century?

   ✯ What are the destructive uses of technology?

   ✯ Which forms of technology are you using at home/office ?

   ✯ What is the future of technology?

3. ***If the Cue-Cards are related to shopping, then in part 3, a follow on concept will be applied, i.e., all the questions are related to youngsters, males and females trends.***

   JUST FOLLOW THIS EXAMPLE

   ✯ Do you like shopping?

   ✯ Do you think window shopping is wastage of time?

   ✯ What are the benefits and drawbacks of consumerism?

   ✯ What are the advantages and disadvantages of credit cards?

GUIDELINES FOR SPEAKING MODULE

THE DAY Of INTERVIEW

SUCCESSFUL TIPS FOR STUDENTS

- **BE LOUD & CLEAR**
- **MAINTAIN THE RATE OF SPEECH**
- **TAKE A DEEP BREATH & RELAX**
- **STRICT TO INTERVIEW ETIQUETTES**
- **POSITIVE BODY LANGUAGE/DRESS PROPERLY**

COMMON ERRORS

BEING EXCESSIVELY POLITE

Explanation: Foreign Examiners can become uncomfortable when the candidate is overly respectful.

Example of Error: Saying sir or maam, and waiting to be asked to sit down on the chair by the candidate.

How to Avoid this Error: Be polite and respectful, but not excessively so. Say "Hi" instead of "Good morning sir/maam."

THINKING THAT THE IELTS EXAMINER IS A STRANGER TO YOUR COUNTRY

Explanation: The IELTS Examiner almost certainly lives in the same country as you and has done so for some time.

Example of Error: Saying things such as, "Welcome to the my country!"

How to Avoid this Error: Showing that you know that the examiner is familiar with your country by saying, "In my country, as I am sure that you are aware..."

NOT SPEAKING LIKE AN INDIVIDUAL

Explanation: Although it is common to think as being in part of a group for many people, most IELTS examiners come from backgrounds where they expect and prefer individuals to give their own personal answers to questions.

Example of Error: For example, answering a question by saying, "Of course, I am from.. , so I like.."

How to Avoid this Error: When giving your own opinion say: "In my personal opinion....

USING STEREOTYPES

Explanation: Describing one ethnic or national group as unique and deserving, special treatment is offensive to many people.

Example of Error: For example, answering a question by saying, "---- people are the most hospitable people in the world."

How to Avoid this Error: Recognizing that there are many different types of people in the world and that no one country or ethnic group can be the best at anything. So saying something, such as the following would be acceptable:

"My people have a reputation for being very hospitable..."

TRYING TO BEFRIEND THE EXAMINER

Explanation: Trying to find out information about the examiner, such as "So your name is..?" or "Where are you from?"

Example of Error: Be polite and smile only.

How to Avoid this Error: Remember that you are taking part in a test, not a social activity.

DRESSING INAPPROPRIATELY

Explanation: The IELTS speaking exam is a formal exam. You should dress formally and thereby gain the respect of the Examiner.

Example of Error: Wearing casual clothes.

How to Avoid this Error: Dress like you were going to a job interview.

TRYING TO MAKE PHYSICAL CONTACT WITH THE IELTS EXAMINER

Explanation: This is usually through trying to shake hands with the Examiner. It is a formal exam, so physical contact between the Candidate and the Examiner is inappropriate and may make the Examiner feel uncomfortable.

Example of Error: Trying to shake hands with the Examiner.

How to Avoid this Error: Avoid it unless the examiner chooses to shake your hands. Then you probably should do so, so as to avoid being disrespectful to the IELTS Examiner.

INTRUDING ON THE EXAMINER'S PERSONAL SPACE

Explanation: Most Examiners are from countries where it is important to respect people's personal space; which is around a handshake distance from another person (30 cm). Many people, especially native English speaking Examiners, frequently feel uncomfortable and offended when strangers intrude into their area of personal space.

Example of Error: Leaning across the interview table into the examiner.

DO'S AND DONOT'S FOR IELTS SPEAKING EXAM

DO'S FOR IELTS

- ✯ Give extended responses.
- ✯ The IELTS instructor gives more weightage to comprehensive and complete answer.
- ✯ Be concise and to the point.
- ✯ Don't beat about the bush in front of the IELTS examiner.
- ✯ Be grammatically correct
- ✯ Try to use correct tenses and connectors.
- ✯ Speak in simple, small sentences.
- ✯ Usage of appropriate English words.
- ✯ Don't use slang language like wanna, gonna, etc.
- ✯ Usage of proverbs, phrases, idioms and metaphors
- ✯ Troubleshooting
- ✯ If the question is not clear, use words like sorry/pardon.
- ✯ Speak in a nice and pleasant tone.
- ✯ Use synonyms by substituting meanings.

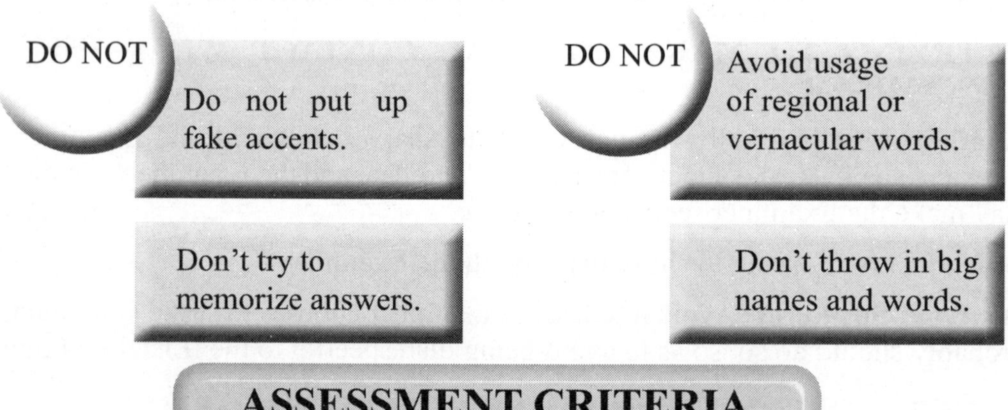

ASSESSMENT CRITERIA

FLUENCY | COHERENCE | LEXICAL RESOURCE | PRONUNCIATION

(All these terms are thoroughly discussed in our 3rd book of IELTS TECH i.e. VOCAL COSMETICS)

Chapter 7 : Part I – Interview Session

MOST POPULAR 50 QUESTIONS (INTERVIEW SESSION)

1. What is your full name ? What should I call you?

Ans. My name is …… Ankit Bhardwaj. You can simply call me ANKIT.

2. Can I see your ID?

Ans. Sure …. Please.

FAMILY

3. Tell me something about your family?

Ans. Well….. I belong to a simple, small and nuclear family. I am living with adorable parents and two small sisters. All coordinate with one another and live happily. I must say God has blessed me with "A CLOSE KNIT FAMILY"

4. What do you like doing most with your family?

Ans. I like to have long meals, amusement, fun and frolic, would like to tease my sisters, sharing griefs and sorrows with them. These is a common saying – "The family which eats together, lives together and laughs together is truly a close knit family."

5. Who are close to you in your family?

Ans. Well… I am very close to my mother, "A true picture of maternity". She cooks what I wish to eat. She loves and teaches me what is good or bad for me. She is really a very virtuous lady with the blend of passionate feelings of a child. I wish to salute this real role model and admire this wonderful creation of God on this planet.

6. In what way is your family important to you?

Ans. My family is everything to me. My family members are my best friends and they support me in every real challenge of my life. I know they are always with me, no matter what. They are not only my best friends, but we truly are tied with strong bonds of respect, unity and strength. That's why I used to say my family is my real earned wealth and strength.

WORK

7. Do you work or are you a student?

Ans. I am a very hardworking person. Presently, I am doing both the tasks simultaneously. In the morning hours, I usually go for my orientation classes of language as I am fond of learning linguistics and in the afternoon, I am working as an executive in a reputed company.

8. What are your responsibilities at work ?

Ans. My responsibilities include keeping an eye upon the junior executives for maintaining organisational goals and objectives and so keeping supervision over them, checking their targets as well as maintain coordination and proper communication is my main work. Thorough commitment to work is my first and last responsibility towards work.

STUDY

9. Do you work or are you a student?

Ans. I am a student at the moment. I am studying English Linguistics and literature together and hoping to get more and more excellence in this field.

10. Why do you choose that course or job?

Ans. Honestly speaking, as everyone knows English is a global language. It serves both socially as well as professionally. Because what I believe socially, it is the order of the day and professionally it is 'A Bag of Handsome Perks & Incentives.'

11. What is the most difficult thing about your studies or job?

Ans. The most difficult thing about my studies is its grammatical rules and lexical part. Its really difficult to remember high profile words and proverbs. Moreover, grammatical rules limits my tendency to learn the things.

12. What type of study most of the students prefer these days?

Ans. Very interesting question, see...... The ultimate goal of every education is to earn good, so most of the students these days tend to fall upon more professional studies despite of academic ones. Because these types of vocational studies widen up their empirical outlook and open their arenas for the professional world.

HOBBIES

13. What are your hobbies?

Ans. There is no one thing I'm fanatical about. I have various interests. I am a keen cook and love to make new dishes. I love reading books. I am creative too and love to follow new tracks ever day. Frankly speaking, hobbies add charms to life and pull out the hidden talents and abilities.

14. What do you like about your hobbies?

Ans. Well....the thing that really fascinates me about my hobbies are that it pulls out my hidden talents and abilities. It brings positive changes in my life. It proves to be a creative utilisation of time. It is the best way to refuel your body and mind.

15. What type of hobbies are popular among teenagers in your country?

Ans. Actually, hobbies are personal tastes of every individual. As far as my country's teenage hobbies are concerned, I must say that among boys hobbies like getting involved with online friends, regular visitor of Orkut, Facebook and Twitter, Net surfing, health resorts, gyms and spa, sending SMS, etc. and among Girls are STORIES, Puzzles, Chatting, Tidbits, Creative Arts, etc.

FREE TIME, LEISURE

16. What are the best ways to utilise your free time?

Ans. A 'Hobby a day keeps the doldrums away.' So the best way to utilise your free time is to get completely involved in doing which you like the most. It is really beneficial for everyone to cultivate a suitable hobby to help in the proper channelization of free time.

17. Do people have more free time now than in the past?

Ans. It's really quite ironical to say, as we are living in the gadgetry and luxurious world where labour saving machines, such as washing machines and dishwashers are prevailing yet people are too busy in the rat race of earning and spending money. They don't have time to spend with their relations. But in the past, almost all the work was done manually, still people had time to eat and laugh together.

18. What is the impact of leisure activities on society?

Ans. The impact of leisure activities on the society is spectacular. It becomes a pattern or style of living for the entire society. Everyone follows the same pattern of living and they coordinate their lives accordingly. They can plan their schedules and programmes as per each other's conveniences.

FRIEND, FRIENDSHIP

19. How do you usually contact your friends?

Ans. Well... I usually get very less time to contact my friends, but I always try my every level best to call them or chat with them online.

20. Are friends as important to you as your family?

Ans. Friends and family, both are invaluable and no doubt, both act as a four-leaf clover, hard to find and lucky to have...

21. Do you think friendships change as we get older?

Ans. Very true. Gone are those days when friends used to truly love each other. Nowadays, fake friendships are in the air via various technological advancements like the Facebook or Twitter. Nobody remembers his/her childhood friends.

22. Whom do you call best friend?

Ans. According to my opinion, a Best Friend is much beyond roaming together and sharing good moments. It is about friendship with someone who comes to rescue you from the worst phase of life. Friendship with your best friend is eternal.

HOMETOWN

23. Describe your hometown. (Individual Opinion, because candidates have to answer according to the place where they are residing.)

24. Is your hometown in the grip of problems?

Ans. Undoubtedly, the general problems of my city these days are overpopulated streets, pollution, traffic embezzlements, etc. Some problems shiver down my spine like the evils of female foeticide and hooliganism.

25. What changes would you like to have in your hometown?

Ans. Very interesting question. Well if I am given an opportunity to change my hometown, my first priority will be to provide homes to the slums, then encourage every student of the city to be literate and educated, and last but not least, to bring technical back up for my city.

TRAVEL

26. Do you think it is true that travel br\ idens the mind?

Ans. I do, yes…it is true. Travel and change of place impart new vigour to the mind. Travellers never think that they are foreigners. Rather, you see, different ways of living, such as, eating, drinking, interacting with others,etc. allows you to analyse your own culture more objectively.

27. Do young people and older people get benefits from travelling?

Ans. Well ……for youngsters, travelling is an adventurous experience but for older people, it is more of relaxation than enjoyment because while travelling, they get switched off from their regular duties and routine work. Moreover, it is advantageous for both the generation to go for travelling, as it is an eye opener when we observe people of different states or countries and are familiarised with their lifestyles. There's a common saying – 'The World is a book, and those who do not travel, read only a page.'

28. How do you usually travel to work or college?

Ans. Well……The Metro or Bus is the best means of transport in our city from one place to another. Generally, I travel to the place of my work via Metro, as it is the cheapest means of transport as well as it saves time and is petrol savvy.

29. Which place do you like to visit the most?

Ans. My country, India is a tourist's paradise. Well…if I get an opportunity, I would like to visit Kashmir, the real paradise on earth. It is a completely blend with natural beauty, ethnic splendour and cultural diversity. It is the 'CROWN HEAD' of India.

ENGLISH LANGUAGE/LANGUAGE LEARNING

30. How do people in your country feel about English being the world language/?

Ans. There is no such feeling in learning the English language. Everyone knows it is a global language, so learning is automatically inevitable and everyone has to embrace this global lingua franca not only for communication, but also for their economic benefits.

31. Do you think the culture of English Speaking Countries as well as the English language dominate the whole world?

Ans. Undoubtedly… I do believe the usage of Internet really allows the scope of English on international grounds. It becomes a trendy language these days. No doubt, these days it has becomes the wine upon the lips.

32. When & where you began studying English? Do you face any problem while studying English?

Ans. As you know, I belong to India so English is not my mother tongue… As it my native language.. I began learning this language in my school when I was 5 years old. Learning the English language for the first time can be difficult. However, when done in an exciting and humorous way, learning English vocabulary and grammar are less confusing and more enjoyable.

33. Which is the most effective way of learning English ?

Ans. The best way of learning English is to Listen properly. It can be with any source like English Native Speakers, Some English Audio DVD's or CD's, Watching English Movies, etc.

FESTIVAL

34. Which is the most important festival of your country?

Ans. AHHHH…. The festival of lights, i.e., Diwali is the most important festival of my country. It comes in the month of October or November. It is related to the Hindu and Sikh history. It brings everyone together under one roof of happiness and prosperity. It provides an opportunity to meet friends and relatives. It strengthens our social bonds. It breaks the monotony of hectic and engrossed life.

35. Can you define festival, how is it celebrated, and why is it celebrated?

Ans. Festivals act like vehicles that carry our culture, religion and history to the new generation. Well, I must say it is an occasion where everyone enjoys fun and fiesta. During festivals, we meet our friends, sit and share with them meals and laugh for long hours. It is celebrated as a symbol of our conventions and customs.

CULTURE

36. Do you think the culture of your country influences you?

Ans. Yes..I do… it reflects in your personality the way you eat, the way you dress, the way you adopt different lifestyles, its values & beliefs, etc. It is the widening of minds and spirits. It teaches you how unity can be maintain in the diversities of culture.

37. Which culture is the best, 'Indian' or 'Western'?

Ans. Well… the culture never teaches you anything wrong. It is the thinking capacity of the person that allows you to think this is Indian or Western. The Indian culture is already enriched with values and that's why it is incredible and the Western culture is completely based on Facts of those values, so I think no comparison exists between both of them. Both teaches the real virtues of life.

38. How has your country'culture changed in 50 years time?

Ans. Change is the law of nature, but sometimes, it's frightening to accept the change. Culture does not change because no doubt it is accepted by the society in different ways but its values and norms always remain the same. Earlier, it was limited to customs, but now it is influencing our deportment, etiquettes, mannerisms, food habits, etc. It would not be wrong to say that it is our 'Signature's style' these days.

LIFESTYLE, HEALTH, KEEPING FIT

39. Why do some people think that modern lifestyles are not healthy?

Ans. See, people have a valid reason for thinking so. People today love comfort and luxury, and they want to satisfy their appetites at any cost. Rather than cooking at home, they love to eat out at restaurants and fast food joints. Fast food may be tasty, but contains a lot of fat that is not good for health. Previously, people used to walk or engage in some kind of manual work. That is not the case today. Personal vehicles and modern devices have made their life easy and people have a great aversion towards sweating their bodies. This lifestyle naturally invites diseases.

40. Why do some people choose to lead unhealthy lives?

Ans. The simple answer is laziness. Today many people do not have the discipline to lead a healthy life. They love comfort and convenience in everything that they do. In fact, they don't realise that their comfort and luxury are going to end soon. They need to face the reality sooner or later.

41. Should individuals or governments be responsible for making people's lifestyles healthy?

Ans. It is the individuals themselves who are responsible for making their lifestyles healthy. It is one's personal freedom to lead a healthy lifestyle. The government has nothing to do with it. No government can interfere into such personal affairs. The government can't ask people to eat this or that. The only thing that government can do is to spread awareness about this issue. Nothing more than that.

42. What could be done to encourage people to live in a healthy way?

Ans. The best way to encourage people to live in a healthy way is to spread awareness about the consequences of an unhealthy lifestyle. This can be done through the media like television and newspapers. At an early age, children should be given education about the importance of a healthy lifestyle. It should also be included in the curriculum. Moreover, sports should be made compulsory in schools. Another effective way is to give gym and sports facilities in factories and offices.

MUSIC

43. Which instrument do you like to listen most? (Why?)

Ans. My favourite musical instrument is the flute. (I love listening to the flute, the most). I have always wondered why I like flute. Maybe, it is because of its simplicity or because of its sweet sound. Flute has a very soothing music and it goes directly into your heart. I think it is very easy to learn flute, but I am not sure. Anyway, I like it.

44. Have you ever learnt to play a musical instrument?

Ans. Not really, I don't think I have the talent for it. So I have not seriously tried. When I was small, I just used to play with the harmonium, but actually, I could never play any proper notes. Even now, I love to press the keys of the electric keyboard and I like to hear the sound or the music. But I have never learnt to play any musical instrument.

Children's Games

45. How have games changed from the time when you were a child?

Ans. Games have changed tremendously over the years. When we were children, the standard of the game or the players were not as good as it is today. Moreover, newer rules have been introduced to make it more appealing to the television audiences. I think the speed of the game has considerably increased. There is much more money in sports and games today, so more and more young people are interested in making it a full time career. That was not the case when I was a child.

46. Do you think this has been a positive change? Why?

Ans. Yes, it has definitely been a positive change in all ways. Games have become more popular and players get much better rewards. Televised games have made it possible for people to watch games in the comfort of their homes rather than going to a stadium. Watching games have become a very easy affair. Overall, the standard of the game has improved.

47. Why do you think children like playing games?

Ans. Children are physically very active and you can't keep them idle for a long time. They always like to be with their friends, playing some games. Psychologically, at their age, they can't think of engaging in a serious activity for a long time. Playing games would occupy them in a very effective way; otherwise, they are going to create some mischief at home.

BOOKS

48. What kind of books do you like to read?

Ans. I mostly like to read biographies for example Hellen Keller – The Story of My Life, Anne Frank – The Dary of Young girl. I'm not sure why, but it is interesting to read about people's real lives, especially when they have had interesting lives and have had to deal with many problems. I do read fictions as well, but I often find it difficult to get hold of a book that I really like. I also like reading about books dealing with current affairs.

49. Do you read the same kind of books now that you read when you were a child?

Ans. Not really, no. Actually, with I didn't read that much when I was a child, but if, I did it was mainly fiction books, such as fairy tales. Things like The Lion, The Witch and the Wardrobe, and othe such fantasy books.

50. When do you think is the best time to read?

Ans. I think any time is ok, but when I read I like to concentrate, so I can't read for a short time like on a bus ride like some people do. I like to put time aside to enjoy it. So if I have some free time at the weekend, I might read for a few hours. And I nearly always read before I go to bed – this really helps me to sleep.

MOST POPULAR CUE-CARDS FOR IELTS TEST

CUE-CARD - 1 : LANGUAGE LEARNING

– Let us talk about learning English

– How long have you been learning English?

– Where did you learn?

– Is it easy/difficult?

– Is English important in your job?

I have been learning English ever since I was about 10 years old, when I was studying in my fifth grade. I learnt the alphabets and basic words at that time. I studied in a vernacular medium school, but English was a subject throughout my school years. I did not take English very seriously during my school days, and I scored comparatively poor marks for it. Well, English was the most difficult subject for me; and to be frank, I hated this subject at that time. One of the reasons that I did not like English was that we did not have any good teachers.

It was after I joined college, I started studying English seriously. I had a wonderful English teacher who laid a sound foundation in English Grammar. Since then, I started loving this subject and began reading books in English. Now I am in my forties and the more I study English the better I love it.

Since I am an English teacher, I need to improve my English all the time, learning new vocabulary and reading more and more books. I make sure that I update my knowledge of English all the time.

CUE-CARD - 2 : A GIFT THAT YOU PRESENTED

– What the gift was

– What the occasion was

– Whom you gave it to

– Why this gift was very special

My youngest brother was getting married and I wanted to give him a special gift. A couple of days before the marriage, my wife and I went to a Shopping Mall for some shopping. As we were about to return, we just went to my favourite store, 'Wills Life Store'. In fact, this particular shop has the trendiest and the most fashionable clothes for both men and women. I had the gift in my mind when I went into the shop. After spending a few minutes in the store, I spotted an off-white linen casual shirt. It was a designer wear and I put it on, to see how it looked. My wife said, it was the best shirt that had ever decorated my body. I was very happy. It was an expensive shirt but it gave me a great sense of satisfaction.

On the eve of the marriage, we had a party and my brother put this shirt on. Everybody was very appreciative of the shirt and my brother was very happy about it.

This gift was very special to me because I really liked the colour, material and the design of the shirt. Apart from that, it was the first gift that I ever presented to my youngest brother. I was extremely happy that he really liked the shirt. It was the right occasion that I gave him this present.

CUE-CARD - 3 : A GIFT OR ARTICLE YOU TREASURE MOST

- What was the article
- Where did you get it
- How you preserved it
- Why is it very precious to you

Something that I treasure most is my IBM laptop, which was not actually a gift. Although it is quiet old, it never had any serious technical problems, except a few software crashes, ever since I bought it about 8 years ago. Well, I bought it from a friend of mine who has a computer business. He suggested the brand and I think I made the right choice by buying an IBM laptop. Technically, the components of my computer are of very superior quality and therefore, in spite of my constant use, I have never changed any parts.

Although I have a leather laptop container, I rarely use it now. I used to put it in a leather bag initially, but later, due to my laziness, I just left it on my study table. Sometimes, it gathers a lot of dust and occasionally, I wipe it with a towel. I would say my laptop is very untidily kept but by God's grace, it keeps working.

My laptop is very precious to me because I type my notes in it and use it for presentations in my class and meetings. Sometimes, I watch movies in it. I also have stored a lot of data and personal information in my computer. After my office hours, I spend long hours in front of my computer, either browsing the net or studying.

CUE-CARD - 4 : DESCRIBE A WEDDING YOU ATTENDED

– You should say: When it was, who got married
what happened at the wedding,

– And explain, whether it was a typical wedding ceremony

Happy and sad events are a part and parcel of our lives. The happy event I am going to talk about here is the wedding of my cousin. I attended this wedding on 15th January. My cousins name is Priya. She is my maternal aunt's daughter. All our friends and relatives were invited. Actually, the whole week before the 15th, was busy in the pre-wedding celebrations like *Tilak, Sangeet, Mehandi, and Haldi*. On the day of wedding, the marriage palace was decorated like a bride. My cousin also looked beautiful in her sequin spangled *lehanga*. The *baraat* came at 5 p.m. High tea was served in which there were lots of cakes and snacks. Then there was the *Jai Mala*. The Bride and the Groom exchanged fresh flower garlands. Then we all danced and enjoyed to the beat of the music. After the sumptuous dinner, all the guests departed and only the close family was left. Then the priest set a small fire and the remaining ceremony took place around the fire. The *doli* took place early in the morning. It was a very tearful moment for all of us but we were all very happy from deep inside as my cousin was beginning her new phase of life. Such celebrations are very common in my country.

CUE–CARD - 5 : DESCRIBE A GAME OR SPORT YOU ENJOY PLAYING

You should say:

– What kind of sport it is

– Whom you play it with

– Where you play it, and explain why you enjoy playing it.

I enjoy playing various kinds of brain games online. There are a number of different websites I visit on a regular basis in order to play these games by myself. The objective of the games is to exercise different areas of your brain so that you preserve and enhance your memory and also expand and develop your brain capacity.

The games are of various kinds. Some enable you to practise your verbal skills. Others test logical reasoning, spatial skills and visual memory. I can keep a track of my scores, so that each time I play, my goal is to do better than the past – to outdo myself, so to speak. In addition, if I want, I can compare my scores to others who play online. This aspect is intriguing, but frankly, it doesn't interest me much. I don't regard this as a competition with anyone else. It is something I do simply to sharpen my mental abilities and improve myself.

In fact, one of my favourite games is supposed to be the best for brain fitness. It involves solving a number of simple math problems using *addition, subtraction, multiplication* and *division* as quickly as possible. I really hope these games will enable me to preserve my intellect and my memory into old age.

CUE–CARD - 6 : DESCRIBE SOMEONE IN YOUR FAMILY WHOM YOU LIKE

– You should say:

– How this person is related to you

– What this person looks like

– What kind of person he/she is and explain why you like this person.

The person in my family whom I really like and also love is my mother. She is a very special person and I cannot imagine what I would be without her.

Physically, my mother is petite. She is only about 5 feet tall, and weighs about 110 pounds. She has fine, black hair and a fair complexion. One thing people often notice is that my mother always takes pride in her appearance. Even now, at the age of 80, my mother is a well dressed, well-groomed and elegant woman, with her fine choice of clothes and matching accessories, jewellery and shoes.

Intellectually, my mother always loves learning. Even after her busy day, she won't go to bed without reading the newspaper. She is one of the few members of her family who completed her university education. She also has many creative and cultural interests, such as literature, music and dance, and passed on this love of culture to all her children, including me.

Emotionally, my mother has a heart of gold. All her life, she has been ready, willing and able to help anyone who needs anything, with a smile on her face. She is of the old school – she remembers to wish friends and relatives on their birthdays and anniversaries, she attends their weddings, dinners and parties, and she visits them when they're hurt, unwell or in mourning. In fact, my mother has always been a kind soul and people of all ages love her as soon as they meet her. I think this is because she is good-hearted from her core, and her authenticity is what everyone relates to. She has taught me the meaning of being compassionate, loving, kind, helpful, supportive and so much more. In fact, thanks to the unconditional love of both my wonderful parents that I feel I've been truly blessed in this lifetime.

CUE-CARD - 7 : DESCRIBE YOUR FAVOURITE BOOK

You should say:

– Which book is it

– Where did you read it

– Why do you think it would be useful in future

I have read many books in my life. In my view, books represent a way to get away from boredom of life and it helps me to be more creative by helping me excercise my own imagination. Books also help me to increase my knowledge as well as vocabulary. It also increases my reading skills.

The book here I would like to talk about is 'THE SECRET'. It is written by Rhonda Byrne. She is a very famous writer. A movie has also been made after the success of this book. The secret contains the wisdom of modern day teachers, men and women who have used it to achieve health, wealth and happiness. By applying the secret, they bring to light compelling stories of eradicating diseases, acquiring massive wealth and overcoming obstacles.

They have achieved so many things which one would regard as impossible. In this book, you will learn how to use the secret in every aspect of life, i.e, money, health and relationships. You will Begin to understand the hidden untapped power that's within you and this revelation can bring joy to every aspect of your life as there is also a very famous quote written in this book that 'if you really think of achieving something then the whole world conspires in your favour.'

So I think I would definitely like to read this book again as it evokes positive feelings within me and every time, I feel motivated and revitalised whenever I go through this book and I would rather suggest my friends also to read this book.

CUE-CARD - 8 : TALK ABOUT A SITUATION WHEN YOU WERE ANGRY

– What was the situation

– Where was it

– Who was there

Normally, I do not lose my temper easily. My friends say that I am as cool as a cucumber. However, there have been times when I was a little angry. I remember one such time when I was angry with my friend.

I had to go for a job interview to Jalandhar, and I was very nervous. It was a walk-in-interview for a call centre job and I requested my friend Roshni to accompany me. I somehow feel very confident when she is around.

She has a great sense of humour and never lets me feel sad or depressed. She also promised to accompany me but on the day of the interview, she did not turn up. Her phone was also switched off. I had to go alone.

I was very hurt and angry too! I appeared for the interview and after coming back home, I went straight to her house. I wanted to shout at her and give her a piece of my mind. However, when I reached her home, I came to know that her father had taken ill suddenly and was admitted in the ICU. Her phone was also switched off because she was in the ICU attending her father. Everything had happened so suddenly that she did not get the time to call and inform me.

All my anger vanished and I felt ashamed of myself. I should have known that she would not ditch me for some trivial reason. I should have had more faith in her. This incident strengthened our ties of friendship even more.

CUE-CARD - 9 : TALK ABOUT A COLOUR THAT MATTERS TO YOU

You may say:

– What colour it is

– When this colour became important in your life

– Why this colour matters to you

– How your choices are affected by this colour

Colours are very important in everyone's life. It adds charm and spice to life. A world without colour would be dull and boring indeed. I like many colours such as red, blue, yellow, green and black. But my all time favourite is red. I don't exactly remember when this colour became important to me, but once in school I, took part in a fancy dress competition and wore something in red.

Then I won the first prize. Since that day, I consider it my lucky colour. Even my school bag used to be red. Even today, my wardrobe is full of shades of red. This colour matters to me because I look good in red.

Whenever I wear red, I get many compliments. My choices are also affected by this colour. I buy accessories, such as bags, sandals and jewellery also in different shades of red. [For boys – My bike (car) is also of red colour] Red has a lot of importance in our culture.Hindu brides usually wear red. Red is also the symbol of love. It also symbolises danger. Red is also used as a traffic signal.

Blood is red in colour. Fire engines are also red. Basically, red is a *primary colour*. We can make many colours by mixing red – for example, we can make orange by mixing yellow with red. We can also make pink by mixing white with red. Therefore, red is my favourite colour.

CUE-CARD - 10 : DESCRIBE AN OLD PERSON THAT YOU KNOW

You should say:

- What your relationship is to this person
- How often you see him
- What people think about this person
- Explain why you like him

Ok, I'd like to tell you about an old person that I know. His name is Harsh, and he is the owner of a small convenience store at the end of my street.

I would say that my relationship with him is as a friend. I know him because I regularly go to the shop in order to buy things when I don't have time to go to a supermarket. He's quite friendly and I always have a chat with him. I've known him now for about five years – since I've lived in the area, in fact. That's why I'd now call him a friend.

I'd say that I see him fairly regularly. Like I said, I go to the big supermarket out of town sometimes to stock up, but you always need odd things during the week such as milk, or some snack or other. So when this happens, I just have a walk down to his shop. So I'd say I see him every day or two days.

I think Harsh is pretty popular as he's been there for years as far as I'm aware, so most of the locals around the area know him. There will always be someone in the shop having a chat with him. They like him because he's not just a shopkeeper but he's also very involved in activities in the community. For example, I know he helps out at the old people's home some nights, and he runs the quizzes at the local pub. He also helps to organize the fair that is held each year in the town.

The reason that I like him is that he's great to have a chat with. For instance, a while back, I was having problems with my work, and I was really feeling stressed. I didn't really have anyone to talk to at the time as my family is abroad and a couple of my good friends were not around. I mentioned it to Harsh and he was great. He listened and also gave me some really good advice. Generally, he's really welcoming when you go to his shop. He always has a smile on his face.

CUE-CARD - 11 : Describe your favourite dress

You should say:

– What it is

– When you bought it

– Why you bought it and say, why you like it so much

There are various kinds of dresses which are available in the market that we can wear on different occasions, but the dress which I think proved important for me was a party wear leather jacket with Italian designs on it. I got this jacket from Chandigarh when I went to my cousin's marriage function. That time I was taken for shopping in the famous market of Chandigarh where I could find the dresses of different brands with some warranty with them. So, I bought this jacket as I liked it most. This jacket was useful to me as I could use it to wear on my cousin's marriage and moreover, everybody praised it when I wore it on the marriage day. It had designing of some mirrors on it which fascinated everybody in the gathering and everybody praised my jacket and my dressing sense.

Yes, of course, I can say this dress is very important to me now also as I sometime wear it on some special occasions and also it was helpful to me fetching some good words from the people present in my cousin's wedding about my dressing sense, So I like this dress very much.

CUE-CARD - 12 : DESCRIBE THE STAGE IN YOUR LIFE YOU HAVE ENJOYED MOST

You should say:

– Which stage it was

– Why it was glorious

– How you enjoyed and say what lessons you learnt.

Normally, everybody passes through various types of situations comprising their weal or woe in life. I remember one stage of my life which was really enjoyable and full of fun for me which came in my childhood period and that was my school days.

Yes definitely, these days were the enjoyable period of my life as I would get up in time and dress up and carry the bag already packed by my mother. Sometime my mother would help me in completing the work which I would get from my teacher in my school. So I can say that I had no tensions in those days and responsibilities were also not on my head. It was a gala time of my life in which I would meet my friends and enjoy their company when we would get together during the break time in school and used to enjoy eating food together. This period was important to me as it taught me how we can work hard in the right direction to accomplish our goals or aims in life. Moreover, this time gave me some lessons about friends that true friendship is based on loyalty and truth spoken by two friends to each other. So this was the most enjoyable time of my life.

CUE-CARD - 13 : DESCRIBE A PHOTOGRAPH THAT YOU REMEMBER

You should say:

- When was it taken
- Who took it
- What is in the photograph and explain why you remember this photograph

I have a collection of many photographs in my album. Here I'm going to describe one such photograph in which I and my cousin are standing with our grandparents in our farmhouse. There is a small round table on which there is a cake. I remember vividly, it was the Golden Jubilee celebration of my grandparents. My aunt baked and iced the cake at home. She's an expert cook. She only clicked the photo.

That's why she is not there in the picture. But her presence can be felt through the cake. Only the four of us were there in the picture. Last year, when I celebrated my parents Silver Jubilee, I wished in my heart that I celebrate their Golden Jubilee too. The table cloth which is spread on the table was embroidered by my grandma. She had a gifted hand in needle and thread work too. Both my grandparents are no more in this world now. I really treasure this photograph as this brings some nostalgic memories of my childhood. Now I have a digital camera in which I capture such precious moments. Maybe, one day my children will also value these photos.

CUE-CARD - 14 : DESCRIBE A HISTORICAL BUILDING YOU VISITED

You should say:

- What is it
- Where is it located
- What did you like in it, and explain what is its singnificance in your country's history.

India is a diverse country. It has a rich historical background. The place I am going to talk about here is the Golden Temple or the Harmandir Sahib or the Temple of God. It is a place of stupendous beauty and sublime peace. It is situated at Amritsar in Punjab.The Sikhs all over the world daily wish to pay obeisance at Shri Harmandir Sahib. Although the 4th guru of Sikhs, Guru Ram Dal had the idea of this temple, but it was made by the 5th guru, Guru Arjan Dev ji. It took 16 years to complete this temple. The temple is surrounded with large lake of water, known as *sarover* which consists of Amrit (the holy water or the immortal vector). There are four entrances which signifies its openness and acceptance. People of all castes, creed, religion and sex are welcome here. However, everyone must cover his/her head as a mark of respect, remove their shoes and wash feet in the small pool of water. People from all the nook and corners of the world flock to see the Golden Temple. I go there once a month to postrate before the God. Whenever we have guests, then a visit to the Golden Temple is surely on our agenda.

CUE-CARD - 15 TALK ABOUT ANY LAW OF YOUR COUNTRY

– What is that law

– Why it is important

– When it is implemented and explain what steps have been taken to implement it.

There are various laws introduced or imposed by the government from time to time. All these laws are meant for the society. Otherwise, there will be the Rule of Jungle prevailing in the society where 'Might is Right' is the slogan of every citizen and chaos and anarchy are the key words that represent its rule. The law I am going to talk about is PNDT, i.e PRE NATAL DIAGNOSTIC TECHNIQUE ACT. This was the first enforced in 1994 and then amended in 2002. In it, there is fine of Rs. 1 lakh, imprisonment and cancellation of licence and registration of the doctor who is caught doing the test.

It is a big disgrace to the Indian society which considers the birth of girl child as a bad investment in the future. She is considered as a consumer than a producer that gives rise to the practice of female foeticide. The situation is quite worst in Punjab where the sex ration is 700 girls per 1000 boys. The decline in sex ratio brings the degeneration of moral values resulting in red rafficking, polyandry, violence against women, etc. Undoubtedly, this law is implemented in a proper way, but it is feared these practices are going on the back street. Only this law is not sufficient, we should take some special measures to implement it, like providing old age pension to old persons, who don't have any son, free and compulsory education for the girls, job reservation for the girls, equal share of the girls in the property of parents, etc. In the end, I must say we all have to join hands to build a gender balanced society.

CUE-CARD - 16 : DESCRIBE A MAJOR DECISION YOU HAVE TAKEN IN YOUR LIFE

You should say:

- What the decision was
- What other choices were available to you
- Why you made the decision, and explain if you think the decision was a good one.

A really important decision I've made recently is to study abroad. No one from my family has ever had the chance to do this before, and my parents were actually hoping I'd start working for the family textile business. I think it's too soon to join the business though. I really want to study marketing – especially, e-marketing – so I can contribute more to my parent's firm in the future. If I study e-marketing in the UK, I can learn how to use the internet to sell our clothes all over the world. As for whether it was the right decision, I'm pretty confident it was and I can't change my mind now anyway because my parents have borrowed money from my uncle to pay for my tuitions. I really can't wait to come back with new ideas that will help expand our business. All I need now is to get a good score in the IELTS exams. So, anyway, that's an important decision in my life.

CUE-CARD - 17 : DESCRIBE AN ACTIVITY YOU LIKE DOING MOST

You should say:

- What the activity is
- How often you do it
- How it helps you forget your routine life
- And say, whether you would recommend other people try the same thing.

OK, I'd like to talk about horse-riding. I'm actually the joint owner of a horse with two of my friends and we take turns looking after it, cleaning out the stable and so on. I don't have a part-time job, so I spend most of my weekends at the stable. Taking care of a horse is quite a dirty business, so it's obviously very different from studying at college. That means I can forget about my classes when I'm at the stable on the weekend. There's quite a large field next to the stable and I just get a wonderful sense of freedom when I'm riding around on my horse. The college seems a million miles away! Do I think other people would enjoy horse-riding? Yes, absolutely. I think everyone should give it a try.

CUE-CARD – 18 : DESCRIBE A LANGUAGE YOU WOULD LIKE TO LEARN

You should say:

– What is the language

– Where is it spoken

– Why are you interested in this language

– And say, if you think you will ever actually have the chance to learn it.

Let me tell you about a language I've always wanted to learn, which is Russian. It's spoken in Russia, obviously, but also in many other countries which have been influenced by Russia including places like Mongolia and Kazakhstan. The reason, I would like to learn Russian is that the energy industry is huge and there are lots of jobs in that industry. A lot of my country's oil and gas come from Russia; so it's really useful to be able to speak that language if you want to work in the energy field. Nonetheless, I know that a lot of Russians can't speak English very well, so there's another reason to learn their language. The problem is I'm already in my 30s and I've spent more than ten years learning English. I don't know if I would ever be able to study Russian because it uses a completely different alphabet and sounds really difficult. But it would be really nice to have the chance to learn it.

CUE-CARD – 19 : TALK ABOUT A JOB THAT HELPS TO MAKE THE WORLD A BETTER PLACE

You should say:

– What job is it?

– Where did you learn about it?

– Why do you think it helps so much?

There are many jobs in the world which help to make the world a better place, such as the job of a teacher, doctor, nurse, scientist, a politician and so many more. In fact, the world can be made a better place by the cumulative effort of all these jobs. Here I would like to talk about a job which helps to make the world a better place. This is the job of a teacher.

Everyone passes through the hands of teachers in school and college years. Teachers are known as nation builders. All other professions, also pass through the hands of a teacher. That is why I believe that teachers can make the world a better place. A teacher is like a candle that burns itself and shows light to others. Since age-old times, teaching has been considered a noble profession. In ancient India, there was the *gurukul system*. Even the king's children stayed in the home of the *guru or the teacher*. They used to do the household chores of the *guru* and in return, the guru imparted knowledge.

Teachers improve the literacy rate of a country. When the literacy rate is high, crime and violence go down. A teacher requires good communication skills and a depth of knowledge on his/her subject.

A good teacher should treat all the students equally. Nowadays, teachers are being paid handsomely by the government. This is to lure the bright students to join this noble profession.

CUE-CARD – 20 : DESCRIBE A PIECE OF FURNITURE IN YOUR HOME

You should say:

– What it is

– Where it is

– What it looks like (or, what it is made of) and explain, how or why you use it.

Furniture is a part and parcel of every home. There is a lot of furniture in my house too. There are beds and sofa sets, chairs and tables, cupboards and dressing tables. But here I would like to talk about a piece of furniture that I use very often. This is a study table.

I have this table in my room. This is a special table which my father made for me by a carpenter in my hometown. The body of the table is made of pure teak wood. The top part is of board which has a grey mica topping. This is bigger than a conventional study table.

It is L shaped. On one side, I have set my desktop PC. There are shelves on the top on which I have set my books. There are drawers on one side in which I keep my stationery materials, CDs and DVDs. A chair can be slid inside the table when not in use.

I find this table very convenient when I have to study or work on my computer. I have a beautiful table lamp on one side. The light falls on my books from the left side. I just love this table. So, this is one essential and important item of furniture in my house.

CUE-CARD – 21 : TALK ABOUT A PLACE YOU HAVE VISITED AT OPEN AIR

You should say:

– Where did you go

– Why did you go there

– What did you do there

I have visited many places in the open air, such as parks and stadiums. But here, I would like to talk about the Rock Garden in Chandigarh. I went there with my college/school trip last year. Our school/college organised an educational tour to Chandigarh. We were 30 students and two teachers.We saw many places, such as the Rose Garden, Sukhna Lake, Mini Zoo and the Rock Garden. The Rock Garden by Nek Chand fascinated me the most. We spent two hours there and clicked a lot of photographs. About 5000 people visit the Rock Garden daily.

It has around 5000 sculptures. It is a unique garden that consists of various art objects.

But the best part about the rock garden is that each of its artwork has been made by using waste materials. The *Rock Garden* has become immensely popular. It has been established in the form of an *open-air exhibition hall.*

The garden has sculptures made by using a variety of different discarded waste materials like frames, mudguards, forks, handle bars, metal wires, play marbles, porcelain, auto parts, broken bangles, etc.

The garden highlights the value of materials many people consider trash. People come from different parts of the world gather here to see this amazing garden. It is located in Sector 1 near the Sukhna Lake. Nek Chand received the Padma Shri in 1983 for his efforts. A sculpture of this garden also appeared on an Indian postage stamp.

The Chandigarh Rock Garden is now acknowledged as one of the *modern wonders of the world.*

CUE-CARD – 22 : TALK ABOUT A SITUATION IN YOUR LIFE THAT MADE YOU LAUGH FROM YOUR HEART

You should say:

– What was the occasion

– When was that

– Who witnessed it with you and why it made you laugh

It has been rightly said that *laughter is the best medicine*. Unfortunately, in the fast paced hectic lifestyle of today, we are forgetting to realise the importance of this free medicine. Even doctors are recommending this therapy for many depressive disorders.

Nowadays, people have again begun to realise its importance. No wonder, we can see many sitcoms on TV nowadays, such as *Comedy Circus and Chhote Miyan*. Laughter clubs have also opened in many cities, where people come to laugh away their worries and stress. I have also faced many situations when I burst into peals of laughter.

Here I would like to talk about one such situation when I really laughed from my heart. It was my cousin's wedding two months ago and we were all dancing on the beats of the DJ. The groom's father, that is my uncle had taken a few pegs of whiskey. He was dancing the maximum. His odd and weird dancing steps were very hilarious and everyone was laughing at him. But he was not at all perturbed. He was thoroughly enjoying himself.

My aunt tried to stop him many times, but he wouldn't listen. He was wearing a silken *dhoti kurta*. Suddenly, he tripped and his *dhoti* came off. That was the most hilarious moment of all. The bride and the groom also had a hearty laugh. The photographer captured it all very nicely in his video camera.

Even today when we see that video we all have a hearty laugh. So this is the situation when I laughed from my heart.

CUE-CARD - 23: AN ADVERTISEMENT THAT CAUGHT YOUR EYES

You should say:

- Which advertisement it is
- Why you like it
- What this advertisement is all about and explain what message it wants to convey

You know now that some commercials are better than the TV programmes. In the past, we did not have so many TV commercials. Now, we have a plethora of them – before, in the middle and after each program. I think TV commercials add variety to the program because sometimes, the program becomes very monotonous.

Some TV commercials also give you a chance of refreshment. The TV advertisement I am going to talk about here is of *Vodaphone Telecom*. It is a very humorous commercial. A 6-7 years old girl is shown to be getting ready for school. She can't find her socks. Her very cute puppy obliges her by finding her socks. Then she is shown sitting in her school bus. She has forgotten her school tie. Then they show the cute puppy running after the bus with the tie around its neck.

What the vodaphone people want to convey is that their network follows wherever they go. They also want to show that they are always willing to help. I changed my phone connection from cell-one to vodaphone after seeing this advertisement Cell-one was giving me a lot of problems with network, but now, I have no such problems.

CUE-CARD - 24 : YOUR FAVOURITE CUISINE

You should say:

– Which dish it is

– How is it made

– Who made it and explain where is it available

I like all the cuisines, such as Chinese, Indian and Mexican, but my all time favourite is Indian cuisine. This cuisine has a lot of diversity. The North Indian and the South Indian cuisines are poles apart. Although I like both, but I really relish the North Indian cuisine. Green vegetables, pulses, lentils and a variety of desserts are part of the North Indian cuisine.

My favourite dish is *Makki di Roti* and *sarson da saag*. You know ma'am, *makki di roti* is a loaf made of maize flour and *sarson da saag* is a dish made of mustard leaves to which spinach leaves can be added. My mother cooks very delicious *saag*. It is a winter dish, but now you can eat the tinned *saag* at any time of the year. Good marked company markets the tinned variety.

CUE-CARD 25 : MY FAVOURITE SHOPPING MALL

You should say:

– Which mall it is

– How does it look

– What type of stores are there and explain who maintains it

Many new shopping malls have come up recently in my hometown. The Arjun Mall and the Ansal Plaza are the two major ones. Here I am going to talk about the Ansal Plaza.

It is in the suburbs of Phagwara. It is a modern shopping mall built with the state-of-art technology.

The Ansal Plaza has four storeys. It has a huge parking in the basement that can hold more than a 100 cars. The Ansal Plaza has escalators and 4 lifts and the Plaza has 3-4 food courts including McDonalds which is my favourite place to eat out.

The Ansal Plaza is a joint venture of some businessmen of Delhi and has many branches in India.

The Ansal Plaza being on the highway is flocked by countless hordes of people. It also has many branded stores like *Reebok* and *Nike*.

CUE-CARD - 26 : YOUR FAVOURITE PLACE OF EATING OUT

Describe a restaurant you know

You should say:

– Where this restaurant is

– What type of food the restaurant serves

– How often you go to this restaurant, and explain why you would recommend this restaurant.

There are many restaurants which I visit frequently, but here I am going to describe the Haveli.

It is on the national highway between Jalandhar and Phagwara. Actually, it falls in the suburbs of Phagwara.

I like it because of the delicious and quality food, quick and prompt service and a friendly atmosphere. It is always swarming with people and brimming with activity.

The food is priced at very normal rates. It is a huge place with a seating capacity of about 200 people. The interior is decorated to simulate a traditional Punjabi village scene. Handicrafts adorn the walls which give the place a very ethnic look. The food served is mouth watering and delicious. The restaurant is very clean and hygienic.The waiters are amicable and friendly.

In the evenings, the Punjabi cultural songs and dances are performed by various artists.

It is a must-visit place for one and all. It is so interesting that one can never feel bored there.

CUE-CARD - 27: YOUR FAVOURITE MAGAZINE/PERIODICAL/JOURNAL

DESCRIBE A MAGAZINE YOU THINK IS INTERESTING

You should say:

– Why you like this magazine

– What are its features

– What it contains, and explain why you think this magazine is interesting

My favourite magazine is 'The Reader's Digest'. It is a monthly international magazine. The editor of the magazine is Mohan Sivanand. I like this magazine because it is not a magazine to be read and thrown away. It is a collectible.

I have collected many past issues of the magazine in my personal library. There are many regular features of the magazine. The feature I like the most is 'word power'.

It gives me 20 new words of English every month with their meaning and antonyms.

It helps me to improve my vocabulary.

The other regular features are – 'laughter is the best medicine', 'life is like that' and 'humour in uniform'. All these articles contain jokes and humours which are always fresh.There are also many quotable quotes in this magazine.

Another article I like is 'The Reader's Choice'. It runs for about 15-20 pages. It contains a true story or an abridged form of a novel. All these articles are very inspiring.

Reading this magazine relaxes me. This magazine is entertaining and educative. Everybody in my house reads it. This magazine has something for everybody.

CUE-CARD - 28 : YOUR FAVOURITE NEWSPAPER

You should say:

– Why you like this newspaper

– What are its features

– What it contains, and explain why you think this magazine is interesting.

There are many newspapers published in my city in different languages. My parents have subscribed to one Punjabi newspaper, *Ajeet* and one English newspaper, that is *The Tribune*. I like to read *The Tribune*. It is a complete newspaper according to me.

It has many pages that cover important topics, national and international news and also local news from my state and city. The editor's page is called the 'Opinion'. I read the editorial daily.

It touches topics of daily interest. Different social, political and international topics are discussed in this section.

Only the other day, I read about global warming. There is a supplement every alternate day.

On Wednesday, it is *Jalandhar Plus*. In this supplement, local news of my hometown, Phagwara is also there. I have been reading this newspaper for quite some time now. I don't think there is any room for improvement but then a technology section would add a feather in the cap of this paper.

CUE-CARD - 29 : YOUR FAVOURITE CHANNEL

You should say:

– Which channel you like

– What are its features

– Why you like and explain what you learn from this channel

Nowadays there is a multitude of channels and a plethora of programmes on TV.

As I am an animal lover, my favourite channel is the *Animal Planet*. The Animal Planet is a very informative channel.

I like this channel because I have learnt a lot from this channel. It provides me with a new word of English every 20 minutes. So it has improved my vocabulary a lot. It is an offshoot of the discovery channel. My favourite programme is *Animal Safari*.You can learnt about animals, birds and reptiles from it.This channel can never get boring. Some programmes are real eye-openers.

I learnt many facts about the animal world from this channel.

CUE-CARD - 30 : YOUR FAVOURITE ANIMAL

You should say:

– Which animal you like

– Why you like

– Where it resides and explain its habits of living

The animal I like the most is the elephant. The elephants are the biggest land animals. They are herbivorous and can be identified because of their trunks. The trunk is the projection of their noses and the upper lips. There are two types of elephants – the Indian and the African. The African elephants are bigger than their Indian counterparts.

They have comparatively larger ears. Among the African elephants, both the males and females have tusks whereas, only the males among the Indian elephants have tusks and so they are called *tuskers*.

The back of the Indian elephants are convex, whereas that of the African elephants are concave. The Indian elephants can be tamed and they are more beautiful. Elephants are gregarious animals and live in herds headed by tuskers. They have a well-structured family life. The young ones, called the calves, are looked after by the cow elephants. Their cry is called the trumpet.

In India, elephants are captured, tamed and used for various purposes.

Elephants are among the few animals whose existence are not endangered till now.

CUE-CARD - 31 : YOUR FAVOURITE POET

You should say:

– Which poet he/she is

– What you like in his personality

– His/her talent features and explain his/her works

My favourite poetess is Amrita Pritam. She's no more now. She died at the age of 86 on 31st October, 2005. She was a charismatic personality. She was very beautiful with almond-shaped eyes, fine features and a fair complexion.

She began composing poetry in her teens. Amrita's father was a man of letters and encouraged Amrita to read and write. She published her first book of poems when she was just fourteen.

After the Partition in 1947, Delhi became her home. Her talents blossomed in the capital of independent India, and writing in Punjabi, her mother tongue, she was to take the language places. Her poem *Aaj Aakhaan Waris Shah Noo* made her reach the pinnacles of fame. She often wrote on the condition of Indian women and her writings reflected their neglect and suppression in the Indian society.

She has to her credit 15 novels, numerous short stories and poems. She witnessed the Partition of India and portrayed it in her works. Her works have been widely translated. She has received many awards, including India's highest literary award, *Jnanpith, in 1981.* Films have been made on two of her novels – Daaku and Pinjar (skeleton). Her other famous novels are: *Kachchi Sarak* (HINDI), *Lal Dhagee ka Rishta* HINDI) *Raseedi Ticket* (HINDI), *The Revenue Stamp – An Autobiography*. Her other famous poems are *Khamoshi Se Pahle* (HINDI) *Aawazen* (HINDI).

CUE-CARD - 32 : YOUR FAVOURITE FILM STAR

You should say:

– Which Filmstar he/she is

– What you like in his/her personality

– His/her talent features and explain his/her works

I like many film stars like Shah Rukh Khan, Aamir Khan, Salman Khan, but here I am going to talk about Amitabh Bachhan. He is my all-time favourite.

He is a versatile actor and really lives the role he is given. He is the *Shehanshah of Bollywood* and the superstar of the millennium. He is the apple of millions of Indian. He has appeared in more than 180 films. His debut film, 'Saat Hindustani' did not succeed in the box office, but his 1970s films, *Zanjeer, Deewar* and *Sholay* took him to the pinnacle of his career.

He met with a near-fatal accident while shooting for *Coolie* in 1983.

He has a strong will power. He took ill once again in 2005 and underwent a major surgery of intestine, but again recovered because of his will power. He has won many awards. He has even hosted a TV show, called the *KBC (Kaun Banega Crorepati).*

He is a legend.There is no one else who can replace this legend. I like his movie, *Baghban* the most.

CUE-CARD - 33 : A STORY YOU HAVE HEARD AS A CHILD

You should say:

– Which story it is

– What is the story all about

– Why you like it and explain what moral lessons you have learnt

The story I've heard as a child is of a thirsty crow. Once upon a time, there was a crow. The crow was very intelligent. One day it became very thirsty. It wanted to quench its thirst. It looked for water everywhere. But nowhere, could it find the water. Then it found a pitcher with a little water at the bottom.

The crow could not reach the water. It pondered and immediately hit upon an idea. It gathered pebbles and dropped them into the pitcher. The water level rose. It drank the water and quenched its thirst. This story is very easy to learn and most popular during the childhood days. The moral of the story is that at the time of adversity, you've to use your wits.

CUE-CARD - 34 : YOUR LAST DAY AT SCHOOL

You should include:

– Which day it was

– How did you celebrate

– What you did, and explain, how it became memorable for the whole of your life.

An unforgettable incident in your school days. An unforgettable incident in your life. My last day at school was a very memorable one. I remember vividly the date also. It was the 6th of February. Our juniors had organised a farewell party for us. We all were very excited about that day. In fact, most of us had bought new clothes for that day. Our principal and all the teachers were also invited.

Our juniors had many surprises for us up their sleeves. They also had many awards for us. We all were asked to perform on the stage. It could be a mono-acting or a joke or a song. Everyone was doing rather well. When my turn came, I became very nervous. It was a stage fright. I had never performed on stage before. My legs were shaking. As I went up the stage I tripped and fell face down on the stage.

Everyone burst into peels of laughter. It was the most embarrassing moment for me.

I too started laughing. I realised that if you have the courage to laugh at yourself, others don't laugh at you anymore and that's the best way to overcome embarrassment. I told them all a joke. As I began speaking, I realised that all my nervousness flew away and everyone enjoyed my performance.

Guess what? I won the best boy/girl award too. It was the happiest moment of my life and the most unforgettable one too.We had a lot of refreshments too and danced a lot on that day. It was very painful. It was as if one of my limbs had been amputated.

CUE-CARD - 35 : YOUR FAVOURITE FESTIVAL

You should say:

- Which festival it is
- Why you like this festival
- How it is celebrated and explain what activities are prominent during this festival

Diwali or Deepawali is a Hindu festival of lights.The word 'Deepawali' literally means rows of *diyas* (clay lamps). It is a family festival. It is celebrated 20 days after Dussehra. It is celebrated to commemorate the return of Lord Rama to his kingdom after 14 years of exile. It is also meant to celebrate the destruction of arrogant tyrant Bali at the hands of Vishnu.

Another reason for the celebration of Diwali is that the 6th guru of the Sikhs, Guru Hargobind Ji, was set free from the Gwalior jail along with about 52 kings on this day.

On this very day, twinkling oil lamps or *diyas* light up every home and there are numerous firework displays. Lord Ganesha, the elephant-headed God, the symbol of auspiciousness and wisdom, is worshipped in most of the Hindu homes.

Goddess Lakshmi, who is the symbol of wealth and prosperity, is also worshipped. Spring cleaning and whitewashing of houses are done. *Rangolis* (decorative designs) are painted on the walls and the floors. New clothes are bought and family members and relatives gather together to offer prayers, distribute sweets and to light up their houses.

There are some bad practices also followed on this day. Some people resort to drinking and gambling which is not good at all.

CUE-CARD - 36 : A VISIT TO A MUSEUM

– When did you visit it

– Describe the museum

– How did you feel after going there

Last month, my cousins came over to my house and they were insisting on going to a museum. I was not interested in going to the museum because I do not like museums at all. They finally persuaded me to go there and when I entered the museum, I was mesmerised by the beauty of the museum.

The Museum was divided into sections. The first section was related to the great inventions, whereas the other section was mainly concerned with the paintings and all other stuff. I was more inclined towards the inventions, so I went to the first section. As I entered the area, I could see a huge computer. The computer was made in 1960s and it was of the size of the room. I was amazed to see its size and I realised that the computer engineers of today would have made a lot of effort to reduce the size of the computer. I also saw the first bulb and other stuff.

My cousin came to me and told that there was some interesting stuff down there on the other section, so I decided to give it a look. The other section consisted of paintings of the Mughal era. The paintings were very beautiful and they were depicting the beauty of that period. There was also a huge food court in the museum, so we went to eat something.

The overall experience of the museum was simply fantastic. I saw a lot of things and I came to know about my country's culture. I think that if I had not visited the museum, I would have regretted this decision for the rest of my life. I feel that everyone should pay a visit to the museum because it keeps him or her well informed about the culture and we should all applaud the efforts of our ancestors as they made many sacrifices to make our life easier.

CUE-CARD - 37 : SADDEST MOMENT IN YOUR LIFE

– What happened

– How did it change your life

– How did you cope with it

I have had a lot of sad moments in my life, but the saddest moment was when I failed my Math exam. It was in grade 9. I was struggling a lot with my math so my father came to my rescue and he taught me. He used to teach me well but I never revised the concepts. I got 49% in the math exam and I came back home. My father asked me about the result as he had great expectations from me, but I told him that I had failed the exam.

At that moment, I saw his face. It showed as if he was blaming himself for my failure. He did not even scold me and went straight into his room. That moment I realised that not taking my studies seriously was not only hurting me, but also my parents. I did not make any fake promises this time and I made a true promise to myself that no matter what happens I will work very hard for my exams, and will try my best to achieve good grades in the exams.

I stopped watching movies and I started concentrating on my studies. I don't know what was happening. I was getting a kind of strength to work harder and I was fully determined to show to the world that I was capable of something good and ultimately, I passed the next math exam with an A grade.

CUE-CARD - 38 : YOUR FAVOURITE MUSIC

– What kind of music do you like?

– When do you listen to it?

– How does it change your mood?

Music is a very important part of every human being's life. Some people like hip hop, some like rap and others like jazz. Different people have different tastes for music, but there is one thing common amongst all these people, which is that almost everyone in this world is madly in love with music.

I am very fond of music. I like all types of music, but my favourite type of music is the Indian music. I like to listen to sad Indian songs because I feel that I can relate to them. My life has not worked according to the plan, and I have been sad for most part of my life. So I think that these songs are made for me.

I like these Indian songs because they are in my native language and the music in those songs is very melodious. Whenever I am sad, I play the songs so that I feel better. I know it seems weird but I kind of like it when a song is telling my story. I also listen to sad songs when I am driving a car and my time is spent in a very good manner.

I really like the songs in which the piano is played. I also know how to play the piano so I also play the same tunes on my own piano.

As I told you earlier that if I am sad, I listen to sad songs so that I could become more sadder, but when I am happy, I do not listen to these sad song. On the contrary, I listen to happy songs which make me more happy. So I would say that sad songs make me sadder, whereas happy songs make me happier. Once I recalled a day when I was sad and my cousin turned on a rap song. This actually infuriated me and I went out of the room, banging the door.

CUE-CARD - 39 : THE MEANS OF COMMUNICATION

– What are the different means of communication

– What is your favourite means of communication

– What are the advantages and disadvantages of using it

Communication is very important to impart information from one person to another. In the medieval times, people used to communicate via birds, signs and fire. Now the means of communication have changed, but the purpose of communication is the same. Languages were made to facilitate communication and people learnt languages to make communication better.

There are many means of communication in this world. I would like to tell you about the means of communication which I generally use. I use phone, laptop, e-mails and letters. I personally feel thatthe mobile phone is the best means of communication. I remember that once I met with an accident as I was travelling alone in a rainy night. I did not know what to do, but I had my phone and I straight away called for help. I was able to get the help because of the phone.

There are many advantages of using a mobile phone as I mentioned earlier that it can help a person in emergencies. Other than that, the phones are operating as mini-computers these days, as they have all the features which are available in a computer. We can catch up with a friend without actually meeting the friend personally. Mobile phones tend to save time if they are used properly, for instance, if I have to cancel a class, I simply send a message to the students and they come to know that I won't attend the class today. This would apply if you are a teacher too.

There are also some disadvantages of using mobile phones. The most obvious ones are that people waste a lot of time and money by talking on the phone for hours. I also hate the ring tones of mobiles, so I certain mostly keep my mobile silent.

CUE-CARD - 40 : THE MEANS OF TRANSPORTATION

– The means of transportation in urban and rural areas in your country

– Which means of transportation do you use

– What are the advantages and disadvantages of using it

There are many means of transportation in my country. People in the urban areas usually have their own cars, or they use the public transport, whereas people in the rural areas tend to travel on bicycles and tractors. People in this world use those means of transportation which are suitable for them. The previous mentioned means of transportation are used to travel within the country, whereas airplanes are used to travel from one country to another.

My favourite means of transportation is a car. I got this car when I was 19 years old. First I used to travel by bus, but after getting the car, my life became a lot easier and felt that a car was a necessity rather than a luxury. First, I used to travel by bus and I never reached my destination on time. There was a day when I missed a bus and due to that I also missed my exam. So I got a zero in my exam. I think that the use of a car enables a person to reach on time and it also protects a person from bad weather. There are also some disadvantages attached to the use of car as it is very expensive to keep a car and a person also has to pay for the maintenance charges. Cars also create pollution and traffic congestion.

I still feel that the benefits of using a car outweigh the drawbacks and more and more people in this world are trying to get their own cars.

CUE-CARD - 41 : UNIFORM

– Why do people wear uniforms

– Have you ever worn an uniform

– What role does uniform play in a person's life

We all have seen people wearing uniform. People of different professions wear uniforms in order to distinguish them from other people and to show unity. You can easily observe that different organizations have different uniforms. I personally like the uniform of lawyers. Lawyers wear a black coat in my country which look quite good. Apart from lawyers there are also other people who wear uniforms. The most obvious ones are army men, doctors, students, policemen and people of other law enforcement agencies.

I used to wear a uniform when I was in my school. I used to wear a white shirt and black pant. I was not at all confortable with it. I always thought that my school should have allowed all the students in my school to wear ordinary clothes. I never felt nice after wearing the uniform and I wanted to just take it off. But now that I am an adult and I realise how wise it was of the school to make us wear these clothes. Wearing a uniform just saves us from the effort to try so hard to choose clothes. Now I contemplate the idea behind making the students wear uniform. There are some rich and poor people in a school, so the schools introduce a uniform to promote equality and brotherhood amongst them. A uniform plays a vital role in the life of a person. It promotes unity, discipline and integrity. I can easily say that a uniform has played a very imperative role in my life.

CUE-CARD - 42 : THE TYPE OF MOVIES YOU LIKE

You should say:

- What type of movies do you like
- Compare different types of movies
- How do you feel after watching a movie

I like to watch sad movies. I know that people would consider me as a sad person, but I feel good after watching them. I am mostly interested in watching sad Indian movies. I feel that no one does sad movies better than the Indians and the songs make the entire atmosphere a very unique with a great experience. Two days ago I watched two sad Indian movies and both of them were of Shah Rukh Khan. The actor acted well in both the films.

I go for movies every week with my friends and all of them are interested in action movies. So, on their repeated requests, I decided to watch an action movie and in the end, I was bored to death. The action was so childish and all the people were jumping over buildings as if they were 'spiderman'. It was pathetic and I think that I would never been able to adopt a liking for action movies as I so into sad movies.

I also watch action movies, but I won't be able to connect my feelings with those movies. I get bored after 30 minutes, but there is a whole different story with sad movies. My life has been sad lately. I feel that I am able to relate myself to those movies and I endeavour to find a pattern which matches my life. I know this might be sounding crazy but it is how I feel about the thing.

CUE-CARD - 43 : MY FAVOURITE MOVIE

– Name of your favourite movie

– Why do you like it so much

– What message does the movie convey

I watch a lot of movies and this is what I do in my leisure time. I love to watch movies and there are some movies which I watch again and again. My favourite movie is *The Terminal*. I have watched this movie many times and I am not exaggerating it. I loved the way Tom Hanks acted in the movie, and it was a very well executed movie. The movie is about a person who gets stuck in an airport and he has to live over there for months because the authorities do not let him go outside of the airport. Tom Hanks plays a character of a person who comes to America to fulfil his father's last wish and due to some reason, he is unable to do what he has to do.

In the movie, Tom Hanks lands at the airport and at the same time, there is a mutiny in his country and America stops recognising his country. The movie shows how a person survives all these months and fulfils the wish of his dead father. There is a scene in the movie when the authorities ask him to say that he is afraid of his country, but he says no.

You would not believe what I am going to tell you now. Once I was travelling and I was stuck in the Schipol Airport for 2 days, and I had to face similar kind of situation because my ticket had expired. I just felt as if the whole movie was going to be played again and I was to play the main character this time.

The movie shows that no matter what happens a person should never compromise on his or her love for his country. The movie also gives a message that no matter how long the wait is, people with strong determination always achieve their goals.

CUE-CARD - 44 : AN INCIDENT WHICH CHANGED YOUR LIFE

– What happened

– Who was involved in it

– How did it change your life

It was about 3 years ago when I was going to my friend's house. I was driving the car really fast. Speed always thrilled me and I always felt good by driving the car very fast, so I was driving the car fast when a car passed by me. It was faster than me and I reckon it would be travelling at a speed of 200km/hr. First I thought, I was going at the same speed but then I stopped. After about 30 seconds, I saw that the car had hit a truck and the driver of the fast car was dead.

I was not directly involved in the accident, but it had an overwhelming effect on my life. It changed everything. I never took life seriously and I never considered driving to be a hazardous activity, but the killing of the person had a devastating effect on my life. I realised that the thing which I considered to be fun could even take my life away and could destroy others too.

I made a strong determination that day that I would end this kind of behaviour and try to avoid these things. I thought that doing this stuff could also take another person's life for which I would have never been able to forgive myself.

Now when I drive, I drive the car at a slow or average speed, and even if I have to reach a place urgently I decide to drive slow because it is better to reach late than never.

CUE-CARD - 45 : THE HAPPIEST MOMENT OF MY LIFE

– Describe it

– Why do you regard it as the happiest moment

– How did it affect your life

The happiest moment of my life was when I passed my Grade 12. It was a crazy day. I was behaving like a maniac as I was so stressed out. I had to go to my school to get my result and I was panicking. My admission in the college was solely dependent on whether I pass or fail the exam, so it was very important for me to pass the exam.

I reached my school and I was trembling with fear because I thought that I would fail in one of the subjects. After a long wait, I was asked to pick my result, and with trembling hands, I opened the envelope.

I had passed the exam. It was the happiest moment of my life. The main reason for the happiness was that I had not worked for the exam, but still I passed the exam. Somewhere in my heart, I thought that I did not deserve the passing marks, so getting it was a bonus for me!

If I compare this situation to other events in my life, I can say that I have had better marks in other exams, but this was the most important one. After, I got admission in the college and began my higher studies. I remember that most of the students in my class had not gotten it and they had to sit for the make-up exam; however, I was damn lucky and it also helped me realised that luck was not always going to work and in the future I will have to put up some real effort to get success in life.

CUE-CARD - 46 : THE MOST EMBARRASSING MOMENT IN YOUR LIFE

– Describe the event

– Why did you feel so much embarrassed?

– Can we avoid these kinds of incidents?

The most embarrassing moment of my life was when I went to school without my book. I was studying really hard all night. Actually I was pulling an all-nighter, and I forgot to bring my books to school. As I was sitting in the class, my math teacher asked all the students to take out their books, and as the students were taking their books out, the principal entered the class.

I put my hand in the bag and realised that I had forgotten the books at home. Everyone in the class had brought the books and I was the only one who had not brought it. The principal approached me and asked that why had I not brought the books? I told him that I was studying late, so I forgot the books at home. He told me that the only reason you have to study at home is that you do not bring your books to school and you do not study over here. It was such an embarrassing moment for me that I felt like crying. The entire class started laughing at me and I was the new dumbo of the class.

I do not think that we can avoid these embarrassing moments in our life. They are beyond our control as in my situation, my hard work for the night was not acclaimed and a slightest mistake just turned out to be a blunder as I had to face embarrassment in front of the whole class. Some people say that we can avoid certain things to avoid these incidents, but I do not think in a similar way.

CUE-CARD - 47 : MY FAVOURITE ELECTRONIC DEVICE

– Name of the device

– When do you use it

– How do other people regard this incident

My favourite electronic device is a laptop. I am not exaggerating by saying that I cannot live without it. When I did not have it, I never thought it would become such vital thing in my life, but when I started using it I realised that I could not live with it. I use a Dell laptop and it is very beautiful. Apart from being beautiful, it has a lot of other functions and features which have made my life easier.

I carry my laptop all the time. The main reason I use the laptop is that I am running my own website and for that reason, I have to look at the website statistics at all times. If I do not use my laptop, I would not be able to operate my website. I also use the laptop when I have to talk to my friends, or when I have to check the e-mails. I have some friends who live in other cities so when I feel that I am missing them, or I feel that I should keep in touch with them then I talk to them on skype.

A Laptop is an electronic device which has not only made my life better, but also the lives of many people better. People have been able to communicate in a much better and faster way and the communication done via the laptop or internet is almost free. At first, it was considered to be a luxury, but thanks to the modern technology, it has now become affordable for everyone.

CUE-CARD - 48 : MY FAVOURITE SPORTS EVENT

- Why did you attend it
- Describe the sports event you attended
- What was the best part about the sports event

It was about 9 years ago, when I went to the Annual Sports Day of a school. It was a very grand event; more than 600 students were participating in different games. I had to attend it because my cousin was playing in the hockey team. I had come to watch the hockey match because I wanted to support my cousin.

It was a magnificent event. Things were organised incredibly well and the head boy of the school was organising everything by himself. I was really impressed by the look of the event, and it would not be wrong to compare the event to the Olympics. There was a massive display of fireworks at the beginning of the hockey match and then the teams came for the match. I must say that it was a very interesting encounter.

The best of the sports event was when my cousin scored the goal. He had been working really hard to get a place in the team, and when he used this opportunity in the best way by scoring the only goal of the match, the entire crowd was cheering for my cousin and it was a moment to cherish. I was feeling proud of my cousin and I realised that he was not a celebrated person at the school. After the match was over, I congratulated my cousin and told him that the entire sports event was a blast and I have enjoyed a lot by coming to the event, and by watching the match.

CUE-CARD - 49 : FAVOURITE FOOD

– What kind of food do you like

– How do you feel after eating it

– Do you know how to cook it

My favourite food is the Pakistani food and my favourite dish is Biryani. I like to eat Pakistani food because I have been eating it since my childhood and I am fond of eating spicy food. I have been to many countries in this world and I have tried many things, but still I consider the Pakistani food to be my favourite. Some people like to eat things which are expensive and they feel that the things which they eat or like are recognised worldwide, but I have different opinion. I like to eat things which are delicious and the food which I have been eating since my childhood.

I remember that once I was feeling very sad, and I did not want to eat anything at all. But then as I saw Biryani I began feeling hungry. There are times when I am not even feeling hungry, and I start eating Biryani the moment I look at it. I feel very good after eating Biryani. It is so mouth-watering and sumptious that sometimes, I eat it in high quantities.

Some people think that only girls should be the one who cook, but I think boys should also know how to cook food. I learnt making this dish and it was a unique kind of experience. I never thought that cooking was so fun, and now whenever, I want to eat Biryani, I prefer to make it myself. I believe that you should also try it out someday as most people in my country love it so much.

CUE-CARD - 50 : MY FAVOURITE DRINK

– Name of favourite drink

– Tell me something about the taste

– When do you drink it

My favourite drink is Mountain Dew. I drink it every day and you can say that I am almost addicted to it. I cannot live a day without it. My fridge is always stuffed with chilled cans of Mountain Dew. It was 5 years ago when I saw the ad of Mountain Dew. I was really impressed by the adventurous ad of Mountain Dew and I thought of trying it out. The surprising thing is that I liked it the first time, I tasted it and the entire feeling was incredible.

It is easy to tell about the taste of the drink. It has a unique taste and it feels as if there is a lemon taste in the drink. The drink tastes the best when it is chilled. I cannot describe the taste, but you could get a good idea of its taste if you try it yourself.

I drink it every day. This is the reason why I have been putting on a lot of weight. Mountain dew has a lot of calories, but I just ignore the calories as I am a slave to its taste. I drink 150-ml bottle almost everyday and prefer to drink this while I am having dinner. I do not get angry at people and it is very difficult to annoy me, but once I had put my Mountain Dew in the fridge, and my cousin drank it all. This episode irritated me so much that I shouted at him. I am just so possessive about Mountain Dew that I cannot tolerate anyone else drinking my drink and getting all the pleasure.

CUE-CARD - 51 : MY FAVOURITE WEBSITE

– Why is it your favourite website

– How often do you use it

– What would your life be without it

My favourite website is *youtube.com*. A lot of people in this world regard *youtube* to be their favourite website and I feel in the similar way. This is a website in which a person can watch or upload videos for free, and the best part is that the user can even create his or her channel and then earn money by the videos he or she has uploaded. We can find almost everything on *youtube* and everything is available over there free of charge.

I started using *youtube* 4 years ago, and it has been a really great experience. I spend most of my lesiure time on *youtube*. I have uploaded my own video lectures on *youtube* and these video lectures are provided to people for free. I also stay on *youtube* to watch trailers and songs. You can find almost every song of this world on *youtube*. There was a day when I missed a cricket match because I was busy in something, but because of *youtube* I was able to watch the entire match again because someone had uploaded the match and it made me very happy.

My life would be hell without *youtube*. I would not be able to function without it. I am running an educational institute in Pakistan, and I provide free online video lectures to everyone irrespective of the fact that they are my students or not. If *youtube* goes out of my life, I would not be able to provide this free service and it would be bad not only for me, but also for all the people who are benefitting from it.

CUE-CARD - 52 : SINGNIFICANCE OF EXERCISE

– When do you exercise

– What exercise do you do

– How do you feel after doing exercise

I do not think that anyone in this world can deny the significance of exercise in their life. I have seen that people who do exercise live a healthy and wealthy life. I would even consider obesity as a disease which deserves to be eradicated from this world.

I definitely know about the importance of exercise because first I used to be very fat. I weighed 200 pounds and I was obsessed with junk food. I got so much fat that I began hating myself. One day, I made a commitment to myself that I would lose weight and that could only be done through exercise.

I started off with jogging on the treadmill, but as the time progressed, I also began weight training. The exercise which I like the most is *running*. After running, I feel as if I am in the air and I feel very light-weighted and good. I run for about 30 minutes every day and it is a very good experience. Last month, I had to go out of town for a business meeting. As I was attending the meeting, I did not get a chance to do exercise and I felt so bad. Some people say that they feel tired after doing exercise, but that is not the case with me. Whenever I do exercise I feel energetic and I am able to perform my other tasks in a very efficient manner. I would recommend everyone to indulge in some kind of exercises or the other because it would make a person both mentally and physically fit.

Chapter 9 : Part 3 Follow-up Queries

MOST POPULAR DISCUSSION TOPICS

The topic of discussion is related to the topics of the second part (a Speech/Cue Card), but the difference is that here you should EXPRESS AN OPINION and explain why it is, and what it is. This is the part where you should compare two opinions, present several points of view, say what your perception is, and what future developments might follow, etc.

This part usually takes 4-5 minutes.

It's difficult to predict exactly what questions we will get asked in the third part of the exam, but usually they will have a close connection to the topics we discussed in part 2 of the exam. In addition, the following functions may be tested:

1. Comparing (time/objects/concepts)
2. Predicting
3. Advantages
4. Disadvantages
5. Problems
6. Solutions
7. Opinions (why)

1. Comparing

Do you think people were smarter in the past?

What is the difference between learning skills and knowledge?

2. Predicting

Do you think people will be more intelligent in the future?

Do you think technology can replace teachers in the future?

3. Advantages

What are the main advantages of studying online?

What are the main advantages of studying abroad?

4. **Disadvantages**

What are the main disadvantages of studying online?

What are the main disadvantages of studying abroad?

5. **Problems**

What are some of the main problems that students often encounter with learning English?

What problems do students often have with their classmates?

6. **Solutions**

[for above "How could we solve these problems"]

7. **Opinions**

Why do you think some people enjoy learning new things?

What are some useful ways to remember things?

1. **Comparing:** Try to use language of comparison (cheaper, more expensive, more/ less than)

   Opening: Well, obviously, there are a variety of possible differences here; Well, undoubtedly, they are like chalk and cheese.

   The First Difference: However, I (guess/ suppose) that the most striking difference is ~; whereas in contrast... But I would say the most fundamental would be that (S+V). On the contrary,

   The Second Difference: In addition, a subsequent contrast could be that (S+V). Conversely, moreover, a further distinction might be that (S+V). While on the other hand, ...

Practice Questions for Part 3 of the IELTS EXAM

- ☆ In what ways do the magazines are different from newspapers?
- ☆ How could we deal with the problems of Internet?
- ☆ Are people travelling more now than in the past?
- ☆ Who make better teachers – men or women?
- ☆ How have family values changed over the years?

2. **Predicting:** Try to use future tense (will, going to + verb)

   Opening: I am sure that in years to come, we will see a number of changes related to this; I imagine that in the near future, we will witness some major changes with regards to (N).

The First Prediction: To begin with, I would predict that we will most likely to have (N). Primarily, it looks quite possible that we are going to have (N).

The Second Prediction: As well as, some people claim that we will probably start to see (N). Likewise, I would imagine that we may even be able to see (N).

The Third Prediction: And who knows, there is even a chance that we will have (N). And I know it is a bit of a crazy thought, but one day we may even have (N).

Practice Questions for Part 3 of the IELTS EXAM

- ☆ What will schools be like in the future?
- ☆ What will cars be like in the future?
- ☆ Do you think people will have to conserve water in the future?
- ☆ Do you think we will get the news in different ways in the future?
- ☆ What will your country be like in 50 years?

3. **Advantages (merits, benefits, rewards)**

Opening: Clearly there are a number of obvious merits; Obviously there are a number of positive features.

The Main Advantage: But I would probably say that for the most part, the one thing that really stands out is that~. This is obviously favourable because (S+V). However, I guess that the most evident would be that (S+V). This is surely a positive feature as (S+V).

The Second Advantage: Besides this, a second plus point could be that (S+V). This is undoubtedly favourable and at the same time, a second bonus might be that of (S+V).

Practice Questions for Part 3 of the IELTS EXAM

- ☆ What are the advantages of living in an old building?
- ☆ What are the advantages of living in big cities?
- ☆ What are the advantages of owning an up-to-date mobile phone?
- ☆ What are the advantages of advertising?
- ☆ What are the advantages of studying abroad?

4. **Disadvantages (drawbacks, shortcomings)**

   Opening: I am sure most people would agree that there are some drawbacks; Of course, there are a couple of shortcomings.

   The Main Disadvantage: I suppose the most unfavourable quality might be that (S+V). This is a weakness obviously because of (S+V). I guess the most impractical characteristic would be that of (S+V). This is a clear limitation because of (S+V).

   The Second Disadvantage: At the same time, another stumbling block might be that ~. And the trouble with this is that... Correspondingly, an additional weak point may be that (S+V). And this can be a hassle as~...

Practice Questions for Part 3 of the IELTS EXAM

- ✯ What are the disadvantages of living in an old building?
- ✯ What are the disadvantages of living in big cities?
- ✯ What are the disadvantages of owning an up-to-date mobile phone?
- ✯ What are the disadvantages of advertising?
- ✯ What are the disadvantages of studying abroad?

5. **Problems**

   Opening: Obviously, we can say that there are quite a lot of dangers with regard to this issue. It is universally accepted that there are a few hazards involved with (N).

   The Main Problem: Essentially, one fundamental concern is probably that ~. This is clearly alarming because~.

   The Second Problem: Equally worrying is the suggestion that~. And the underlying repercussions of this are...

Practice Questions for Part 3 of the IELTS EXAM

- ✯ What problems are associated with eating fast food?
- ✯ What problems are caused by a lack of physical exercise?
- ✯ How is our busy lifestyle contributing to health problems?
- ✯ What problems are associated with global warming?
- ✯ What problems are associated with violence being shown on TV?

6. **Solutions:**

   Opening: In my view, there are a few ways to tackle this problem.

The First Solution: When dealing with _________, the easiest way to solve it out would be ~.

The Second Solution: I also think that we could ________________

Practice Questions for Part 3 of the IELTS EXAM

- ✯ How could we deal with eating fast food?
- ✯ What would you do to get more physical exercise?
- ✯ How can stress from our busy lifestyle be relieved?
- ✯ What steps could be taken to tackle global warming?
- ✯ How could kids be prevented from seeing violence on TV?

7. Opinion (why)

Opening: Well in my opinion, there are undoubtedly a variety of justifications for this. I suppose I would say that (S+V). There are probably a number of factors involved. Well generally, it is my belief that (S+V). There are obviously a number of motives surrounding this idea.

The First Reason: The chief cause might be that (S+V). The key explanation is possibly because of (S+V).

The Second Reason: As well as this, a subsequent factor could be because of (S+V). At the same time, a secondary motive could be that of (S+V).

Practice Questions for Part 3 of the IELTS EXAM

- ✯ Why do people like travelling to foreign countries?
- ✯ Why do so many people move from the countryside to cities?
- ✯ Why is it important for children to play sports?
- ✯ Why do young people spend so much time on the Internet?
- ✯ Why is watching TV so popular all over the world?

POPULAR DISCUSSION TOPICS

GIFTS

1. **What are the positive/negative aspects of giving and receiving gifts?**

Ans: Giving and receiving gifts have both advantages and disadvantages. On one hand, it is an expression of one's love or appreciation for someone, and on the other hand, it strengthens relationships. It can also create a good feeling in the minds of people.

On the other hand, giving and receiving gifts today has become a commercial activity. Sometimes we are forced to give and receive gifts. A lot of time and money are involved in buying gifts. For example, if someone calls you for a birthday, you are compelled to give a gift. Sometimes, it can become a burden on your budget.

2. **What are the different types of gifts that women, men and children would like to receive?**

Ans: Women are usually fond of ornaments and clothes. They also like to receive household appliances and handicrafts. For special occasions, like birthdays, they receive a lot of such gifts. Children are usually attracted to toys and dolls. They love chocolates and sweets too.

3. **What changes have taken place in giving and receiving gifts in the last 50 years?**

Ans: A number of changes have taken place in the way people give and receive gifts, over the last 50 years. In the olden days, gifts were not very common and it was exchanged only during rare occasions like marriages. Today, giving and receiving gifts have become a very frequent affair. Exchanging gifts have become very common on a number of occasions like birthdays, anniversaries and success in an exam.

4. **Whose gifts do you treasure most?**

Ans: I treasure the gifts of my loved ones. For instance, I always cherish the gifts that my wife has given me. In fact, she gives them to me with great love. I greatly value gifts from my parents too. Gifts from close friends or colleagues also give me great pleasure.

5. **Do you think people have become more or less materialistic in the last 25 years?**

Ans: What I feel is, people's attitude towards material things have not changed over the last 25 years. The only difference is that today we have greater access to comforts and luxuries unlike in the past, and we have enough money to buy them, so we enjoy them. For this reason, many people tend to say that materialism is on the increase. Actually, that is not the case. If people in the past had access to such things and if they had as much money as we have today, they would have definitely enjoyed luxuries. The only difference is the economic progress that we have made. The attitude towards materialism remains the same always.

I feel that people have definitely become more materialistic during the last 25 years. Formerly, comforts and luxuries were not available to people as much as we have today. Maybe, people were more idealistic and they had better human relationships. Especially in rural communities, people maintained traditional values in families and social life. Whereas, today the situation has changed. Urbanisation has forced people to be more individualistic and achievement-oriented. Material achievement has become a major purpose in life and therefore, I think, other values of life have taken a back seat.

6. What kind of gifts children usually like?

Ans: Children usually like chocolates, toys and electronic games. You know, for example, if you go to a shop with your children, you will see them running to the toy corner or the chocolate rack. These days, a lot of children have a great liking towards electronic games. There are many children who like cartoons and story books too. So when you plan to give a gift to a child next time, think of these things.

7. What kind of things give a sense of prestige to people today?

Ans: From my personal experience, I feel, material possessions can give a great deal of prestige to people today. For example, if you have a luxurious car or a beautifully designed house it can give you a sense of pride. Another important criterion for prestige is political power at different levels, which can make you popular and accepted by the society. Superior positions in government services can also definitely give you prominence in the society. What I mean is, senior police officers, judges and similar officials have great prestige in the society. Apart from that, superior education can give you a lot of honour among the people. Certain professionals like doctors, engineers and teachers are respected in the society.

8. What kind of things were status symbols in your grandfather's time?

Ans: Although I am not very sure, money and other material possessions were status symbols even in my grandparents' time. I think, people who had a lot of land were considered honourable in the society. Superior education and political power were also considered status symbols at that time. I believe, basically, the status symbols of people of all ages are generally the same.

9. What kind of things are women usually attracted to?

Ans: Women are generally fond of good clothes and ornaments. If you go to a textile store or jewellery shop, the majority of the shoppers are usually women. This means that there is a certain vanity in women and they love to flaunt their beauty. They are also attracted to cosmetics. Many women buy a lot of house hold appliances and crockery.

10. Do you think people purchase a lot of things for prestige and not because of genuine need?

Ans: Certainly, today if you have money to spare, you certainly buy things that can show off your wealth. Although you may not need such luxurious items, you buy them because you want others to look upon you. For example, one of the considerations for many people, when they choose a car, is whether a particular car is used by the elite in the society. Or, even if the family is a small one, people build huge houses and many of the rooms are unused for years. Prestige is a serious consideration for many people these days.

11. What will be the kind of things that will give a sense of prestige to people in future?

Ans: Even in the future, wealth will be a major determining factor which is a sense of prestige to people. Education, the expertise in technology and communication abilities also give a sense of pride to the people.

FAMILY

1. In what ways can people in a family be similar to each other?

Ans: People in a family can be similar to each other in many ways. They usually resemble each other in their physical appearances. For example, children look like their parents, in their facial features, colour, type of hair and so on. They can also be alike, in their character and behaviour.

2. Do you think daughters are always more similar to mothers than to the other male relatives?

Ans: Not always! There are many daughters who look more like their fathers or other male members of the family than mothers. That includes their colour, face, hair and so on. But I do think that most daughters look like their mothers in physical features.

3. What about sons and fathers?

Ans: I think it is the same with them as well. There are many sons who resemble their mothers more than their fathers or other male members of the family.

4. In terms of personality, are people more influenced by their family or friends? In what ways?

Ans: People are usually more influenced by their family than friends, because as children, most people live with their families. And that is when an individual's personality is developed. Even after that, people spend more time with their family members and interact with them more closely than their friends. This intimacy with the family members has a great influence in their character formation. On the other hand, friends also have a significant influence on one's personality, but not as much as family members.

GENETIC RESEARCH

1. Where can people in your country get information about genetic research?

Ans: There are many sources in my country where people can get information about genetic research. I think the most common source is a book. You can find books on genetic research in public libraries or in bookshops. Apart from that, there are a number of universities and institutes that do research in genetic studies. There are lots of scientists and professors who can give information about this subject. I think the internet is a wonderful source to get information about genetic research. If you search on Google, you will come across many websites that will give you, at least, the primary information about genetic research.

2. How do people in your country feel about genetic research?

Ans: In general, I think people in my country have a positive attitude towards genetic research. They know it has a lot of benefits in terms of better agricultural production and prevention of many genetic diseases. However, some people are worried about genetically modified foods. They fear that it can be dangerous to human health.

3. Should this research be funded by the governments or private companies?

Ans: I think both government and private companies should jointly or separately fund genetic research. It should not be the monopoly of either of the parties. If private companies alone fund genetic research, the benefits of the research may not reach the common man, because of their profit motive. So the government also has the responsibility to fund it, so that everybody enjoys the benefits.

TRAFFIC WHERE YOU LIVE

1. How do most people travel to work where you live?

Ans: Most people in my place travel to work using the public transport system. We have both government and private bus services that are very efficient and frequent. The bus fares are also quiet moderate, and that makes it the favourite mode of travel for ordinary people to go to work. People, who go to longer distances to work, usually make use of trains. We have a number of short distance trains, which are very inexpensive. A lot of people also have their own private vehicles to go to work. Most young people have their own motorbikes. The more affluent go to work by car.

2. What traffic problems are there in your area?

Ans: Traffic problems are quite frequent in my area, especially during the peak hours of morning and evening, when people travel to work or study and come back. Many roads are very narrow and cannot hold the increasing traffic volume at a time. So traffic moves at a snail's pace, especially during the rush hours. There are also a lot of puddles on the roads, particularly during the rainy season and manoeuvring them would further slow the traffic down. There are constant repairs on the roads which are both slow and ineffective and traffic is often diverted through narrower roads making the situation still worse.

3. **How do traffic problems affect you?**

Ans: Traffic problems affect me very badly. I need to reach work on time and very often, the unexpected traffic snarls and jams do not let me do it. I have made it a point that I start a bit earlier from home, so that these unexpected delays do not affect me much. Another problem is that driving in high gear in the traffic jam exhausts my fuel tank very fast.

4. **How would you reduce the traffic problems in your area?**

Ans: The first thing that the government should do is to widen the roads with immediate effect and that can definitely reduce the problems drastically. Another area that the authorities can look into is to engage a big company to construct roads that can last for a longer period of time. It would definitely reduce the constant repairs on roads. People should also be made to obey traffic rules very strictly.

PARTY

1. **What types of parties do people have, and why are parties important?**

Ans: People have parties to celebrate special occasions like birthdays, weddings, or the beginning of a new year. I think it's important to celebrate these things because they are landmarks in our lives. Parties are a good way to bring people together, and they're an opportunity to let off some steam.

2. **Why do you think some people like parties but others hate them?**

Ans: Most people like parties because they have a good time at them – eating a nice meal, chatting to friends, or dancing. People who don't like them might find social situations difficult because they are shy, or maybe, they don't enjoy making small talk with people they don't know.

3. **Do you think parties will become more popular in the future?**

Ans: No, I don't think anything will change. People have always had parties, and I'm sure they always will in the future. Humans need to socialise and enjoy themselves, and parties are one of the best ways to do that.

DECISION

1. **Is it better to make important life decisions on your own or is it better to consult other people?**

Ans: There are good reasons for both, I suppose. Ultimately, it's your life so I suppose you should make the decisions. On the other hand, any decisions you make can affect other people, so it seems only right to discuss things with others first. Like many philosophical questions, there's no simple answer, I'm afraid.

2. Do you think good decision-making can be taught?

Ans: Well, if you go to a bookstore, you'll see lots of self-help books that claim to teach decision-making. I'm not sure any of them are effective though. I suppose it depends on the type of decision you mean. If it's a business strategy, then I'm sure some decisions are better than others and business schools teach this. But if it's a moral issue then I'm not sure anyone can claim to know the right decision, so how can anyone teach it?

LEISURE TIME

1. Is watching TV a good way of forgetting about work or study?

Ans: Absolutely, yes. These days there's so much choice available that we can completely immerse ourselves in entertainment. I mean, you can turn on a good drama or comedy show and pretty soon, you forget about everything that happened that day. I think that without TV we'd all go a little crazy.

2. Should coworkers also spend their leisure time together?

Ans: I'm completely against this. The problem with people going out together after work is that they just gossip about certain people in the office or factory, and this can hardly be a good thing for the company, can it? Another thing is that there's always the risk that you will say something you regret after a few drinks and then you have to face your colleagues again the next day. So, in short, I would definitely advise people to think twice about socialising with colleagues.

TOURISM

1. What do you think are the preferred places for tourism in your country?

Ans. My country, India is a tourist paradise. We have all sorts of destination for people of varied tastes. From Kashmir to Kanayakumari, India is blend with natural beauty, ethnic splendour and cultural diversity in the form of hill stations like Mussorie, Dalhousie, Shimla, Ooty, etc. The natural paradise on earth is KASHMIR.

2. What are the negative impacts of tourism?

Ans. Well, I've seen areas where large number of visitors have had a detrimental effect on local habitats. Excessive use of natural resources, danger of epidemics and excise or imports issues including threats of terrorism can't be ignored.

3. How do you think can we make tourism better for the local community?

Ans. Undoubtedly, the local economy really uproars if the tourism is promoted in a better way. It does not only increase the Gross Domestic Product (GDP) of the place but rather, it adds value to the national Exchange. But the need of the hour is to preserve and protect it.

4. How has tourism changed in your country over the last 10 years?

Ans. Tourism has changed manifold. Tourism brings investment and better infrastructure to poorer communities. It brings the improved quality of life for the local people. It also brings greater work opportunities for the local people. For example, earlier they are limited to fishing and farming but nowdays, it offers high earning jobs.

5. How do you think will it change in the future?

Ans. Well..I must say in the coming years, our economic development largely depends upon the tourism sector. It will strengthen universal brotherhood, fraternity, international world peace and exchange of cultural values.

6. How well equipped is your country to deal with tourists?

Ans. Ahhh…Very interesting, but I must say presently, we are under the grip of loopholes as most of the tourist centres like Taj Mahal…the Seven Wonders of the World, are facing a severe threat of pollution. Similarly, wildlife sanctuaries are also facing the problem of *extinction, poaching and hunting*. Historical sites are losing their charms due to faster means of globalisation and communication. So catering interest among tourists for visiting these places seems to be a hard nut to crack.

EDUCATION

1. What do you think are important skills for a teacher?

Ans. A teacher is the milestone that plays an indispensable role in building up of a nation. For a student is a mirror where the transparent picture of a subject can be easily seen. So it is quite essential that the teacher should be well educated, cultured, disciplined, most important is up-to-date with the present scenario in his/her subject of teaching. Here I must say, he/she should be an *Encyclopaedia of knowledge*.

2. What facilities should a school have?

Ans. Giving and getting Smart Education is the order of the day. Gone are those days when teachers were restricted to chalk and blackboard. Today in this smarter world, the teacher and student both need to be smarter to get the best and practical education. Each and every school should try to facilitate the system of *Smart Education* in the form of *Online Education.*

3. **What are the problems with the education system in your country?**

Ans: Education is the gateway to success. But if steps are not proper, it may lead to ignorance and darkness. Our education system is also in the grip of a number of problems like Utopian Education (Imaginary), more stress on examination rather than putting efforts for building up of attitude and aptitude in knowledge. Undoubtedly, it is flexible and experimental these days but sometimes, it is all Greek to those who are unable to answer it.

4. **What can be done to solve these problems?**

Ans. More stress should be laid down upon Smart and Practical Education to improve its standards. *Time Immemorial Syllabus* should be immediately banned, i.e., the quality of curriculum should be changed according to the the times, so that students become more updated to the present scenario.

5. **What do you think the typical classroom will look like in 20 years?**

Ans.The typical chalk-blackboard classroom will be converted into high profile online classrooms where the creation and proliferation of the personal computer, the globalization of ideas and other human acts, and the use of technology in exchanging ideas and providing access to more people will be done.

SKILLS

1. **How important is it to have a skill?**

Ans. Keeping and having skills are the indispensable requirement in the vocational, professional and occupational world. Gone are those days when degrees or diplomas are sufficient to get any job but these days, it is necessary to possess skills like language, communication, IT, man power, techniques, etc.These skills are even highly lucrative as far as monetary aspect is concerned.

2. **What is the most useful skill you have?**

Ans. Well ..I do believe possessing skills is the inherent requirement of the present scenario. The most useful skill what I have is that of Communication. I do believe that this skill is the need of the hour as the world is governed according to this skill. Possessing good command over language not only enhances your language skills, but also allows you to interact with the world.

3. **How can children learn different skills?**

Ans. Children are the nation builders of tomorrow. It is highly essential for them to possess skills like communication, IT, techniques, dance, acting, swimming, etc. They can learn these skills while doing their academic education in school. Moreover, it is the moral responsibility of the schools to open avenues for children to adhere to these skills, so that they should not academically be brilliant but also talented and skilled in the art of doing some practical work.

4. Can anyone be a good artist/singer, etc.?

Ans. Yes..of course, why not. I know talent and skill both are different terms but if we try to polish the talent, then it becomes a good skill that helps anybody to achieve higher in life. For example, anybody can be a good artist or singer if he/she is learned and practised in a right way because possessing talent is not sufficient enough until or unless it is polished to form a skill.

THE ENVIRONMENT

1. How can we teach people to care more about the environment?

Ans. Undoubtedly, it is the next generation who will have to bear the burden of saving the planet. So it is necessary to alert them with the havoc of environmental problems like Global Warming, Depletion of Natural Resources, Scarcity of Water, Pollution, etc. For this, they should be given proper statistics and survey details of all these problems so that the coming generation should understand its urgency and take proper repercussions to improve the environmental problems.

2. Are people in your country aware of environmental problems?

Ans. To be honest, no... I think the middle and upper classes are mad in the rat race of earning and spending money, and there are many people in my country, who live below the poverty line and they quite literally can't afford to worry about the environment when they are struggling to put food on the table and just survive.

3. What is the biggest environmental issue in your country at the moment?

Ans. Global warming is the major issue in my country at the moment because it results not only in the depletion of the ozone layer but also responsible for creating suffocation and congestion in the environment.

4. Does the responsibility for protecting the environment lie with the governments or with the individuals?

Ans. In my view, the responsibility lies with all of us. However, individuals, at least in my country, aren't taking action of their own accord and nor our businesses, they are just out to make profits. The government also fails to force people to be more green, for example by fining companies or factory owners that release toxic waste into our rivers or incentivising us to recycle.

BOOKS

1. How important are books to you?

Ans. Books are my best friends which never demand and never complain. It is the *Store house of Knowledge*. It directs us towards our goals. It also improves our Focus and Vision towards Life.

2. Do you think that children don't read enough these days?

Ans. Yes..certainly in the world of e-books, reading habits are dashed into the ground in the children's world. They love to do Net Surfing instead of getting engrossed into the bookish world. But those who are fond of reading still love reading novels at length.

3. How can we make sure that children should keep reading?

Ans. Well, here I must say children of present day are more observatory and experimental rather than theoretical.We can make sure children should keep reading by using the art of creativity to cater their interests because reading simple text without graphics seems to be cumbersome and a hard nut to crack for them. So it is better to have animated, creative and fantasy based books to maintain their art of reading.

4. What impact has new technology on books and reading?

Ans. New technology brings revolutionary change on books and reading. It brings the era of e-books. Nowdays, with the mushroom growth of science and technology, media, television channels, etc., its scope becomes more widened and broad. Now online oriented material takes the place of manual text.

5. How do book preferences now compared to preferences in the past?

Ans. Well, earlier people were fond of reading Religious Books.They were more inclined to books related to philosophy. But today in the era of E-books, students are more aware of experimental knowledge. They become more factual than value based.

6. Do you think in the future paper books will disappear all together?

Ans. Certainly..Here I must say not in future, rather even in the present education system too, the era of smart books has invaded the global education system. It has replaced paper books to a great extent. Even the school infrastructure is designed on behalf of giving smarter education to children for this purpose. Smart screens are used for providing online education in place of chalk Blackboard pedagogy .

TECHNOLOGY

1. Do you like the new technology/gadgets?

Ans. Yes… why not ..of course..it is the order of the day. Without it life is indispensable. I love the gadgetary world and its equipments as it makes life more comfortable and pleasant to live. It removes the definition of isolation from the world and allows the networking of social sites which brings revolutionary change in the culture of socialisation.

2. How important is technology in your life?

Ans. To be very frank, I must say life will be burdensome if technology is not in my life. It is one of the cheapest and best source to lead a comfortable life. It has excelled the field beyond one's expectations. Whatever area it may be, whether it is medical, communication, insurance, education, science, etc..it leaves its blueprint remarkably.

3. Which device has had the biggest impact on daily life?

Undoubtedly, the Internet has the biggest impact on our daily lives. It is the revolutionary invention of the 21st century. With the advent of internet, the world has been converted in to a global village. It is the house of information, door of social networking sites, education package for youngsters, package of games and leisure time activities for children.

4. How does communication these days differ from communication 10 years ago?

Ans. Well, earlier communication took place in the form of postal letters and telephonic conversation, but these days, the mode of communication has completely changed. E-mails, the fastest mode of transportation, has excelled the field of communication beyond one's expectations. Earlier television was the only media of knowing information. Nowdays, in the era of gadgetary world, mobile devices like cellular phones, tablets, I-pads, etc. have improved the modes of communication.

5. What are the disadvantages of all this technology?

Ans. We are becoming the servants in thought, as in action, of the machine we have created to serve us. Technology... is a queer thing. It brings you great gifts with one hand, and it stabs you at the back with the other. It makes your life more lethargic. It offers a sedentary life style where there is no physical exercise of the body.

LEARNING A LANGUAGE

1. How hard do you find it to learn a language?

Ans. Yes, it is true. Sometimes, its tough to learn the phonetics of alphabets of the second language, as it is not our mother tongue. So the best way to understand the second language is to meet the same folk of people belonging to that language for regular communication and only exchange of words in the same language enchances your language capacities. Learning the English language for the first time can be difficult. However, when done in an exciting and humorous way, learning English vocabulary and grammar are less confusing and more enjoyable.

2. **What aspects do you find the most difficult?**

Ans. Language is the medium of communication. If the individual excelled in the art of speaking a language, then it understands how to communicate in the same language with, other people. So I think communication in the same language is the most difficult aspect.

3. **Is it necessary to learn the culture of a country to understand its language?**

Ans. Every language is a temple, in which the soul of those who speak it is enshrined. *Language is the mirror of every culture.* The way we communicate becomes our caste, colour and creed. As you know, I belong to India which is a multilingual state, with unity in diversity, so language becomes the most significant factor that distinguishes one culture from other which later united us into one nation. For example, Punjabi belongs to Punjab people, Marathi belongs to Maharashtra the but together, we are only Indian. So I think, one can easily learn about the culture of a country by the way we communicate.

4. **Is it possible to get a good job these days without knowing a second language?**

Well.... these days .., I must say... no...It is tough for Indians to get a job on behalf of their mother tongue. As we are living in the environment of MNCs and corporates which work with English based nations requires employees who know English to communicate their business. So undoubtedly, it is very hard to survive on mother tongue alone these days.

5. **How can people best learn a language?**

The best way to learn any language is to communicate with those people who are using that language as their means of communication. The other ways to learn a foreign language is to watch movies in that language, listen to audio CDs /DVD's all of these one can enjoy in the language one wishes to.

Abstract

LISTENING MODULE

In the listening module, we endeavour to help the candidate to know the pointers, tips and common errors in the listening section and for practice, we enlist for candidates.

Chapter 10 : Listening Strategies & Skills

LISTENING MODULE IELTS

Duration & Format:

- First Module IELTS test of 30 minutes
- Test is played once only
- Approximately 30 minutes + 10 minutes Transfer Time
- Total 40 Questions

STRUCTURE OF THE TEST

	No. of Speakers	No. of items (Questions)
Section One	Conversation between two speakers	Ten (10)
Section Two	One Speaker	Ten (10)
Section Three	Conversation between two and four speakers	Ten (10)
Section Four	One speaker	Ten (10)

Question Types

- ✯ Short Answer Type
- ✯ Multiple Choice
- ✯ Matching
- ✯ Classification
- ✯ Summary Completion
- ✯ Sentence Completion
- ✯ Diagram Completion
- ✯ Table Completion
- ✯ Form Completion

Factors in the Assessment

- ✯ Proper understanding of the foreign accent
- ✯ Recognising the role of speakers
- ✯ Understanding and identifying numbers, dates and names
- ✯ Understanding the general meaning of the conversation

TEST TIPS FOR LISTENING TEST

TIP NO. 1: ENCIRCLE THE KEY WORDS

In the beginning of the test, 40-45 seconds are allotted to the candidate. During that time, try to encircle the key words of the listening sections.

TIP NO. 2: BE CAREFUL OF THE 'W' Family

Focus what type of questions the speaker is talking about, i.e., What, Where When, Why, Whom.

TIP NO. 3: DONOT REPEAT THE INFORMATION

Do not rewrite the word which is already written in the question paer.

TIP NO. 4: LISTEN TO INSTRUCTIONS CAREFULLY

TIP NO. 5: AVOID CHECKING YOUR ANSWERS

While attempting the test avoid checking your answers, otherwise, you will miss the rest of the questions.

TIP NO. 6: QUERIES ARE IN CHRONOLOGICAL ORDER

TIP NO. 7: DO NOT EXCEED THE WORD LIMIT

Chapter 11 : Listening Practice Tests

Listening Test 1

Section One

Listen to the journey of the 44th Black President of America, 'BARACK OBAMA' and answer the following questions, (1-7) on your answer sheet.

Circle the appropriate letter from (A-D).

1. **Barack Obama took office on**
   A. 20th January, 2009
   B. January 20, 2009
   C. Jan 20, 2009
   D. 2009, Jan 20
2. **Barack Obama is the ____________________ of the Harvard Law Review.**
   A. Attorney
   B. President
   C. African
   D. Community Organizer
3. **Barack Obama served the senate for three years as**
   A. Community Organizer
   B. Civil Rights Attorney
   C. President
   D. Teacher
4. **He was the Lecturer of ____________________ in the University of Chicago Law School.**
   A. Law
   B. Constitution
   C. Constitutional Law
   D. None of these
5. **Barack Obama is not successful in the House of**
   A. U.S. Senate

B. U.S. House of Representatives
C. Democratic National Convention
D. Harvard Law School

6. **Barack Obama RIVAL/Running Mate is**
A. Joe Biden/Mc Cain
B. Mc Cain/Delaware
C. Mc Cain/Joe Biden
D. Joe Biden

7. **Barack Obama won with**
A. 70 % of votes
B. 46 % of votes
C. 53 % of votes
D. None of these

BARACK OBAMA
PRESIDENT OF THE UNITED STATES

Section Two

Listen to the profile of Barack Obama and answer the following questions (8-20) on your answer sheet.

- ✯ Born **8.** ____________________
- ✯ Youth Name **9.** ____________________
- ✯ Met Michelle Robinson, Wife of Obama in **10.** ____________________
- ✯ Married on **11.** ____________________1992
- ✯ First Daughter **12.** ____________________ in 1998
- ✯ SECOND DAUGHTER, 'Sasha' in **13.** ____________________
- ✯ Family is just like **14.** ____________________
- ✯ Second Husband of Mother belongs to **15.** ____________________
- ✯ Favourite Sport **16.** ____________________
- ✯ Obama left the habit of **17.** ____________________
- ✯ Religion **18.** ____________________
- ✯ 'Dreams from My Father' released in **19.** ____________________
- ✯ In 2007, he released the **20.** ____________________

Section Three

Listen to the description of the 'Umbrella' by the narrator and answer the following questions from (21-28) on your answer sheet.

21. ____________________ 22. ____________________ 23. ____________________

24. ____________________ 25. ____________________ 26. ____________________

27. ____________________ 28. ____________________

Section Four

This section gives a brief idea of the courses offered for studying abroad in graduate and post-graduate classes in countries like, UK, Canada, Australia and New Zealand.

Listen the tapescript careful and tick (✓) mark the following answer from (29-36) on your answer sheet.

Graduate Courses

	A	B	C	D	E	F	G
Country Name	Arts	Science	Business	Medicine	Commerce	Mathematics & Science	Engineering
29. U.K.							
30. Canada							
31. Australia							
32. New Zealand							

Post Graduate Courses

Country Name	Medicine	Business	Arts	Social Sciences
33. U.K.	A	B	C	D
34. Canada				
35. Australia				
36. New Zealand				

Complete the following blanks:

37. PHD in Social Science offered in ____________________.

38. Canada offered ____________________ courses.

39. Australia offered PHD in ____________________ courses.

40. Degree/Diploma offered by ____________________.

Answer Sheet for Listening Test - 1

1.
2.
3.
4.
5.
6.
7.
8.
9.
10.
11.
12.
14.
15.
16.
17.
18.
19.
20.

21.
22.
23.
24.
25.
26.
27.
28.
29.
30.
31.
32.
33.
34.
35.
36.
37.
39.
40.

Listening Total ____________________

Listening Test 1

Answers

Section One

1. B
2. B
3. B
4. C
5. B
6. C
7. C

Section Two

8. Aug, 4, 1961
9. Barry
10. June, 1989
11. October, 3
12. MaliaAnn
13. 2001
14. Mini United Nation
15. Indonesia
16. Baskct Ball
17. Smoking
18. Christian
19. 1995
20. State of Black America

Section Three

21. G
22. A
23. C
24. F
25. B
26. H
27. D
28. F

Section Four

29. B, D
30. E, F
31. A, B, C
32. A, B, E, F, G
33. A, B
34. C
35. B, C, D
36. B, D
37. UK
38. Vocational
39. Arts
40. New Zealand

Listening Test – 2

Section One

Listen and tick (✓) A, B, C or D to indicate which picture in (1 – 8) questions is being discussed.

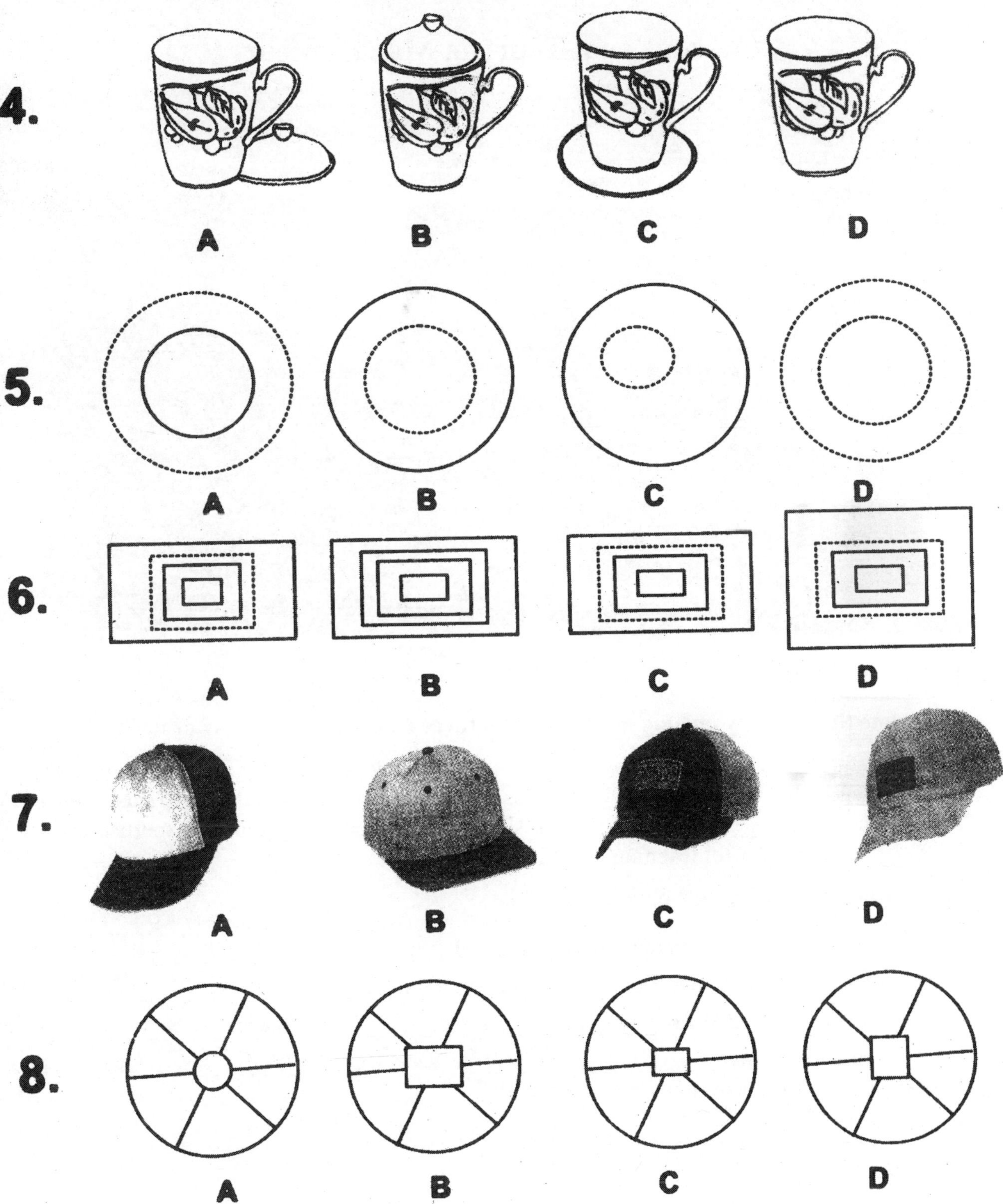
4.
A
B
C
D
5.
A
B
C
D
6.
A
B
C
D
7.
A
B
C
D
8.
A
B
C
D

International Tourism Management

Section Two

Complete this form by putting not more than three words for each answer in (9 – 17).

ITM: International Tourism Management course is a new course in the field of Tourism Management. This course not only includes teaching, research, industry expertise, but also business. **9.** ________________ Scottish Centre of Tourism provides expertise **10.** ____________________ for teaching the students.

Opportunities: Students get opportunities like

- ✯ Planning and Implementation of tourism **11.** ______________________
- ✯ Thorough understanding of contemporary tourism **12.** ____________________
- ✯ Proper handling of **13.** ______________________________ issues.
- ✯ Learn to get **14.** ________________________ and **15.** ________________________

Skills: Students will learn transferable skills like

16. _____________________________

17. ______________________________

Independent learning ability

Circle the appropriate letter from (18 –22)

Benefits

18. ITM can be studied:
    A. Full time
    B. Part time
    C. Both
19. ITM gives:
    A. Academic Qualification/Professional Qualification
    B. Professional Qualification/ Industrial Qualification
    C. Academic/ Professional/ Industrial Qualification
    D. Industrial Qualification

Subjects Offered:

20. ITM offers subjects like:
    A. E-business
    B. E-business and IT application
    C. Case Studies & Decision Making
    D. All of the above

Career Opportunities:

21. ITM candidate get career in the field of Public Sector Tourism like:
    A. Leisure Organisation
    B. Tourism research
    C. Regional Tourist Boards
    D. Visitor attraction
22. Customer Focussed Organisation gets:
    A. Leisure Organisation
    B. Travel Organisation
    C. Business Tool-kit
    D. Tourist Research

Section Three

Listen the tapescript and lable the diagram from (23 – 29) recycling of aluminium. Write not more than three words for each answer.

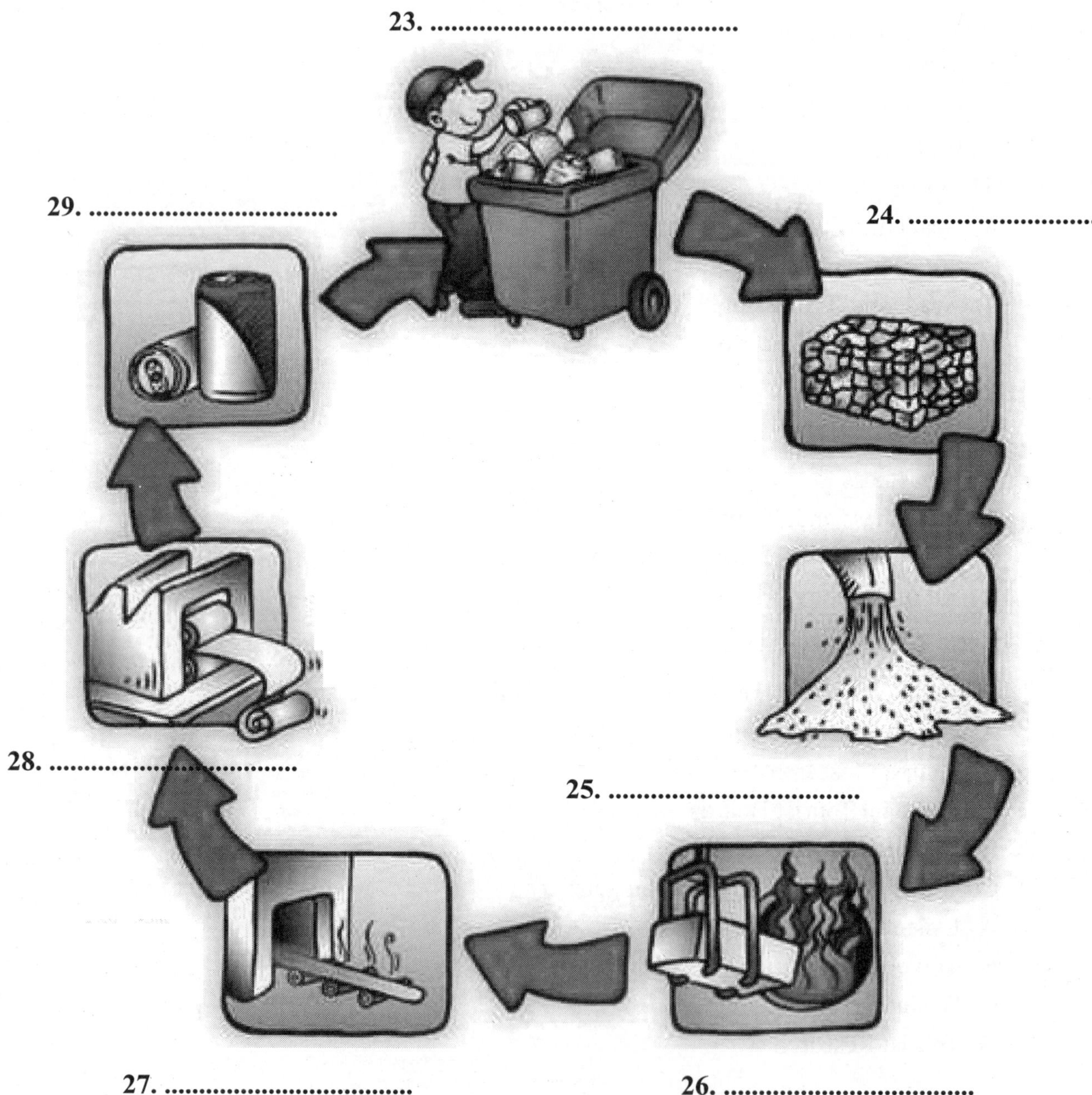

Recycling of Aluminium

Section Four

Complete the following summary from (30 – 40). Use words from the box. There are more words in the box than you need. Some may be used more than once.

rest	relaxed	angry	warm
stress	work	hunger	45 degrees
chew	exhaustion	desk	40 degrees
noise	tense	study	crowded
speak	smoky	relaxtion	long-term
tired	exercise	raised	

The most usual cause of headache is 30. ______________________ Headache can also come as a result of excessive 31. ______________________. Some people say that they get a headache when they 32. ______________________. This is probably because they get very 33. ________________. It may also be because they are working in poor light which makes them very 34. ______________________. It is helpful if your reading material is on a booke\rest at 35. __________________ to the desk. It is also important to 36. ________________________ in bed. You may even get a headache because you 37. ________________ too hard. The best advice is to try to eat regular meals, get enough 38. ________________ and avoid 39. ______________________ places. These places can also do you serious 40. ______________ damage.

Answer Sheet for Listening Test - 2

1.		21.	
2.		22.	
3.		23.	
4.		24.	
5.		25.	
6.		26.	
7.		27.	
8.		28.	
9.		29.	
10.		30.	
11.		31.	
12.		32.	
14.		33.	
15.		34.	
16.		35.	
17.		36.	
18.		37.	
19.		39.	
20.		40.	

Listening Total ________________

Listening Test 2

Answers

Section One

1. C	2. A	3. B	4. A
5. D	6. B	7. C	8. C

Section Two

9. Management Skills	10. Staff	11. Strategies	12. Issues
13. Complex	14. Autonomously	15. Professionally	16. Initiative
17. Decision-making	18. C	19. C	20. D
21. C	22. C		

Section Three

23. Unused, not thrown	24. Collected and crushed		25. Large bale
26. Molten aluminium	27. Thin sheet	28. Punching of cans	
29. Decorated and filled			

Section Four

30. hunger	31. noise	32. study
33. tense	34. tired	35. 45 degrees
36. relaxed	37. chew	38. exercise
39. smoky	40. long-term	

Listening Test – 3

Section One

Listen to the Japanese Culture of 'Go-game' and complete the following blanks from (1 – 10) by putting not more three words on your answer sheet.

1. OTHER NAME OF 'GO'

   ____

2. ORIGIN IN

   ____

3. INTRODUCED IN

   ____

4. IN CONTEMPORARY TIMES 'GO' IS AN

   ____

   ☆ Indoor game

   ☆ Outdoor game

5. In earlier times, 'GO' is an

   ☆ Indoor game

   ☆ Outdoor game

6. THEME OF 'GO' GAME ______________________
7. PLAYERS ________________________________
8. TYPES OF STONES ________________________
9. CAPTURING MORE TERRITORY MEANS ____________________________
10. People's Participation

GO-GAME OF JAPAN

Section Two

Listen to the spectacular acts of White Elephants of Thailand delivered by the narrator and complete the following summary using not more than three words for each answer. Now answer the following questions (11 – 26) on your answer sheet.

WHITE ELEPHANTS of Thailand is a symbol of 11. ______________________ and 12. ______________________ . The King of THAILAND is honoured with the highest Order of 13. ______________________. Thailand white elephants are appreciated because of its 14. ______________________ on the field of sport foot movement, agility. Racing and tactics are the special skills of Elephants. By getting the signal of take off elephants 15.______________________ immediately. OFTEN Elephants are competitive. They play obstacle race elephants football, sparying 16. ______________________ are quite common Elephants loved music. They are 17. ______________________ in the rock Jazz and 18. ______________________ categories. By getting command from their trainer they sway and prance of the 19. ______________________ trunk 20. ______________________ feet keeping time with 21. ______________________ and heads 22. ______________________ Elephants are best friends they even have their 23.______________________ and 24. ______________________ Elephant's friendship becomes most obvious when the female is above ready to give 25. ______________________ she solicits help in 26. ______________________

Section Three

Listen to the tapescript and lable the process of paper making. Write not more than three words for each answwre (27 – 31).

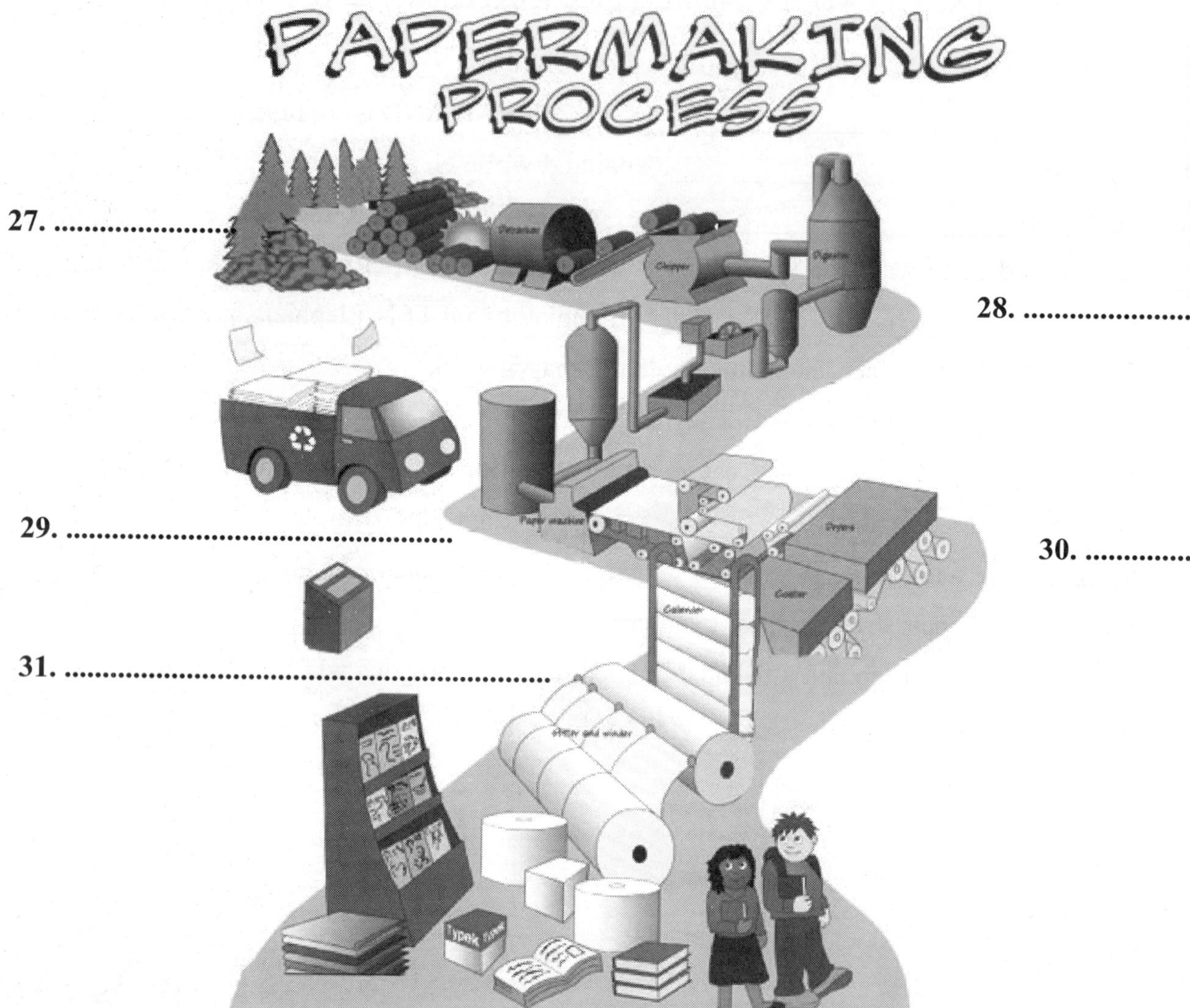

27. ....

28. ....

29. ....

30. ....

31. ....

Section Four

This section will tell you about the detailed description of the process of paper making. Listen to the tapescript and complete the summary by using words from the box. There are more words in the box than you need. Some words are used more than once. Now listen carefully and answer the following questions (32 – 40) on your answer sheet.

25	Wire
Water	Wood
Trees	Finished
Web	Cooked
Bark	Dyes
Coatings	Logs

Forest product companies and 32. ___________ for paper making. In the process of paper making, debarker is used for removing 33. _____________ and chippers are used to cut the 34. _______________ Then in the mixture of water and chemicals these chips are pressure 35. _______________ . Later pulp is bleached and pumped into a moving 36. _____________ screen. When the pulp travels down the screen, 37. ________________ is drained away and recycled. The semidry 38. ____________ is passed through heated dryer to remove the remaining water. 39. ________________ paper is wound into large rolls whose weight is around 40. _______________ tons.

Answer Sheet for Listening Test - 3

1.		21.	
2.		22.	
3.		23.	
4.		24.	
5.		25.	
6.		26.	
7.		27.	
8.		28.	
9.		29.	
10.		30.	
11.		31.	
12.		32.	
14.		33.	
15.		34.	
16.		35.	
17.		36.	
18.		37.	
19.		39.	
20.		40.	

Listening Total ________________

Listening Test 3

Answers

Section One

1. Go/Go Board Game
2. China
3. Japan
4. Indoor game
5. Outdoor Game
6. Winning Territory
7. Two
8. Black & White
9. Winner
10. Seven million

Section Two

11. Power
12. Place
13. White elephant
14. Intelligence
15. Stampede
16. Water games
17. Trained
18. Folk
19. Rhythm
20. Initiative
21. Beat
22. To and fro
23. Likes
24. Dislikes
25. Birth
26. Delivery

Section Three

27. Forestry
28. Debarking, Chipping/Recycling
29. Pulp Preparation
30. Paper formation
31. Paper finishing

Section Four

32. Trees
33. Bark
34. Wood
35. Cooked
36. Wire
37. Water
38. Web
39. Finished
40. 25

Listening Test – 4

Section One

In this section, listen to the conversation between the coach and a player regarding the equipments required by the players in Billiards and Snooker game. Complete the following blanks (1-12) by putting not more than three words for each answer.

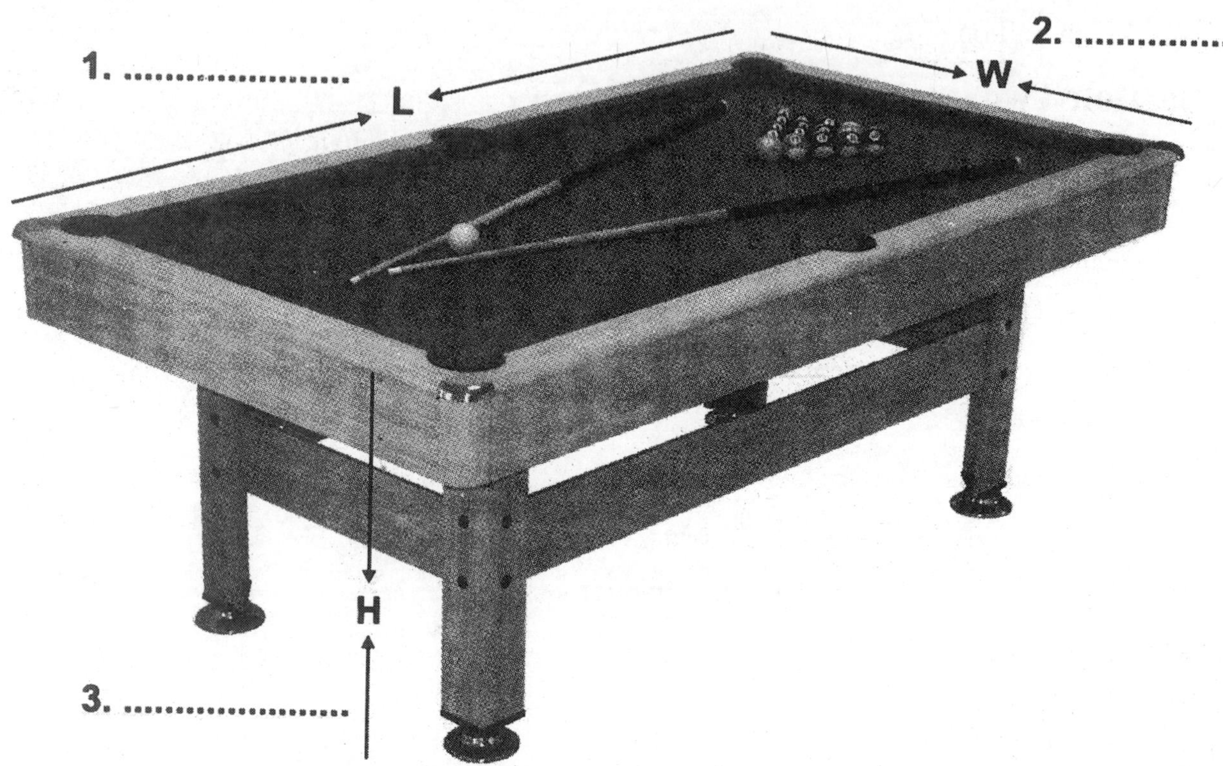

A STANDARD TABLE OF BILLIARDS AND SNOOKER

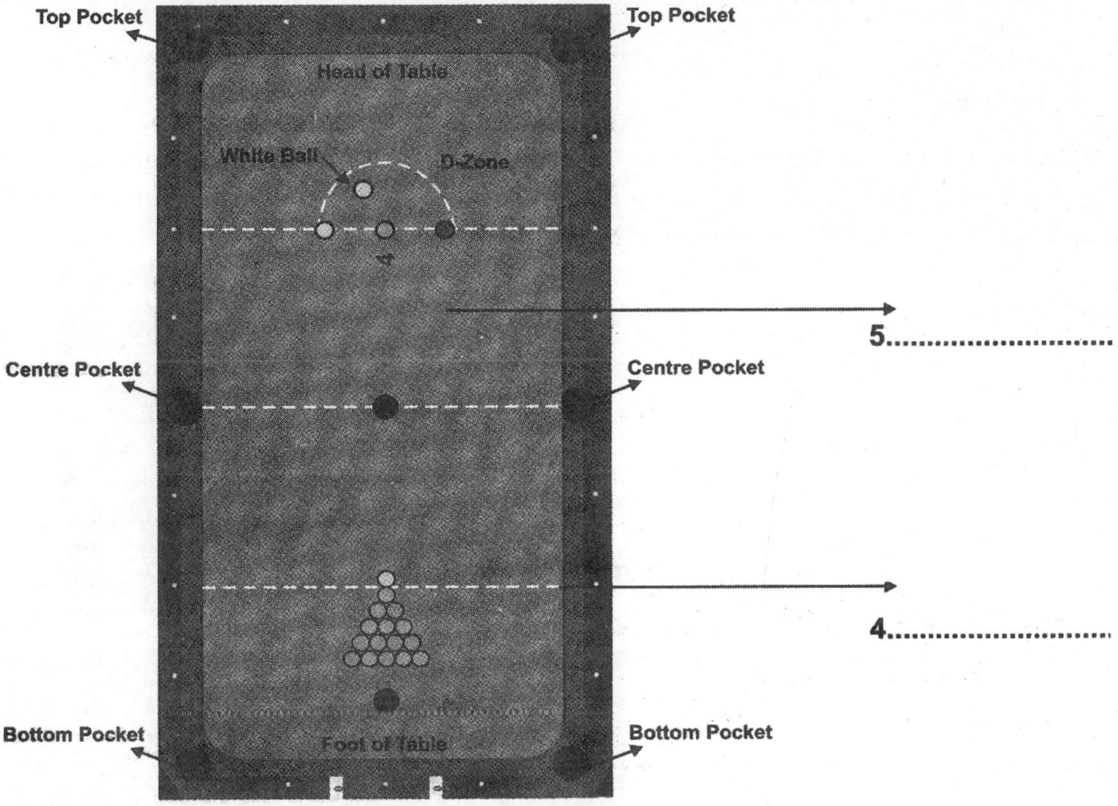

Top Pocket
Top Pocket
Head of Table
White Ball
D-Zone
5............................
Centre Pocket
Centre Pocket
4............................
Bottom Pocket
Bottom Pocket
Foot of Table

11............................
D-Zone
Radius
6............................
12............................
7............................
8............................
9............................
10............................

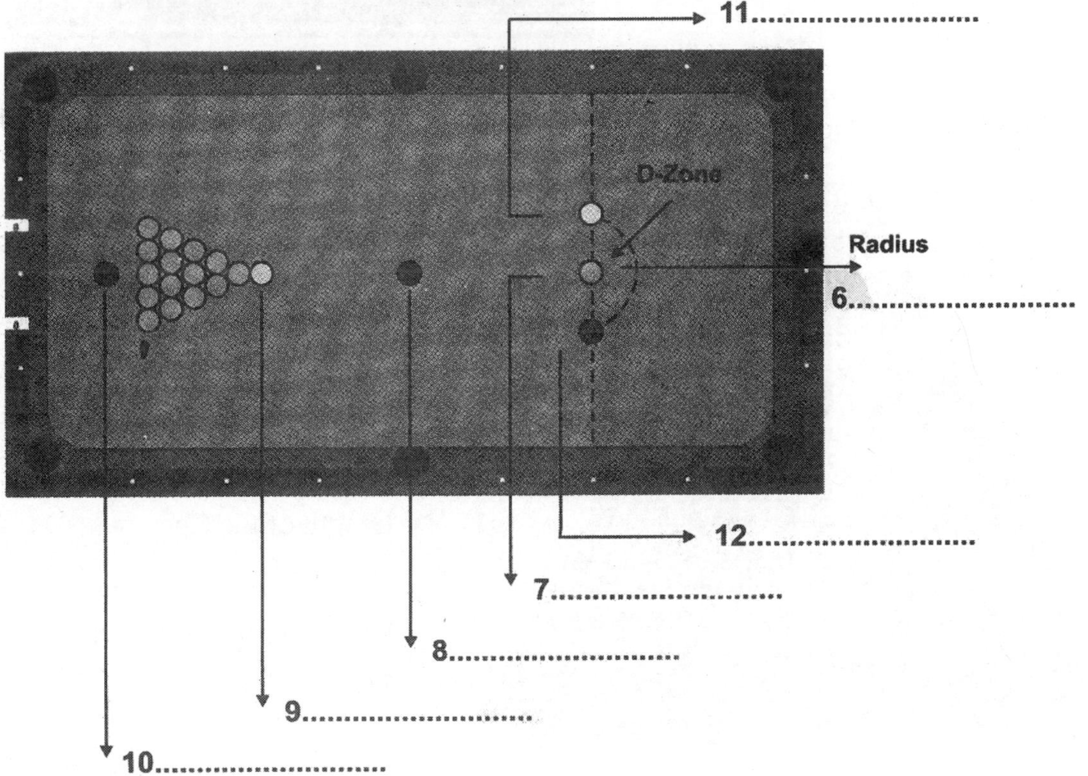

Section Two

Listen to the conversation between the coach and a player regarding the equipments used in Billiards and Snooker game and accordingly, write the value of each ball in front of the following questions (13-19) on your answer sheet.

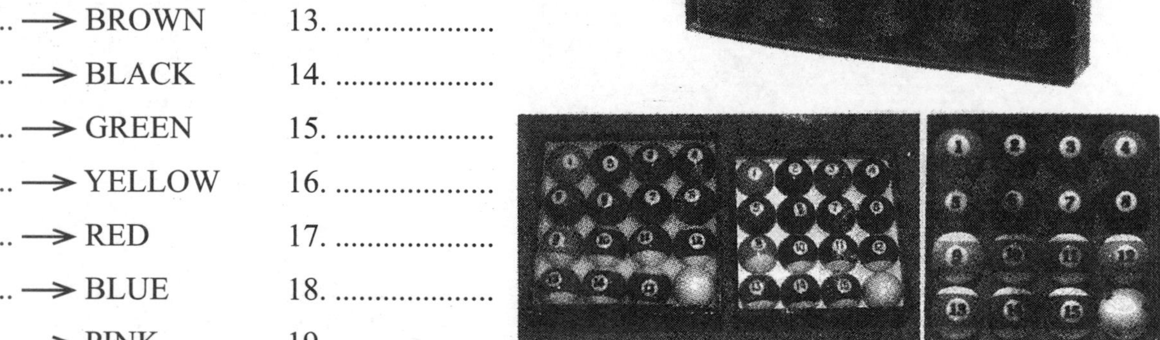

.. —> BROWN 13. ....

.. —> BLACK 14. ....

.. —> GREEN 15. ....

.. —> YELLOW 16. ....

.. —> RED 17. ....

.. —> BLUE 18. ....

.. —> PINK 19. ....

Complete the following blanks by putting not more than three words for each answer (20-21) on your answer sheet.

CUE

Length of the Cue

20. ....

Long Cues are called as

21. ....

Section Three

You will hear an extract from a talk about the problem of 'Dyslexia' among the people. Listen to what the speaker says, and answer the questions (22-29).

Circle the appropriate letter (A-D) from questions (22-29).

22. Diagnostic and Statistical Manual of Mental Disorders classifies dyslexia as a

    A. Writing disorder

    B. Speaking disorder

    C. Reading disorder

    D. Understanding disorder

23. Symptoms of Dyslexia include

    A. Difficulty in recognising words

    B. Difficulty in recognising letter

    C. Difficulty in recognising reading comprehensions

    D. All of the above

24. Diagnosis for Dyslexia can be possible through

    A. Single test

    B. Physician

    C. Medical treatment

    D. Battery of tests by specialists

25. Person with severe Dyslexia can never be a

    A. Bad reader

    B. Good reader

    C. Mild reader

    D. All of these

26. Dyslexia is a condition in which a person is not able to correctly process written words from the

    A. Brain to the eyes

    B. Eyes to the brain

C. Brain to the nerves

D. Eyes to the eyes

27. People with dyslexia have

A. Intelligent deficits and visual impairment

B. Speech and language difficulties

C. Special educational techniques

D. Inability to read and write

28. According to the National Centre, the percentage of people having learning disabilities is

A. 70 percent

B. 80 percent

C. 15 percent

D. 4 and 15 percent

29. According to the International Dyslexia Association, the percentage of students receiving special education services is

A. 80 percent

B. 70 to 80 percent

C. 70 percent

D. 15 percent

30. Complete the following blanks by putting not more than three words. Dyslexia disorders affects

A. ....

B. ....

SECTION 4

Complete the following summary regarding the dyslexia problem. You can use words from the box. There are more words in the box than you need. Some words are used more than once. Answer the following questions (31-40) on your answer sheet.

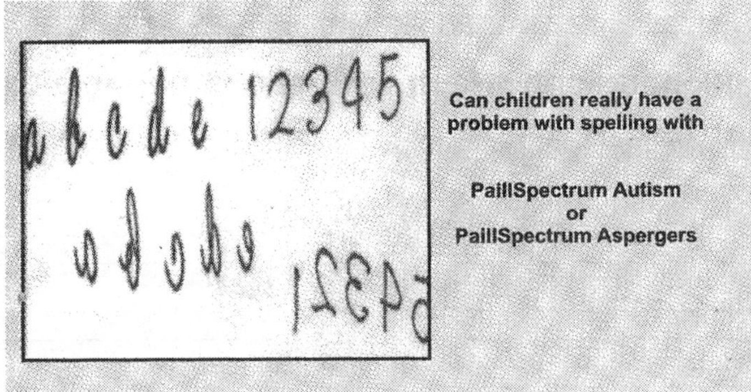

Brain	Phonetics	Memory
Eyes	Impairments	Vision
Language	Heriditary	Basic
Reading	Symbol	Families
Dyslexia	phonology	Active
Phenomena	Nerve cells	

Dyslexia is responsible for improper functioning of the **31.** ....in terms of language. The eyes and the brain play an indispensable role in **32.** .... Any malfunctioning in any part of the brain related to vision, langauge or memory can result **33.** .... A Dyslexia person possesses more **34.** .... brain than normal people. People fail to recognise **35.** .... unit of speech known as **36.** .... They do not understand the nature of sounds known as **37.** .... The studies of these sounds are called **38.** .... Dyslexia always results in speech and **39.** .... problems. It appears to be hereditary and can turn in **40.** ....

Answer Sheet for Listening Test - 4

1.		**21.**	
2.		**22.**	
3.		**23.**	
4.		**24.**	
5.		**25.**	
6.		**26.**	
7.		**27.**	
8.		**28.**	
9.		**29.**	
10.		**30.**	
11.		**31.**	
12.		**32.**	
14.		**33.**	
15.		**34.**	
16.		**35.**	
17.		**36.**	
18.		**37.**	
19.		**39.**	
20.		**40.**	

Listening Total ________________

Listening Test 4

Answer

SECTION 1

1. 3569 mm
2. 1778m
3. 851 mm to 87 mm
4. Baulk line
5. Baulk
6. 11-1/2
7. Black spot
8. Blue spot
9. Pink spot
10. Brown spot
11. Yellow spot
12. Green spot

SECTION 2

13. 4
14. 7
15. 3
16. 2
17. 1
18. 5
19. 6
20. 3ft
21. butts and half butts

SECTION 3

22. C
23. D
24. D
25. B
26. B
27. A
28. D
29. B
30. A males and female

    B. Ethnic and Socio-Economic groups

SECTION 4

31. Brain
32. Reading
33. Dyslexia
34. Active
35. Basic
36. Phenomena
37. Phonetics
38. Phonology
39. Language
40. Families

GRAMMAR RANGE & ACCURACY

S	V	O
Subject	**VERB**	**OBJECT**

S ----- SUBJECT OF ENGLISH

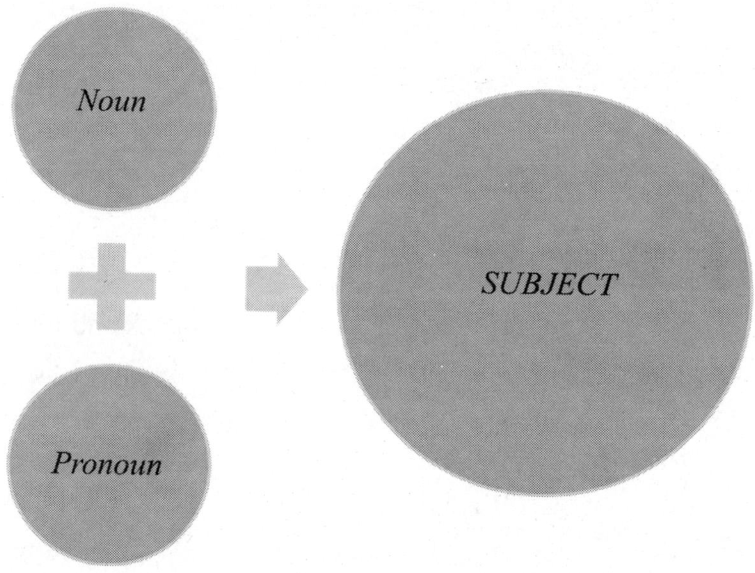

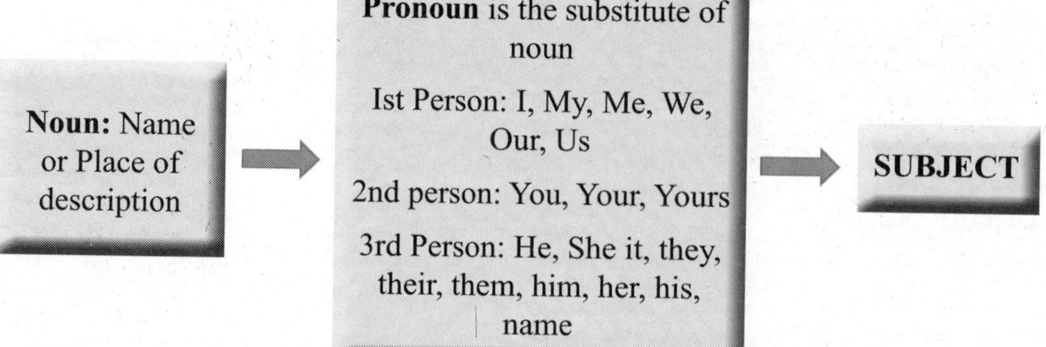

V…..Verb Of ENGLISH

A 'Verb' involves the action of the subject.

O….. Object in English

An 'object' tells about the subject.

English Completes in FIVE Types of Sentences

- Assertive Sentences
- Interrogative Sentences
- Imperative Sentences
- Exclamatory Sentences
- Negative Sentences

WHAT ARE ASSERTIVE SENTENCES

An Assertive Sentence is a simple sentence

WHAT ARE INTERROGATIVE SENTENCES

An Interrogative Sentence involves questioning in sentences.

WHAT ARE NEGATIVE SENTENCES

A Negative Sentence involves 'not' or 'no' in sentences.

S	N	V	O
Sita	Does not	Sing	A Song

WHAT ARE IMPERATIVE SENTENCES

Imperative sentences are those which involve *requests, commands* and advices.

Imperative Words

Please……

May…….

Order…….

Suggestion………

Pardon…….

Forgive……

Wish……

S	O
1. Open	The door
2. Please Give me	Glass of water
3. May	I Come In!

WHAT ARE EXCLAMATORY SENTENCES

An Exclamatory Sentence involves some shocking and surprising aspect.

Hurray!

Alas!

O!

Goodbye!

Sorry!

Wonder!

Wow!

Exclamatory Word	S	V	O
Hurray!	We	Won	The Match

CHAPTER OF TENSES

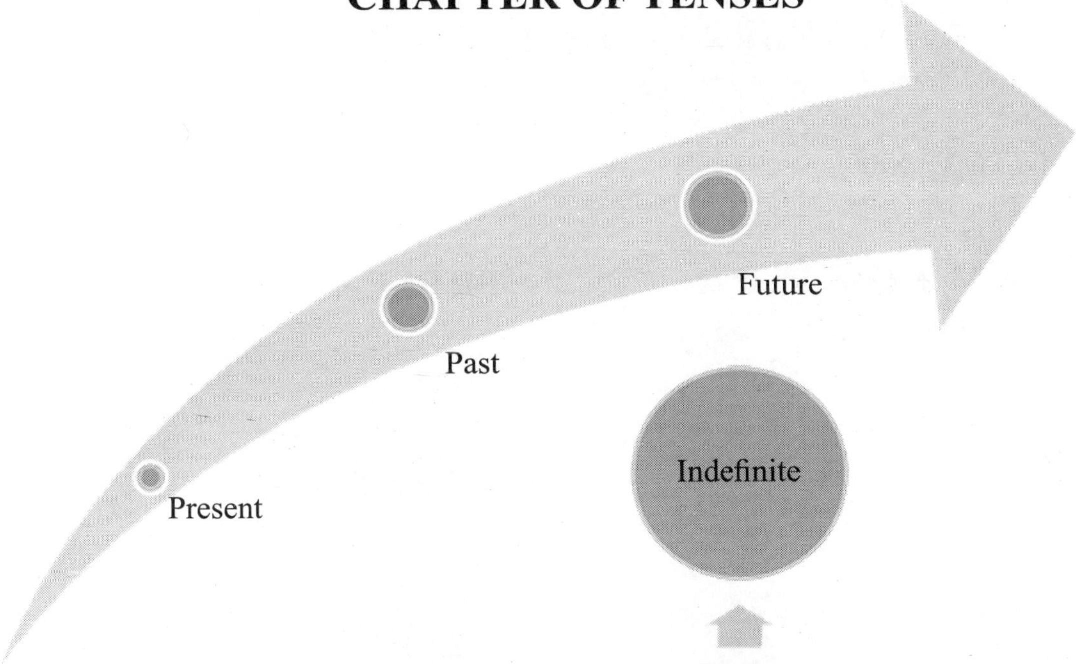

Present

Past

Future

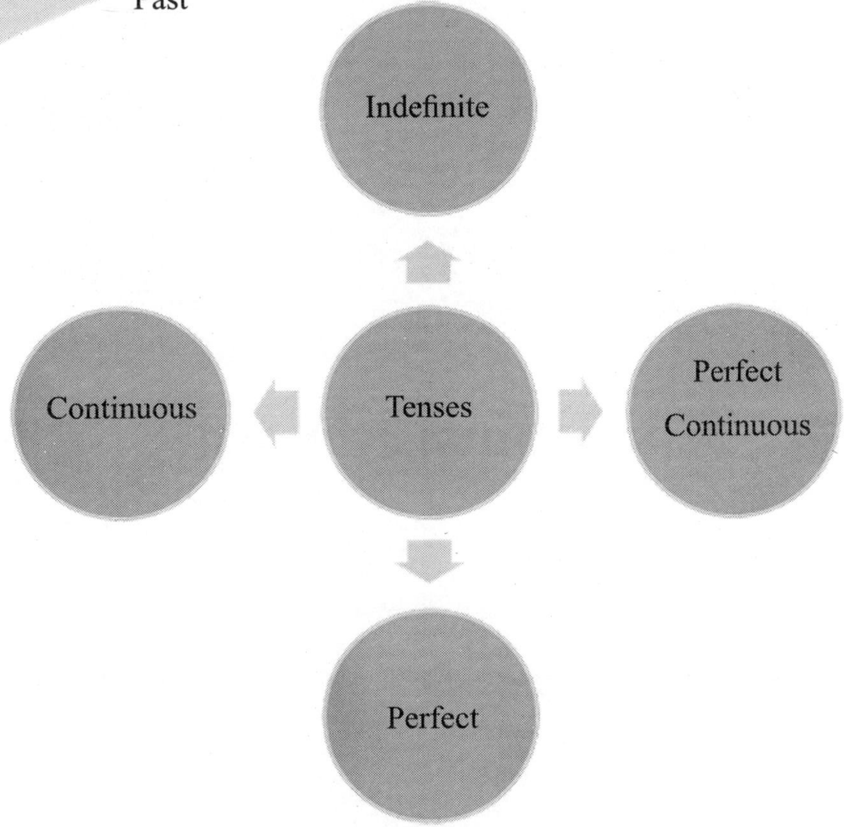

Indefinite

Continuous

Tenses

Perfect Continuous

Perfect

INDEX FINGER

INDEFINITE TENSE

$S + V_2 + O$ → **PAST**

$S +^{\text{Will/Shall}}\ V_1 + O$ → **FUTURE**

MIDDLE FINGER

CONTINUOUS TENSE

$S +^{\text{Is/Am/Are}}\ V_1 + ing + O$ → **PRESENT**

$S +^{\text{Was/Were}}\ V_1 + ing + O$ → **PAST**

$S +^{\text{Will/Shall be}}\ V_1 + ing + O$ → **FUTURE**

RING FINGER

PERFECT TENSE

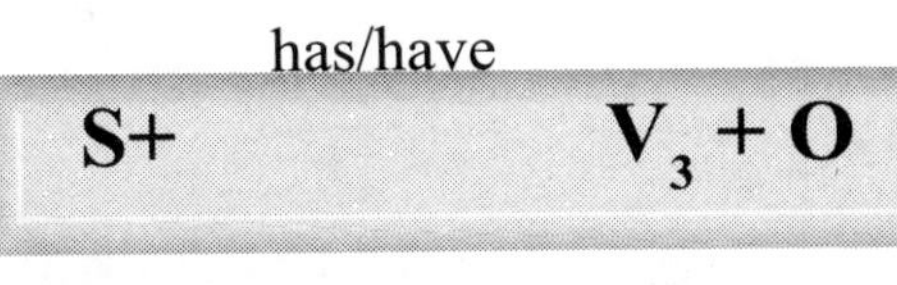

PRESENT

had

S + V_3 + O → **PAST**

Will have/Shall have

S + V_3 + O → **FUTURE**

SMALL FINGER

PERFECT CONTINUOUS TENSE

has/have been

S + V_1 + ing + O → **PRESENT**

Since/for

had been

S + V_1 + ing + O → **PAST**

Since/for

Will have/shall have been

S + V_1 + ing + O → **FUTURE**

Since/for

SELF-IMPROVEMENT/PERSONALITY DEVELOPMENT

Also Available in Hindi

Also Available in Hindi

Also Available in Kannada, Tamil

Also Available in Kannada

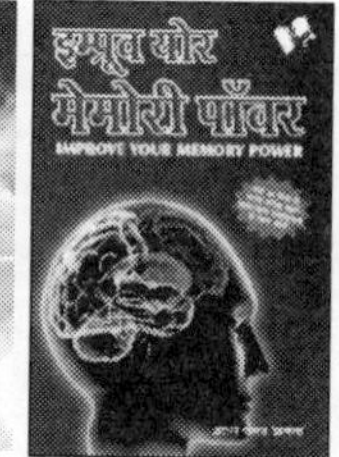

Also Available in Kannada

STRESS MANAGEMEN

All books available at www.vspublishers.com

V&S OLYMPIAD SERIES FOR CLASSES 1-10

MATHS

SCIENCE

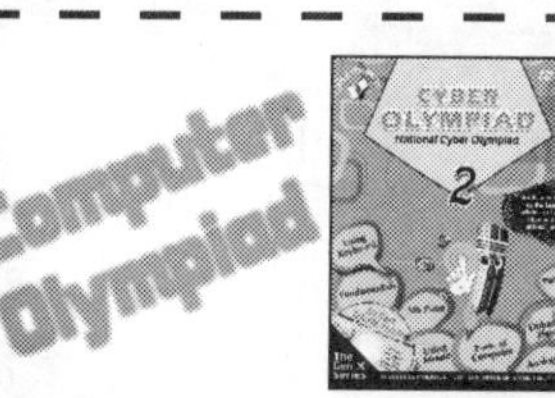

CYBER

ENGLISH

OLYMPIAD ONLINE TEST PACKAGE

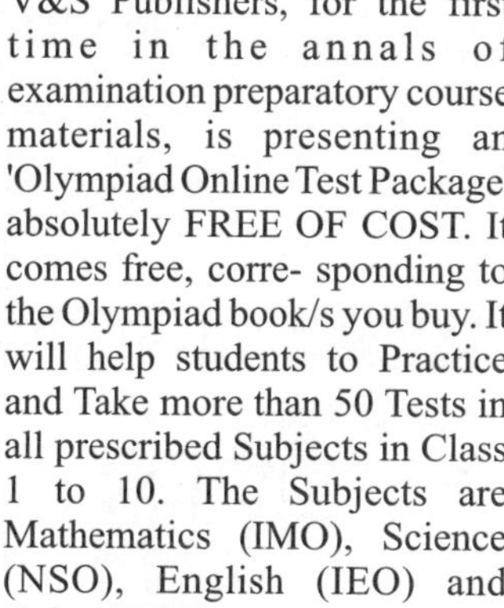

V&S Publishers, for the first time in the annals of examination preparatory course materials, is presenting an 'Olympiad Online Test Package' absolutely FREE OF COST. It comes free, corre- sponding to the Olympiad book/s you buy. It will help students to Practice and Take more than 50 Tests in all prescribed Subjects in Class 1 to 10. The Subjects are Mathematics (IMO), Science (NSO), English (IEO) and Cyber (NCO).

visit our bookstore: **www.vspublishers.com**

STUDENT DEVELOPMENT/LEARNING

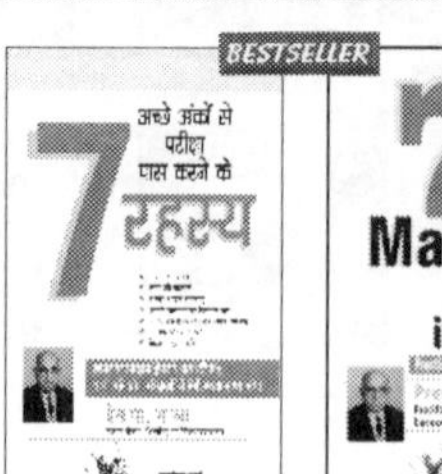

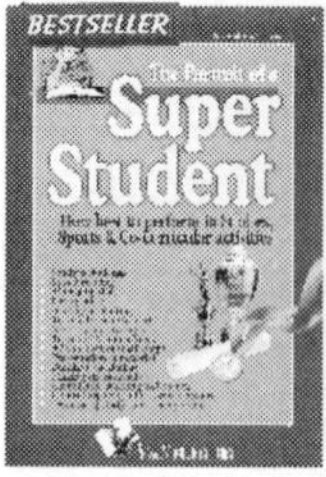

PUZZLES

DRAWING BOOKS

POPULAR SCIENCE

Also Available in Hindi

Also Available in Hindi

Also Available in Hindi

Also Available in Hindi

Also Available in Hindi

Also Available in Hindi

Also Available in Hindi, Tamil & Bangla

CHILDREN'S ENCYCLOPEDIA – THE WORLD OF KNOWLEDGE

Contact us at sales@vspublishers.com

QUIZ BOOKS

ACTIVITIES BOOK

QUOTES/SAYINGS

BIOGRAPHIES

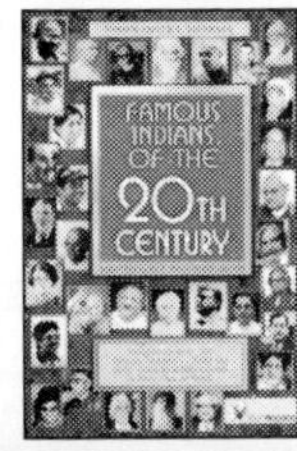

IELTS TECH

ENGLISH IMPROVEMENT

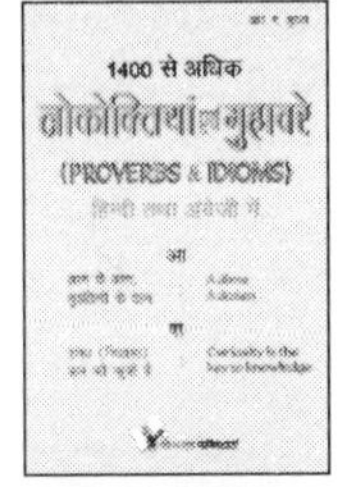

CHILDREN SCIENCE LIBRARY

COMPUTER BOOKS

Also available in Hindi

Also available in Hindi

All books available at www.vspublishers.com

V&S PUBLISHERS
VALUE & SUBSTANCE

HOME EBOOKS BEST SELLERS ACADEMIC BOOKS CHILDREN BOOKS HINDI ENGLISH IMPROVEMENT REGIONAL BOOKS COMBO PACKS

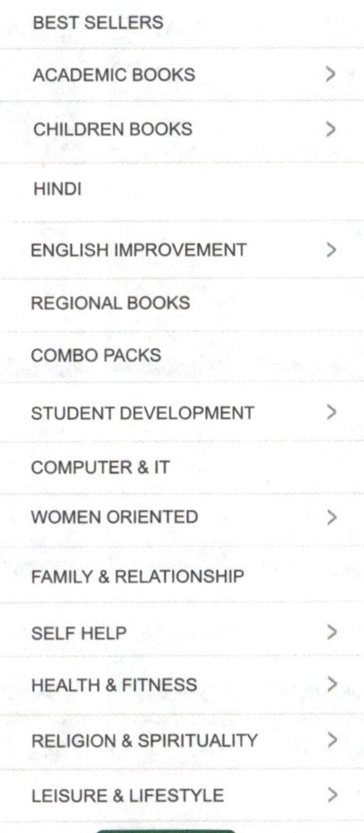

RAPIDEX COURSES | RELIGION | OLYMPIADS | CHILDREN STORIES | ENGLISH IMPROVEMENT | SELF HELP | DICTIONARIES | SCHOOL BOOKS | CRAFT & HOBBY | HEALTH | ACADEMIC | GENERAL KNOWLEDGE

E-books

Bestsellers

Subjects Olympiads

Publishers of Olympiads School Books & General Books

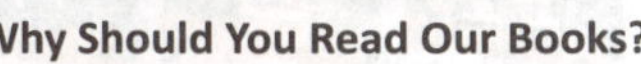

Published by Top Brand
V&S Publishers is a Leading National Level Publisher for Academic & General Books with over 1000 titles published across 50 categories in 10 languages. All books are available as Ebooks on Kindle Worldwide besides being sold as paperbacks through big and small bookstores pan India.

Written by Experts
Each Book is perfectly crafted by Subject Matter Experts & uniquely designed in-house. It offers a rich blended learning & reading experience through simple, quality & informative content. All books are thoroughly edited by experienced editors for grammar, language & factual error.

Assured Production Quality
Production Analysts with decades of experience hand-pick thick, high-quality paper for every book. Each book is machine bound and printed using non-toxic ink at high-end imported printing presses. All books are packaged and singly shrink-wrapped for protection from dust and damage.

On-time Delivery
Each product is exclusively sold by reputed prime sellers & is double-checked for new condition & best in-class packaging standards before despatch. To ensure on-time & rightful delivery, premier courier partners only are chosen for deliveries across all cities.

Buy All Books Online From Our Amazon Brandstore: amazon.in/vspublishers

➤ All V&S Publishers' books are available at best discounts with COD facility on Amazon, Flipkart & Snapdeal.
➤ Search all books by their ISBNs.

➤ अब 'वी एण्ड एस पब्लिशर्स' की सभी लोकप्रिय पुस्तकें COD सुविधा द्वारा Amazon, Flipkart & Snapdeal पर उपलब्ध।
➤ पुस्तक की खरीद के लिए ISBNs नंबर सर्च करें।

Head Office: F-2/16, Ansari Road, Daryaganj, New Delhi-110002, Ph: 011-23240026/27/28 Email: sales@vspublishers.com
Regional Office: 5-1-707/1, Brij Bhawan (Beside Central Bank of India Lane) Bank Street, Koti, Hyderabad-500 095
Ph: 040-24737290 Email: vspublishershyd@gmail.com

V&S OLYMPIAD GUIDE BOOK AND WORKBOOK SERIES (CLASSES 1-10)

ISBN : 9789357940504 ISBN : 9789357940511 ISBN : 9789357940528 ISBN : 9789357940535 ISBN : 9789357940542 ISBN : 9789357942447 ISBN : 9789357942454 ISBN : 9789357942461 ISBN : 9789357942478 ISBN : 97893579

ISBN : 9789357940559 ISBN : 9789357940566 ISBN : 9789357940573 ISBN : 9789357940580 ISBN : 9789357940597 ISBN : 9789357942492 ISBN : 9789357942508 ISBN : 9789357942515 ISBN : 9789357942522 ISBN : 97893579

ISBN : 9789357940405 ISBN : 9789357940412 ISBN : 9789357940429 ISBN : 9789357940436 ISBN : 9789357940443 ISBN : 9789357942546 ISBN : 9789357942553 ISBN : 9789357942560 ISBN : 9789357942577 ISBN : 97893579

ISBN : 9789357940450 ISBN : 9789357940467 ISBN : 9789357940474 ISBN : 9789357940481 ISBN : 9789357940498 ISBN : 9789357942591 ISBN : 9789357942607 ISBN : 9789357942614 ISBN : 9789357942621 ISBN : 97893579

ISBN : 9789357942102 ISBN : 9789357940603 ISBN : 9789357940610 ISBN : 9789357940627 ISBN : 9789357940634 ISBN : 9789357942744 ISBN : 9789357942751 ISBN : 9789357942768 ISBN : 9789357942775 ISBN : 97893579

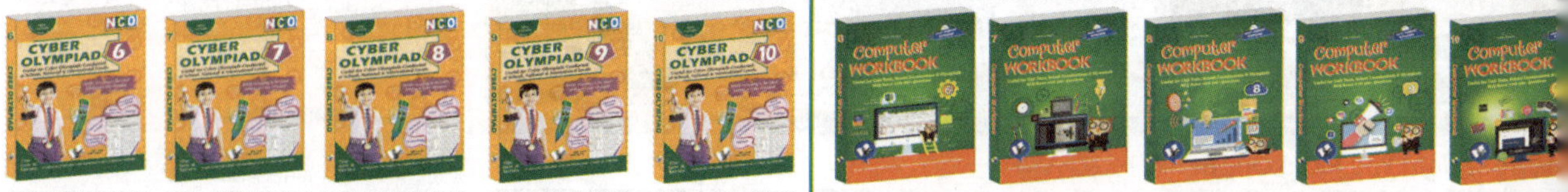

ISBN : 9789357940641 ISBN : 9789357940658 ISBN : 9789357940665 ISBN : 9789357940672 ISBN : 9789357940689 ISBN : 9789357942799 ISBN : 9789357942805 ISBN : 9789357942812 ISBN : 9789357942829 ISBN : 97893579

ISBN : 9789357940696 ISBN : 9789357940702 ISBN : 9789357940719 ISBN : 9789357940726 ISBN : 9789357940733 ISBN : 9789357942645 ISBN : 9789357942652 ISBN : 9789357942669 ISBN : 9789357942676 ISBN : 97893579

ISBN : 9789357940740 ISBN : 9789357940757 ISBN : 9789357940764 ISBN : 9789357940771 ISBN : 9789357940788 ISBN : 9789357942690 ISBN : 9789357942706 ISBN : 9789357942713 ISBN : 9789357942720 ISBN : 97893579

ISBN : 9789357942263 ISBN : 9789357942270 ISBN : 9789357942287 ISBN : 9789357942294 ISBN : 9789357942300 ISBN : 9789357942003 ISBN : 9789357942010 ISBN : 9789357942027 ISBN : 9789357942034 ISBN : 97893579

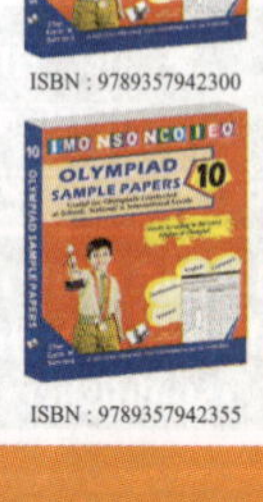

ISBN : 9789357942317 ISBN : 9789357942324 ISBN : 9789357942331 ISBN : 9789357942348 ISBN : 9789357942355 ISBN : 9789357942058 ISBN : 9789357942065 ISBN : 9789357942072 ISBN : 9789357942089 ISBN : 97893579

CAREER & BUSINESS/SELF-HELP/PERSONALITY DEVELOPMENT/STRESS MANAGEMENT

BN : 9789381588789 ISBN : 9789350571637 ISBN : 9789381588512 ISBN : 9789381588963 ISBN : 9789381588598 ISBN : 9789381384039 ISBN : 9788192079622 ISBN : 9789350570753 ISBN : 9789381384396

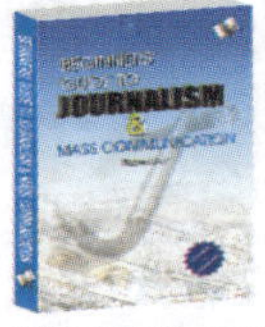

BN : 9789357940115 ISBN : 9789350570968 ISBN : 9789381384527 ISBN : 9789381588666 ISBN : 9789381384541 ISBN : 9789381384107 ISBN : 9789350571187 ISBN : 9789381588574 ISBN : 9789381588277

BN : 9789381588222 ISBN : 9789381384213 ISBN : 9789381588772 ISBN : 9789381588949 ISBN : 9789357940108 ISBN : 9789381384152 ISBN : 9789381384145 ISBN : 9789381448564 ISBN : 9789381384473

BN : 9789381448595 ISBN : 9789381448670 ISBN : 9789381588253 ISBN : 9789381448755 ISBN : 9789381448649 ISBN : 9789381384480 ISBN : 9789350571309 ISBN : 9789381448632 ISBN : 9789381384893

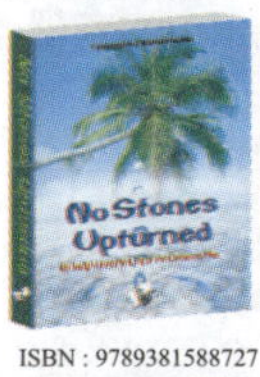

BN : 9789381384091 ISBN : 9789381384176 ISBN : 9789350570265 ISBN : 9789381588727 ISBN : 9789381384411 ISBN : 9789381588246 ISBN : 9789381448687 ISBN : 9789381448786 ISBN : 9789381448533

BN : 9789381448526 ISBN : 9789381384206 ISBN : 9788122310689 ISBN : 9789381384503 ISBN : 9789381588505 ISBN : 9789381448717 ISBN : 9788192079646 ISBN : 9789350570203 ISBN : 9789350570272

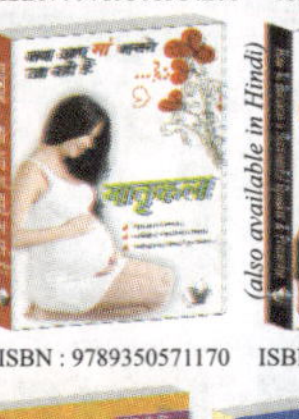

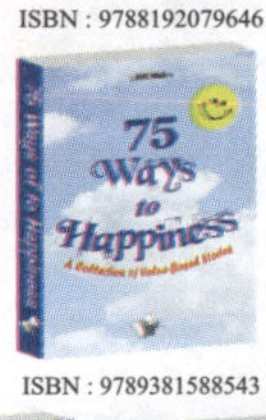

BN : 9789381588741 ISBN : 9789350571170 ISBN : 9789381588215 ISBN : 9789381384763 ISBN : 9789350570296 ISBN : 9789381588284 ISBN : 9789381588543 ISBN : 9789350571880 ISBN : 9789381588765

BN : 9789350570579 ISBN : 9789350571927 ISBN : 9789350571545 ISBN : 9789381384114 ISBN : 9789381384435 ISBN : 9789381448779 ISBN : 9789381448991 ISBN : 9789381384510 ISBN : 9789381384169 ISBN : 9789350570623

BN : 9789381448908 ISBN : 9789381448915 ISBN : 9789381448922 ISBN : 9789381448939 ISBN : 9789381448946 ISBN : 9789357940795 ISBN : 9789357940801 ISBN : 9789357940818 ISBN : 9789357941303 ISBN : 9789357941853

STUDENT LEARNING/QUIZ/POPULAR SCIENCE/BIOGRAPHIES

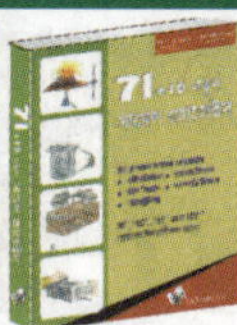

ISBN : 9789357941310 ISBN : 9789357941495 ISBN : 9789357942430 ISBN : 9789381384053 ISBN : 9789381384060 ISBN : 9789381384121 ISBN : 9788122310924 ISBN : 9789381588468 ISBN : 9789381588604 ISBN : 97893505704

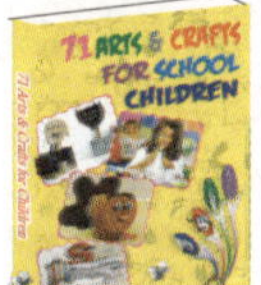

ISBN : 9789350570470 ISBN : 9789350570487 ISBN : 9789350570500 ISBN : 9789350570586 ISBN : 9789350571248 ISBN : 9789350571248 ISBN : 9789350571743 ISBN : 9789381384299 ISBN : 978938144805

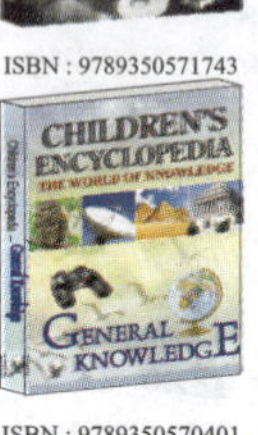

ISBN : 9789381384305 ISBN : 9789381384954 ISBN : 9789381588819 ISBN : 9789350570371 ISBN : 9789350570388 ISBN : 9789350570395 ISBN : 9789350570401 ISBN : 9789350570364 ISBN : 978938158844

ISBN : 9789381448977 ISBN : 9789381384459 ISBN : 9789381384930 ISBN : 9789350571682 ISBN : 9789381588864 ISBN : 9789381588673 ISBN : 9789350570111 ISBN : 9789381384312 ISBN : 978938158868

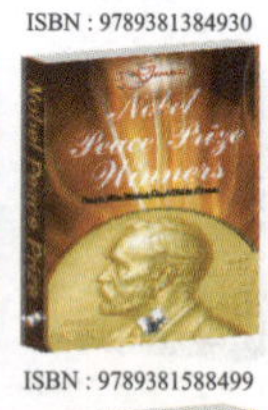

ISBN : 9789350570258 ISBN : 9789350570227 ISBN : 9789381588499 ISBN : 9789381588338 ISBN : 9789381588345 ISBN : 9789381448656 ISBN : 9789381384558 ISBN : 9788192079639 ISBN : 97893505710

ISBN : 9789350571026 ISBN : 9789350571033 ISBN : 9789350571040 ISBN : 9789350571057 ISBN : 9789350570999 ISBN : 9789350571002 ISBN : 9789350571064 ISBN : 9789350571071 ISBN : 978935057108

ISBN : 9789350571101 ISBN : 9789381588321 ISBN : 9789381588307 ISBN : 9789381588567 ISBN : 9789350571163 ISBN : 9789350570517 ISBN : 9789381384183 ISBN : 9789381448625 ISBN : 97893813847

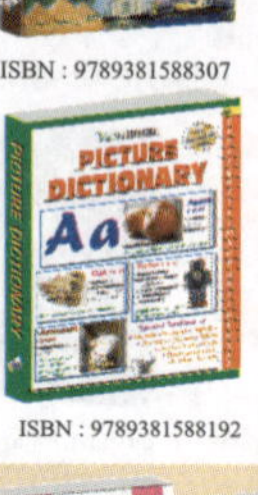

ISBN : 9789381384190 ISBN : 9789381448793 ISBN : 9789381588192 ISBN : 9789381588802 ISBN : 9789381588970 ISBN : 9789350570777 ISBN : 9789381448427 ISBN : 9789350570555 ISBN : 97893505705

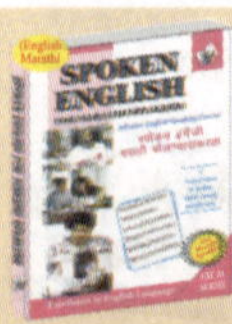

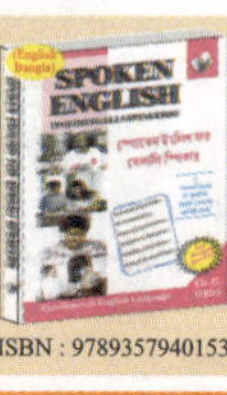

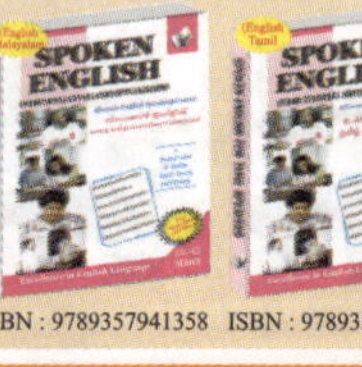

ISBN : 9789357940856 ISBN : 9789357940849 ISBN : 9789357941334 ISBN : 9789357941341 ISBN : 9789357940153 ISBN : 9789357940399 ISBN : 9789357940375 ISBN : 9789357940382 ISBN : 9789357941358 ISBN : 97893579413

FICTION/FUN & FACT, TALES & STORIES/LEISURE READING

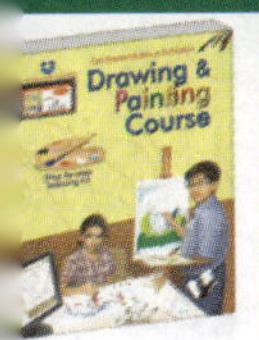   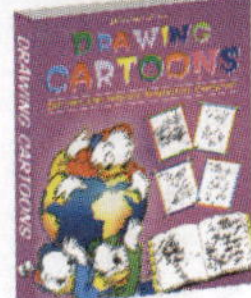 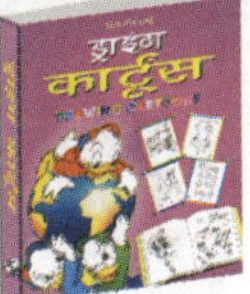    

ISBN : 9788192079660 ISBN : 9788192079677 ISBN : 9789381588659 ISBN : 9789381588840 ISBN : 9789381588857 ISBN : 9789381588871 ISBN : 9789381588888 ISBN : 9789381384336 ISBN : 9789381448069

         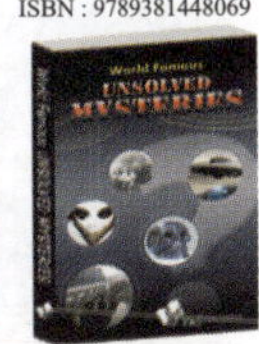

ISBN : 9789381448090 ISBN : 9789381448083 ISBN : 9789381384343 ISBN : 9789381448076 ISBN : 9789381448809 ISBN : 9789381448885 ISBN : 9789350571248 ISBN : 9789350570210 ISBN : 9789381384329

  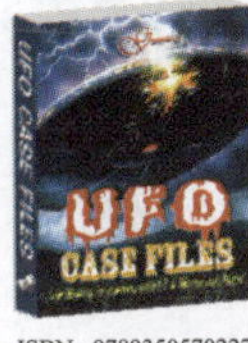      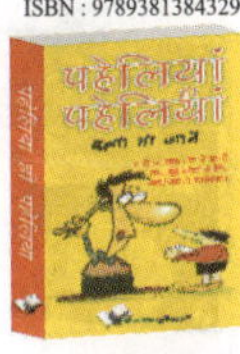

ISBN : 9789381448229 ISBN : 9789381448236 ISBN : 9789350570227 ISBN : 9789381588697 ISBN : 9788192079608 ISBN : 9789350571644 ISBN : 9789381588734 ISBN : 9789350570180 ISBN : 9789381448168

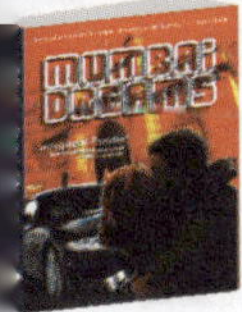  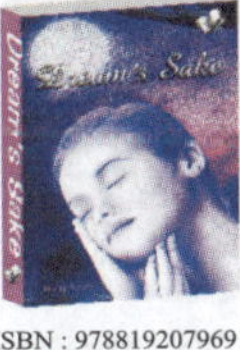  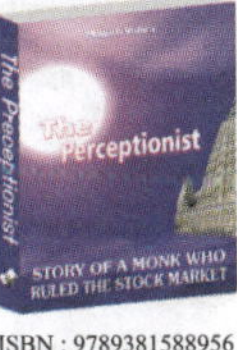    

ISBN : 9789381588314 ISBN : 9789381588260 ISBN : 9788192079691 ISBN : 9789381588291 ISBN : 9789381588956 ISBN : 9789350570852 ISBN : 9789350570906 ISBN : 9789350570838 ISBN : 9789350570883

ISBN : 9789350570845 ISBN : 9789350570890 ISBN : 9789350570869 ISBN : 9789350570913 ISBN : 9789350570821 ISBN : 9783950570876 ISBN : 9789350570920 ISBN : 9789350570937

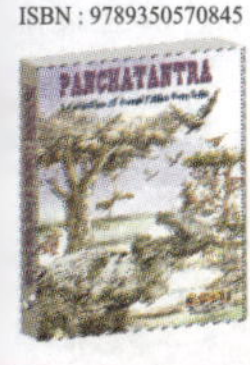      

ISBN : 9789381588987 ISBN : 9789350570005 ISBN : 9789350570012 ISBN : 9789350570029 ISBN : 9789381588994 ISBN : 9789350570036 ISBN : 9789350570043 ISBN : 9789350570050 ISBN : 9789381588406 ISBN : 9789350571552

ISBN : 9789381448182 ISBN : 9789381448199 ISBN : 9789381448144 ISBN : 9789381384404 ISBN : 9789381588451 ISBN : 9789381588581 ISBN : 9789381588529 ISBN : 9789381448137 ISBN : 9789381448106 ISBN : 9789381588178

   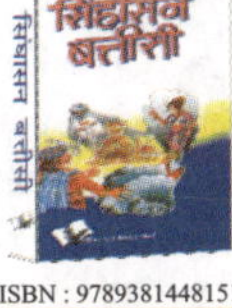   

ISBN : 9789381448175 ISBN : 9789381448113 ISBN : 9789381448120 ISBN : 9789381448151 ISBN : 9789381384701 ISBN : 9789381384718 ISBN : 9789381384862 ISBN : 9788192079615 ISBN : 9789381384015 ISBN : 9789381588185

 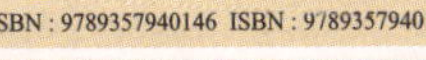

ISBN : 9789350570760 ISBN : 9789350570098 ISBN : 9789350571699 ISBN : 9789350571125 ISBN : 9789357940146 ISBN : 9789357940139 ISBN : 9789350571620 ISBN : 9789350571118 ISBN : 9789350570982 ISBN : 9789350571835

HEALTH & BEAUTY CARE/FAMILY & RELATIONS/LIFESTYLE

ISBN : 9789350570463 ISBN : 9789381588482 ISBN : 9789381448724 ISBN : 9789381448762 ISBN : 9789381448823 ISBN : 9789381384961 ISBN : 9789381384442 ISBN : 9789381448496 ISBN : 9789381588891

ISBN : 9788122307511 ISBN : 9789381448502 ISBN : 9789381384633 ISBN : 9789381448489 ISBN : 9789381384251 ISBN : 9789350570593 ISBN : 9789381384831 ISBN : 9789381384800 ISBN : 978935057061

ISBN : 9789381384220 ISBN : 9789381384817 ISBN : 9789381384572 ISBN : 9789381448694 ISBN : 9789381384824 ISBN : 9789381384565 ISBN : 9789381384909 ISBN : 9789350570609 ISBN : 978938144866

ISBN : 9789381448458 ISBN : 9789381384589 ISBN : 9788192079653 ISBN : 9789381384978 ISBN : 9789381448472 ISBN : 9789381448731 ISBN : 9789350571897 ISBN : 9789381448434 ISBN : 978938144846

(also available in Hindi)

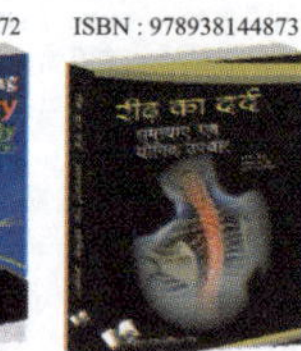

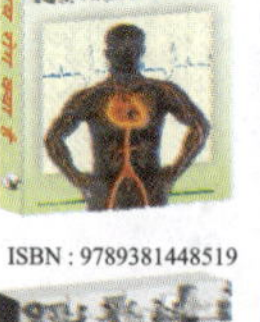

ISBN : 9789381384244 ISBN : 9789381384237 ISBN : 9789381384626 ISBN : 9789381448519 ISBN : 9789381384619 ISBN : 9789381448892 ISBN : 9789381384602 ISBN : 9789381588369 ISBN : 9789381588376

ISBN : 9789381588383 ISBN : 9789381588390 ISBN : 9789381448557 ISBN : 9789381588826 ISBN : 9789381384268 ISBN : 9788122305159 ISBN : 9789381448748 ISBN : 9789381384992 ISBN : 9789381384664

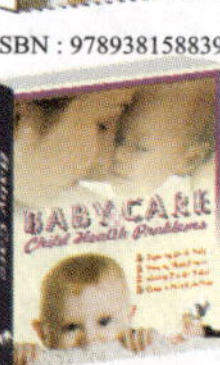

ISBN : 9789381448700 ISBN : 9789381588758 ISBN : 9789381384923 ISBN : 9789350570104 ISBN : 9789381448618 ISBN : 9789381448441 ISBN : 9789381384688 ISBN : 9789381384282 ISBN : 9788122308808

ISBN : 9789381448854 ISBN : 9789381384046 ISBN : 9789381384275 ISBN : 9789381384985 ISBN : 9789381448601 ISBN : 9789381448861 ISBN : 9789381384640 ISBN : 9789381384848 ISBN : 9789381384657

ISBN : 9788122310924 ISBN : 9789357940078 ISBN 9789350570357 ISBN : 9789350571200 ISBN : 9789350570340 ISBN : 9789350570944 ISBN : 9789350570951 ISBN : 9789350571309 ISBN : 9789350571828 ISBN : 9789350571781

SUBJECT DICTIONARIES/IELTS/ACADEMIC/COMPUTER LEARNING

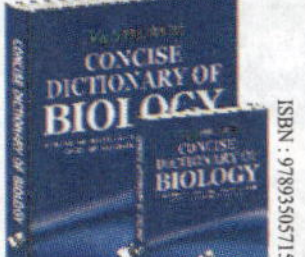

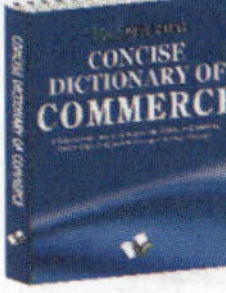
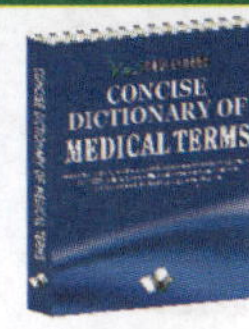

ISBN : 9789350571576 ISBN : 9789350571583 ISBN : 9789350571606 ISBN : 9789350571590 ISBN : 9789350571613

ISBN : 9789381588611 ISBN : 9789381588628 ISBN : 9789381588642 ISBN : 9789381588635 ISBN : 9789381588833 ISBN : 9789350570326 ISBN : 9789350570319 ISBN : 9789350570333

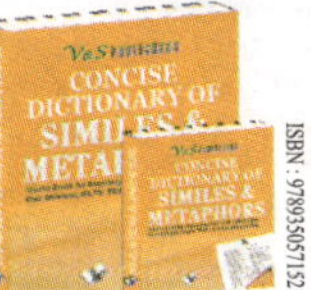

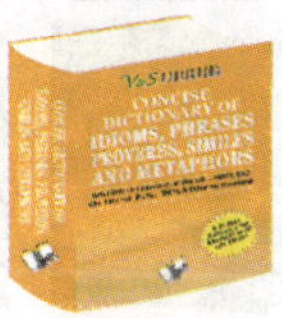

ISBN : 9789350571507 ISBN : 9789350571491 ISBN : 9789350571521

ISBN : 9789350571224 ISBN : 9789350571231 ISBN : 9789350571460 ISBN : 9789350571453 ISBN : 9789350571484 ISBN : 9789350571477 ISBN : 9789350571668 ISBN : 9789350571538

ISBN : 9789350571392 ISBN : 9789350571385 ISBN : 9789350571408 ISBN : 9789350571330 ISBN : 9789350571147

ISBN : 9789350571415 ISBN : 9789350571439 ISBN : 9789350571422 ISBN : 9789350571361 ISBN : 9789350571354 ISBN : 9789350571378 ISBN : 9789350571149 ISBN : 9789350571330

ISBN : 9789357942232

SBN : 9789350571651 ISBN : 9789350571286 ISBN : 9789350571255 ISBN : 9789350571262 ISBN : 9789350571293 ISBN : 9789350571279 ISBN : 9789350571569 ISBN : 9789357940368 ISBN : 9789350571934

ISBN : 9789357942379

ISBN : 9789357942256

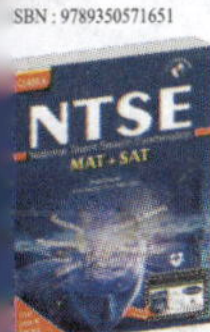

ISBN : 9789350571705 ISBN : 9789350570241 ISBN : 9789350570234 ISBN : 9789350571965 ISBN : 9789357941365 ISBN : 9789357941549 ISBN : 9789357941556 ISBN : 9789357941563 ISBN : 9789357941570

ISBN : 9789357942386

ISBN : 9789357942249

ISBN : 9789357941501 ISBN : 9789357941518 ISBN : 9789357941525 ISBN : 9789357941532 ISBN : 9789357941747 ISBN : 9789357941716 ISBN : 9789357941709 ISBN : 9789357941723

ISBN : 9789357941730 ISBN : 9789350571693 ISBN : 9789357941655 ISBN : 9789357941662 ISBN : 9789357941679 ISBN : 9789357941686 ISBN : 9789350570173 ISBN : 9789381588895

ISBN : 9789357942393

ISBN : 9789357942225

ISBN : 9789350570142 ISBN : 9789381588536 ISBN : 9789350570159 ISBN : 9789350570128 ISBN : 9789350571316 ISBN : 9789350571989 ISBN : 9789350570135 ISBN : 9789350570166

ISBN : 9789357942362

ISBN : 9789357940054 ISBN : 9789357940016 ISBN :9789357940023 ISBN : 9789357940085 ISBN : 9789357940825 ISBN : 9789357940092 ISBN : 9789357940009 ISBN : 9789357940030 ISBN : 9789357940061

ASTROLOGY/PALMISTRY/VAASTU/HYPNOTISM/RELIGION & SPIRITUALITY

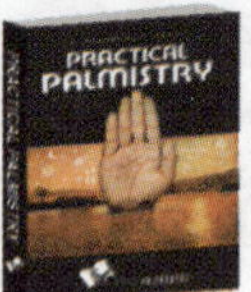

ISBN : 9789381588925 ISBN : 9789381588710 ISBN : 9789381448540 ISBN : 9789381448045 ISBN : 9789381384350 ISBN : 9789381384367 ISBN : 9789381384077 ISBN : 9789357940832 ISBN : 978938138453

(also available in Hindi)

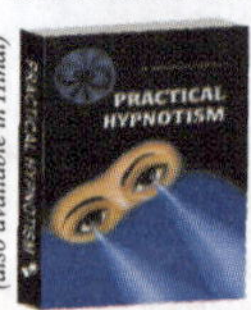

ISBN : 9789381384374 ISBN : 9789350571194 ISBN : 9789381384466 ISBN : 9789381448021 ISBN : 9789381448014 ISBN : 9789381588796 ISBN : 9789381588796 ISBN : 9789381384084 ISBN : 9789381448212

ISBN : 9789381384756 ISBN : 9789381384879 ISBN : 9788122309973 ISBN : 9788122310849 ISBN : 9789381384497 ISBN : 9789381384886 ISBN : 9789381384497 ISBN : 9789381448878 ISBN : 97893813847

NEW ARRIVALS

ISBN : 9789357941471 ISBN : 9789357941457 ISBN : 9789357941419 ISBN : 9789357941433 ISBN : 9789357941464 ISBN : 9789357941402 ISBN : 9789357941396 ISBN : 9789357941389 ISBN : 9789357941372 ISBN : 978935794414

ISBN : 9789357941440 ISBN : 9789350571842 ISBN : 9789350571859 ISBN : 9789357942843 ISBN : 9789357941938 ISBN : 9789350571958 ISBN : 9789350571941 ISBN : 9789350571132 ISBN : 9789350571767 ISBN : 978935057174

ISBN : 9789350571750 ISBN : 9789357941426 ISBN : 9789357942171 ISBN : 9789350571903 ISBN : 9789350571910 ISBN : 9789357940207 ISBN : 9789357940214 ISBN : 9789357940221 ISBN : 9789350571972 ISBN : 978935794017

ISBN : 9789357940184 ISBN : 9789357940191 ISBN : 9789381384770 ISBN : 9789357942850 ISBN : 9789357941983 ISBN : 9789357941990 ISBN : 9789357940313 ISBN : 9789357940320 ISBN : 9789357941976 ISBN : 9789357941960

ISBN : 9789357940306 ISBN : 9789357940276 ISBN : 9789357940283 ISBN : 9789357940290 ISBN : 9789350571873

ISBN : 9789357940269 ISBN : 9789357940238 ISBN : 9789357940245 ISBN : 9789357940252 ISBN : 9789357941952 ISBN : 9789357941945

ISBN : 9789357940047 ISBN : 9789350571811 ISBN : 9789350571804 ISBN : 9789381384138 ISBN : 9789381384121 ISBN : 9789357940870 ISBN : 9789350571798 ISBN : 9789357940863 ISBN : 978935794240